SYSTEMATIC THEOLOGY 1

"I am delighted to be able to recommend this important work. It is well-written, easy to understand and, above all, accurate, standing in the mainstream of orthodox Reformed theology. Each chapter is rooted in careful exegesis of Scripture, paying careful attention to the biblical languages. Dr Bayes writes in the stream of historic Christianity, paying careful attention to the ancient creeds of the Christian church, the confessions of the Reformation and more recent statements of faith. The great debates of the Christian church are considered and careful attention paid to more modern challenges such as Open Theism. Clearly intended for an international readership, its lucidity should make it attractive to readers who have paid little attention to Christian doctrine and even underestimated the importance of the subject."

DR. ROBERT OLIVER
Lecturer in Church History and Historical Theology at the London Theological Seminary, England

"One of the challenges in teaching systematic theology is not only to assert but to demonstrate that systematics grows out of the Bible. Jonathan Bayes has provided us with a first class example of how that can be done. This first part of *Systematics for God's Glory* is refreshing, illuminating and edifying. Scripture comes first; we are then invited to reflection and praise; then the classic confessions and some modern ones from other traditions are integrated; and, finally, key historical and contemporary issues are discussed. A great way to teach and study systematics."

DR. MOSTYN ROBERTS
Pastor of Welwyn Evangelical Church and lecturer in Systematic Theology at London Theological Seminary, England

"*Systematics for God's Glory* is probably the best theology book I have ever read. It is biblical and scholarly yet very readable and practical. I look forward to the next two volumes."

JERRY BRIDGES
Author of *The Pursuit of Holiness*

"I commend Jonathan Bayes for undertaking this major effort in systematic theology. I especially like how he interweaves the Bible as the foundation and major source of his thought with the teachings of the early creeds and modern confessions of faith. He is also concerned to show how various important theologians have thought about these same doctrines. The result is a welcome blend of theology and application in a single, concise volume."

DR. STANLEY E. PORTER
President and Dean, Professor of New Testament, Roy A. Hope Chair in Christian Worldview, McMaster Divinity College, Hamilton, Ontario, Canada

"I cannot speak too highly of *Systematics for God's Glory*. Jonathan Bayes has done the church a great service. His book is lucid, interesting and biblical and combines clear exegesis, historical perspective and devotional warmth while, at the same time, bringing perspectives from non-Western believers on the great truths of the gospel. May the Lord use it to equip a new generation of faithful Bible teachers for the future in our fast changing, global village which so much needs the truth."

DR. JOHN BENTON
Pastor of Chertsey Street Baptist Church, Guildford, England, and Managing Editor of *Evangelicals Now*

SYSTEMATIC THEOLOGY 1

SYSTEMATICS
FOR GOD'S GLORY

God, creation, decrees and providence

JONATHAN BAYES

General editor: Bob Penhearow

CAREY
PRINTING PRESS

CAREY
PRINTING PRESS

Published by
Carey Outreach Ministries Inc., Guelph, Ontario, Canada
www.careyoutreach.org

About us
Carey Printing Press is the publishing arm of Carey Outreach Ministries,
an international Christian organization that provides theological training
to spiritual leaders to shape the church and influence the nations.
General editor: Bob Penhearow

First published 2012

Cover and book design by Janice Van Eck

Also available in paperback: ISBN 978-0-9876841-2-7

Library and Archives Canada Cataloguing in Publication

Bayes, Jonathan F.
        Systematic theology / Jonathan Bayes.

Includes bibliographical references.
Contents: 1. Systematics for God's glory

ISBN 978-0-9876841-1-0 (v. 1) hardcover

        1. Theology, Doctrinal. 2. Bible—Theology. I. Title.

BT75.3.B39 2012   230'.041   C2012-901632-2

Contents

Foreword

We may ponder the question, "Why another book on systematics?" The answer is that Dr. Jonathan Bayes has approached systematics from a solid biblical-theological viewpoint. In other words, great care has been taken, and attention been paid, to work through the biblical text from a historical, redemptive perspective. The overarching theme of grace which permeates Scripture is given its rightful place. Grace permeates God's throne; grace permeates God's acts; grace permeates all that God is and does. This theme of God's grace and how it applies to us in the twenty-first century is both life-enriching and life-changing. God's grace is indeed wondrous to behold!

In this first volume of a systematic trilogy, the reader is confronted with the gracious character of God and the glorious being of God in Trinity. The wonderful revelation of God in and through his Word and creative acts are then examined, followed by the immutable sovereign decrees of God and God's wisdom through providence.

Dr. Bayes is painstakingly careful and thorough in the handling of God's Word. You will not find any "proof texting" here. Scripture after Scripture in context is carefully examined. Sadly, far too many systematic books fall short on solid biblical exegesis and rush to formulate doctrine rather than carefully mining biblical texts. As a result of careful exegesis, Dr. Bayes is able to draw out spiritual insights about our magnificent God that will dazzle the reader.

To help with our understanding of biblical truth, Dr. Bayes has examined the formation of doctrine from the early church creeds such as the *Apostles' Creed* and the *Nicene Creed* to modern creeds and confessions. Creeds and confessions are significant, as they help us to crystallize biblical truth in a systematized format.

Each chapter closes with an emphasis on pastoral application. It is noteworthy that all theology, including systematic theology, has a dual purpose. First, to reveal the wonder of an omnipotent, omniscient, gracious God so that we may delight ourselves in praise and worship: praise and worship for who he is and for what he has done throughout redemptive history. Second, theology is given "that the man of God may be competent, equipped for every good work" (2 Timothy 3:17), good work which is our joy and delight, a natural response to the God of all grace.

Without any reservation, I believe this book will enrich and enhance your understanding and worship of God.

Our prayer is that this book will enable you to gaze upon and then delight your soul in the God of all grace—theology to doxology!

Soli deo gloria.

Bob Penhearow
General editor

Introduction

Imagine four friends enjoying a meal together. They have prepared each course—soup, fish, green beans, tofu, beef, cashew nuts, and rice—and now consume the meal between bouts of laughter and discussion. Abruptly, the meal is over. They clear the table, wash the dishes and put them away. Everything is very tidy.

Systematic theology is an attempt to have a tidy faith. While you are eating a meal there are bowls and plates at various places on the table. Platters hold an assortment of prepared dishes. After the meal, the friends clean and neatly arrange everything.

The only source book for systematic theology is the Bible. However, God did not give us his Word all neat and packaged. In the Bible, God has prepared for us a feast of good things. As we know, a feast requires variety, as a meal among friends requires everything from soup to cashews. Sometimes it can be helpful to bring together all the teaching of the Bible on a particular theme. The task of systematic theology is to arrange tidily the various doctrines taught in the Bible.

Of course, we must not try to make our theology too neat and tidy. We dare not iron out every mystery. God's thoughts are always greater than our own. In Isaiah 55:9, God challenges us to remember this: "As the heavens are higher than the earth, so are my ways higher than your ways, and my thoughts than your thoughts."

As long as we live, we are still just learners. We would be fools if we imagined we could get our faith so neat and tidy that we know it all. Systematic theology always has to be theology in the *process* of arrangement in a tidy system. This book can only be like dipping a toe in the water of the vast ocean of divine truth.

We must repeat: *the only source book for systematic theology is the Bible*. In studying systematic theology, it can be very helpful to look at how other Christians in other places and at other times have tried to arrange a tidy faith, but our only authority is God's Word itself. We must test every opinion about every Christian doctrine by Scripture. As we study each doctrine, we shall take a fourfold approach:

First, we shall do an exegesis of key relevant passages of the Bible. Where appropriate we shall look first at the Old Testament and then at the New Testament. This will help to keep at the forefront of our minds the foundational place of Scripture in sorting Christian doctrine into a tidy framework.

Second, we shall formulate the doctrine in a systematic way. This is the heart of presenting the faith in a tidy format. In this section, we shall look at how our predecessors in the Christian faith summarized the doctrines in their statements of faith. We shall look first at the creeds the early church put together, and then turn our attention to the confessions of faith and catechisms published by the various Reformed churches of Europe during the Reformation period. Finally, we shall look at some examples of modern non-western doctrinal documents. Speaking of the younger churches beyond the western cultural context, John Leith notes, "as yet, these churches have produced few creeds."[1] However, three are available: the *Confession of Faith of the United Church of Northern India* (produced in 1924 as the result of the amalgamation of Congregational and Presbyterian denominations),[2] the *Confession of Faith of the Huria Kristen Batak*

---

1   J. Leith, ed., *Creeds of the Churches* (Louisville: Westminster John Knox Press, 1982), 555.

2   Reproduced in G.C. Oosthuizen, *Theological Discussions and Confessional Developments in the Churches of Africa and Asia* (Franeker: Wever, 1958), 302-304.

Protestant (produced in Indonesia in 1951),[3] and the *Confession of Faith of House Churches in China* (published in 1998 by representatives of four House Church networks).[4]

Third, we shall look at how the tidy formulation of doctrine has developed in the course of the centuries. Our approach here will vary. Sometimes we will take one or two classic statements on a doctrine from different eras of Christian history. When necessary we shall address errors in our own day relating to particular doctrines.

Fourth, each section will be finished with practical, pastoral application. We must never forget that the design of the study of biblical truth is to achieve this goal: "that the man of God may be competent, equipped for every good work" (2 Timothy 3:17). That means every single doctrine in the whole of systematic theology is relevant to the way we live for God in his world today.

This is a course intended for preachers. Each of us needs to ask, *how do I preach this doctrine in such a way that its relevance is clear, whether to unbelievers whom I long to see saved, or to those believers to whom I minister, whether from the pulpit or in personal counselling situations?*

However, before we are ministers of the Word, we are ourselves Christian believers. We need to apply God's truth to our own hearts and lives before we dare preach it to others. Like the apostle, we want to steer clear of the hypocrisy that would mean that "after preaching to others, I myself should become disqualified" (1 Corinthians 9:27).

Although the practical relevance of the teaching will be permeating the whole of our studies, it is useful to draw together the practical application at the end of each section.

---

3 Reproduced in Leith, ed., *Creeds of the Churches*, 556-566.

4 Reproduced in D. Aikman, *The Beijing Factor* (Oxford: Monarch, 2005), 297-303.

1

THE DOCTRINE OF GOD

What does it mean to speak of the glory of God?

The doctrine of God is concerned with God's character. What is he like? This is a vast subject. God is very great. We therefore have to be selective and our aim will be limited. We shall seek to get to the heart of the doctrine of God as he has revealed himself in the Scriptures. We get our doctrine of God largely from the Old Testament. The New Testament takes it for granted that God is as he has already revealed himself to be. How does the Old Testament introduce God? The key word summing up the Old Testament teaching about God is *mercy*. The Lord is merciful, and if our doctrine of God does not centre on mercy and grace, then we are not talking about the God of the Bible.

PART 1: KEY TEXTS

THE BOOK OF EXODUS

In Exodus 3, God addresses Moses out of the burning bush. Moses hears God promise to liberate his people, and receives his commission to go to Pharaoh and demand their release. In verse 13, Moses asks God what he should say if the people of Israel ask him the name of the God he represents. In verse 14 God replies, "I am who I am," and tells Moses to say to the people, "I am has sent me to you." In verse 15, he replaces the phrase "I am" with the name *the Lord*. This name is derived from the verb "to be." The Lord says, "This is my name forever." Alone, the verb "to be" is incomplete. The way the Lord introduces himself to Moses leaves us asking, "You are *what*?" What word or phrase will complete the sense? It is only in Exodus 33 that we find the answer. In verse 18, Moses asks the Lord to show him his glory. The word translated *glory* is *kabod*. Its basic meaning is something heavy. Moses wants to know what is God's weightiest characteristic. In reply the Lord says in verse 19, "I will make all my goodness pass before you." *Goodness* is the translation of the Hebrew word *tub*. This can have two main shades of meaning. It can refer both to kindness and to that which is morally right. The two come together in that God regards it as doing the right thing when he shows kindness. However, in verse 22, he indicates that this is the same as his glory passing by. The glory of God is in his goodness. Goodness is therefore God's most impressive attribute.

The LORD continues in verse 19, I "will proclaim before you my name, the LORD." God is now going to explain the meaning of his name. He is going to complete the sense of "I AM" His name means "I will be gracious to whom I will be gracious and will show mercy on whom I will show mercy." The full meaning of "I AM" is "I am merciful." Mercy is the heart of the divine character.

In Exodus 33, the LORD has been speaking with Moses about what he will do. The event itself takes place in Exodus 34:5-7:

> 5 The LORD descended in the cloud and stood with him there, and proclaimed the name of the LORD.
> 6 The LORD passed before him and proclaimed, "The LORD, the LORD, a God merciful and gracious, slow to anger, and abounding in steadfast love and faithfulness,
> 7 keeping steadfast love for thousands, forgiving iniquity and transgression and sin, but who will by no means clear the guilty, visiting the iniquity of the fathers on the children and the children's children, to the third and the fourth generation."

The first word the LORD uses as he explains the meaning of his name is *merciful*. This translates the word *rahum*. It speaks of a depth of love and tender affection. It connects with the word for the womb. The LORD's feelings for his people compare with the intensity of a woman's emotions as she carries her unborn child. A related term, *raham*, is translated "I will show mercy" in Exodus 33:19. Whereas *rahum* speaks of the intense emotion of mercifulness, *raham* draws attention to the fact that the LORD puts that deep emotion into practice. God's mercy is more than a feeling. It springs into action. It comes to the aid of needy, suffering sinners.

In verses 6–7, a cluster of related terms follow merciful. Each is worth a brief comment. The LORD is *gracious*. The word here is *hannun*. It tells us that the LORD yearns with sympathy towards people in need, and that this sympathy drives him into action to help. In 33:19, "I will be gracious" renders the related verb, *hanan*. The LORD is "slow to anger." This phrase is made up of two words, *'arek*, which means *long*, and *'ap*, the word for *nose*. This is a vividly picturesque description of God. God says that he has a long nose! It means that it takes ages for him to breathe in far enough to begin to smell the stink of sin. He does not flare up at the first whiff of wrong. The LORD is "abounding in steadfast love." "Steadfast love" translates *hesed*. This is a merciful love, a love completely undeserved. The LORD has this quality in abundance. In verse 7, we hear that God keeps steadfast love: he is not fickle and changeable. Therefore, the LORD abounds also in *faithfulness*, a translation of *'emet*. God is true to his Word, unchanging in his commitment to his people, loyal and reliable. This is all summed up in the statement *God forgives sin*. Here is the focus of his mercy. We see God's mercy against the dark background of human sinfulness. It is the LORD's constant delight to forgive. The Hebrew word here is *nasa'*. Its literal meaning is to lift up. To forgive sins is to lift the burden of guilt off the sinner, and consign the memory of his sins to oblivion.

We must make two brief comments on the rest of verse 7. First, there are no Hebrew words corresponding to the words "the guilty." The original simply says that the LORD "will by no means clear." "The guilty" is the translators' guess. The translators assumed that this phrase was talking about God's judgment. However, that does not seem to suit the context. It is perhaps better to insert the word *sin*. God will "by no means clear sin." These words are explaining how God forgives. He does not do it by clearing sin, by treating it as if it does not really matter, or by ignoring it. The word translated *clear* is *naqah*. On a number of occasions, this is translated "leave unpunished."[1] This seems to be the sense here. The LORD does not forgive sin by leaving it unpunished, but by providing a substitute to bear the punishment. There is a hint here of the sacrificial system in which a victim dies in the place of the sinner, and so the sinner is forgiven. This idea points forward to Jesus Christ and him crucified.

Second, the reference to visiting the fathers' sins on the third and fourth generation does not mean that God punishes anyone for their great-grandfather's sins. Such an idea would conflict with Ezekiel 18:20:

> The soul who sins shall die. The son shall not bear the guilt of the father, nor the father bear the guilt of the son. The righteousness

---

1   Prov. 11:21; 16:5; 17:5; 19:5,9; 28:20; Jer. 25:29; 30:11; 46:28; 49:12.

of the righteous shall be upon himself, and the wickedness of the wicked shall be upon himself.[2]

The word rendered *visiting* is *paqad*. A better translation would be *observing* or *reviewing*. These words are emphasizing God's merciful patience. He does not jump in with judgment immediately. In fact, he waits three or four generations before inflicting punishment. He reviews the situation. He observes things to see whether the children and grandchildren will turn away from the wicked ways of earlier generations. He is patient, hoping that he will not have to judge. The Bible reveals an amazingly merciful God. He is a God who judges most reluctantly. He is a God whose delight is to forgive sins because the necessary punishment has fallen on a substitute. John Piper describes the point of Exodus 34:6 as "the contrast between the sluggishness of his anger and the effusiveness of his love." Piper comments like this: "God loves to show mercy. He is not hesitant or indecisive in his desires to do good to his people. His anger must be released by a stiff safety lock, but his mercy has a hair trigger."[3]

This theme runs right through the Old Testament. We see this demonstrated by reference to a number of other Scriptures. We have examined the five terms used in Exodus 34:6–7. As we have seen, this proclamation of the LORD's name reveals what Exodus 33:19 calls the glory of his goodness. On the list of qualities in chapter 34, Robert Gordon writes: "it is as if the light of the glory/goodness of God is passed through a prism to reveal the variegated attributes of deity."[4]

We have seen also that God's mercy comes to practical expression in the forgiveness of sins. A glance at other texts using terms from this cluster of words, and related terms, will demonstrate that this is a dominant emphasis in the biblical doctrine of God. We shall examine thirteen passages that include a phrase like, "The LORD is…," or "God is…," or "You, LORD, are…" followed by a descriptive term connected with God's mercy.[5]

---

2 See also Deut. 24:16; cf. 2 Kgs. 14:6; 2 Chr. 25:4.

3 J. Piper, *The Pleasures of God* (Manila: CGM, 1991), 190f.

4 R.P. Gordon, *"tob,"* in W.A. van Gemeren, ed., *New International Dictionary of Old Testament Theology and Exegesis*, vol. 2 (Grand Rapids: Zondervan, 1997), 355.

5 There are, in fact, two main aspects of God's character highlighted in Scripture—

NUMBERS 14:11-20

Moses is at prayer. The people have rebelled against the LORD's command to enter the land. The unfavourable report from the unbelieving spies intimidates them. The LORD has threatened to destroy them and to start afresh with Moses. However, Moses intercedes for the people. He does so by quoting back to the LORD part of his own description of his character in Exodus 34:6-7. Here are the words of verses 17-20:

> 17 And now, please let the power of the Lord be great as you have promised, saying,
> 18 "The LORD is slow to anger and abounding in steadfast love, forgiving iniquity and transgression, but he will by no means clear the guilty, visiting the iniquity of the fathers on the children, to the third and the fourth generation."
> 19 Please pardon the iniquity of this people, according to the greatness of your steadfast love, just as you have forgiven this people, from Egypt until now.
> 20 Then the LORD said, "I have pardoned, according to your word."

Verse 18 contains three of the terms found in Exodus 34. The LORD is defined as "slow to anger (*'arek 'ap*) and abounding in steadfast love (*hesed*)." These qualities come to expression in the *forgiveness* (*nasa'*) of sins. In verse 19, Moses repeats the words *hesed* and *nasa'*

---

mercy and justice. There are 29 texts where such phrases are followed by an adjective associated with God's justice (Ex. 9:27; 20:5; 34:14; Deut. 4:24; 5:9; 6:15; 32:4; Josh. 24:19; 2 Chr. 12:6; Ezra 9:15; Neh. 9:8,33; Pss. 11:7; 22:3; 92:15; 99:3,5,9; 119:137; 129:4; 145:17; Isa. 6:3; 30:18; Jer. 12:1; Lam. 1:18; Dan. 9:14; Nah. 1:2; Zeph. 3:5; Zech. 9:9). The main adjectives are righteous, holy, and jealous. However, texts where such phrases are followed by mercy terms outnumber the "justice" texts by nearly 25%—there are 36 of them. This implies that the greater emphasis lies here. Ten of these 36 texts (1 Chr. 16:34; 2 Chr. 5:13; 7:3; Ezra 3:11; Pss. 106:1; 107:1; 118:1,29; 136:1; Jer. 33:11) quote the brief ascription of praise to the LORD "for he is good, for his mercy endures forever." A further six (Pss. 25:8; 34:8; 73:1; 119:68; 135:3; Lam. 3:25) also refer to the LORD as good. One text (Deut. 7:9) describes God as faithful, and then defines this by saying that he "keeps…mercy."

as he reminds the LORD how often he has "forgiven this people from Egypt until now." He also uses a different word as he prays, "Please pardon the iniquity of this people." The word here is *salah*. Unlike *nasa'*, which could be used of one person forgiving another, this word is used only of God's forgiveness. God's forgiveness is unique because, unlike human beings, he never needs forgiveness from another. This underlines the astonishing mercy involved in his forgiveness. Moses appeals directly to the character of God. In verse 20, the LORD responds by using the same word. He hears Moses' prayer, and his anger turns away. Verse 17 prefaces this passage by portraying this aspect of the LORD's character as an expression of his great power. The power of God is best seen not in creation or in mighty miracles, but in the mercy by which he overcomes his own anger.

DEUTERONOMY 4:31

Moses now speaks of the LORD as "a merciful (*rahum*) God." He is anticipating a day when the people of Israel have suffered the consequences of falling into idolatry. Then they will seek the LORD again. They will be able to find him, just because he is merciful. The verse goes on to explain what that means: "He will not leave you or destroy you or forget the covenant with your fathers that he swore to them."

2 CHRONICLES 30:1-9

Hezekiah is summoning the people of Israel to join the people of Judah at Jerusalem to keep the Passover. He sends a letter to every part of the country. It urges the people to end their stubborn unfaithfulness, and to return to the LORD. Hezekiah backs up his appeal by reminding the people of Israel of God's character:

> if you return to the LORD, your brothers and your children will find compassion with their captors and return to this land. For the LORD your God is gracious and merciful and will not turn away his face from you, if you return to him (verse 9).

Hezekiah assures the people that the LORD is gracious (*hannun*) and merciful (*rahum*). The word *compassion* is the related verb, *raham*.

NEHEMIAH 9:5-31

The Levites are leading the people in a prayer of confession. They acknowledge the LORD's grace and power: he chose Abram; he liberated Israel from Egypt; he led them through the desert; he gave them the law. Yet constant disobedience marked Israel's history. However, their confident hope now is based on what is said in the second half of verse 17: "But you are a God ready to forgive, gracious and merciful, slow to anger and abounding in steadfast love, and did not forsake them." Here we find the familiar terms *hannun, rahum, 'arek 'ap,* and *hesed.* We are beginning to see that this combination of descriptions is the regular portrait of the LORD running right through the Old Testament.

The phrase "ready to forgive" translates *selihah,* a noun related to the verb *salah,* used by Moses and the LORD in Numbers 14. In this phrase, the people recognize that the LORD is the God of forgiveness. It is his essential nature to be forgiving towards sinners. The prayer continues by pointing to examples from history confirming this as the character of God. Even when they made the golden calf, they found themselves preserved by the LORD's "great mercies (*raham*)" (verse 19). He never withdrew his guidance. He fed them with the manna. They lacked nothing. He gave them the land as promised. He multiplied their numbers. Still the people were disobedient and rebellious. As a result, they suffered at the hands of their enemies. However, when they cried out to the LORD, once again he confronted them with his "great mercies (*raham*)" (verse 27). He sent the judges to save them, only for their hearts to turn away yet again. The pattern of subjugation by enemies, crying to the LORD, and merciful deliverance was repeated time and again. Verse 31 sums Israel's experience up: "in your great mercies you did not make an end of them or forsake them, for you are a gracious and merciful God." Once again, the terms *hannun* and *rahum* come as a pair.

PSALM 86

David cries to the LORD in a time of trouble. Aware of his poverty and need, he prays for preservation and for the restoration of joy. The basis of his confidence in praying like this is in verse 5: "For you, O Lord, are good and forgiving, abounding in steadfast love to all who call upon you." Here we have the words *tob*—related to *tub,* the term that defined

God's glory in Exodus 33—*salah*, and *hesed*. Already in verse 3, David has prayed, "Be gracious to me, O Lord." *Gracious* renders *hanan*. From verse 8 onwards, the psalm becomes more positive in tone. Because the LORD is such a God, he is incomparable. The greatness of his works is destined to be acknowledged universally. For the time being, men who fail to recognize the glory of the LORD are attacking David, but he expresses his confidence again in the words of verse 15: "But you, O Lord, are a God merciful and gracious, slow to anger and abounding in steadfast love and faithfulness."

The same four familiar terms which came in Nehemiah 9 reoccur here: *rahum, hannun, 'arek 'ap*, and *hesed*, along with *'emet*, another of the cluster from Exodus. In fact, these words are an exact quotation of the second half of Exodus 34:6. David has referred to God's *hesed* earlier, in verse 13, and he prays again that God will be gracious (*hanan*) in verse 16.

PSALM 100

This psalm of joy and thankfulness comes to its climax in verse 5: "For the LORD is good; his steadfast love endures forever, and his faithfulness to all generations." Here are two words from the familiar collection: *tob*, and *hesed*, and the word *'emunah*, which is connected to *'emet*. *'Emunah* is used in Exodus 17:12. It speaks of the steadiness of Moses' hands as Aaron and Hur held them up after Moses had grown weary. As long as Moses' hands were raised and steady, Israel prevailed in the battle with Amalek. To speak of the LORD as faithful is to say that he has a safe pair of hands. A sinner who casts himself on God's mercy will never be dropped.

PSALM 103:1-18

This psalm begins by celebrating the many benefits the LORD gives to his people. Amongst these benefits are "steadfast love (*hesed*) and mercy (*raham*)" (verse 4). Verse 8 states the basis of the LORD's kindness: "The LORD is merciful and gracious, slow to anger and abounding in steadfast love." Here are the four familiar terms: *rahum, hannun, 'arek 'ap*, and *hesed*. Apart from the fact that the name "the LORD" is inserted after the word *gracious* in Hebrew, this again is a citation of Exodus 34:6. That verse stated what God really is like. He is so intent that we should understand mercy as his heart that he goes on repeating it. The verses following draw out the implications of the fact that God is like this: he restrains his anger; he deals with us quite contrary to what we deserve; he removes our sins. Verse 11 tells of the greatness of his steadfast love (*hesed*), and verse 13 speaks of his compassion (*raham*). In the context of a world full of uncertainty, "the steadfast love (*hesed*) of the Lord is from everlasting to everlasting…" (verse 17).

PSALM 111

Here the psalmist leads us in praise to the Lord for his wonderful works. The most wonderful of his works are those displaying his kindness to people. In verse 4, we see that "the Lord is gracious (*rahum*) and merciful (*hannun*)." Then we hear of the Lord's provision for his people. Twice (in verses 7 and 8) reference is made to the Lord's faithfulness (*'emet*).

PSALM 116:1-5

In this psalm, the singer's love for the Lord is declared. Our love for him is a response to his love for us. He has heard our cry for deliverance. Verse 5 says that the Lord is gracious and merciful. Here again are the words *hannun* and *raham*.

PSALM 145:1-9

David begins by extolling the Lord for his greatness. This is evident from his works, but as verse 7 indicates, his greatest works are those giving us cause to pour forth the fame of his goodness (*tub*). The next verse makes this statement: "The Lord is gracious and merciful, slow to anger and abounding in steadfast love."

Yet again, the four major terms which sum up the doctrine of God occur together: *rahum*, *hannun*, *'arek 'ap*, and *hesed*. The next verse tells us again that "the Lord is good (*tob*)," and speaks of his mercy (*raham*). The word *abounding* in verse 8 translates a different Hebrew word from *abounding* in Exodus 34:6, Numbers 14:18, Nehemiah 9:17, Psalm 86:5 and 15, and Psalm 103:8. In all those texts, the word is *rab*. It simply emphasizes the vast quantity of mercy God possesses. The word here is *gadol*. This word refers less to quantity than to quality. It is certainly true that the Lord has an abundant quantity of mercy. It is equally true that every particle of his mercy is *of the finest possible kind*. There is richness and splendour to God's mercy, which moves us to wonder and to praise.

JOEL 2:12-14

The first part of Joel's prophecy has spoken about the coming Day of the LORD. That day of darkness and gloom has been foreshadowed in the judgment God's people are facing at the time of Joel's ministry. This passage is an invitation to them to return to the LORD. The second part of verse 13 supports this exhortation with another clear allusion to Exodus 34:6. God's character makes repentance a genuine option: "for he is gracious and merciful, slow to anger, and abounding in steadfast love; and he relents over disaster." Here again we have the four standard terms, *hannun*, *rahum*, *'arek 'ap*, and *hesed*. In practice, a God of such a character is reluctant to inflict disaster, and very eager to bless.

JONAH 3:6-4:2

Why was Jonah so reluctant to go to Nineveh to proclaim God's message there? It was because he knew his God so well. When Jonah finally came to Nineveh, after first running away, his preaching met with a response of general repentance, led by the king himself. As a result, the disaster God had threatened through Jonah did not materialize. This was exactly what Jonah had expected, and it made him angry. In Jonah 4:2, he says this to the LORD:

> That is why I made haste to flee to Tarshish; for I knew that you are a gracious God and merciful, slow to anger and abounding in steadfast love, and relenting from disaster.

Once again the four regular terms appear: *hannun*, *rahum*, *'arek 'ap*, and *hesed*. Jonah knows what his God is like because he knows the Word of God. He is able to quote Exodus 34:6. However, Jonah wants the LORD's mercy to be Israel's exclusive prerogative. He resents the thought of the LORD sharing his mercy with the Assyrian rabble! At the same time, Jonah knows the open-heartedness of God. He knows that the LORD is world-hearted, that his mercy extends to the ends of the earth. Such is the God of the Old Testament, the God of the Bible— and Jonah cannot change him.

NAHUM 1:1-3

A generation after Jonah's time, the people of Nineveh had reverted to their old ways. This time, the LORD called Nahum to prophesy against the wicked city. His prophecy begins with stern words of warning. In the middle of this solemn passage, we come across these words in verse 3: "The LORD is slow to anger." Here is the phrase *'arek 'ap*. Here is a hint even to people who have gone back on their earlier repentance: mercy is still available because the LORD's anger takes so long to ignite.

This, then, is the God of the Bible. Mercy is his lifeblood, his heartbeat, his smile, his embrace. As Micah 7:18-20 says:

> 18 Who is a God like you, pardoning (*nasa'*) iniquity and passing over transgression for the remnant of his inheritance? He does not retain his anger forever, because he delights in steadfast love (*hesed*).
>
> 19 He will again have compassion (*raham*) on us; he will tread our iniquities under foot. You will cast all our sins into the depths of the sea.
>
> 20 You will show faithfulness (*'emet*) to Jacob and steadfast love (*hesed*) to Abraham, as you have sworn to our fathers from the days of old.

Section summary and personal application

REMEMBER

The LORD descended in the cloud and stood with him there, and proclaimed the name of the LORD. The LORD passed before him and proclaimed, "The LORD, the LORD, a God merciful and gracious, slow to anger, and abounding in steadfast love and faithfulness, keeping steadfast love for thousands, forgiving iniquity and transgression and sin, but who will by no means clear the guilty, visiting the iniquity of the fathers

on the children and the children's children, to the third and
the fourth generation."
—*Exodus 34:5-7*

REFLECT

We have seen clearly in Scripture that God is a God of mercy. He is
merciful and gracious, slow to anger and abounding in steadfast love
and faithfulness. He forgives iniquity. These are the weighty characteristics of God as he has revealed himself to us.

1. List ways in which God's mercy has been and continues to be
   evidenced in your life.
2. List ways in which you can cultivate a merciful and forgiving
   attitude in life.

"Be kind one to another, tenderhearted, forgiving one another even as
God in Christ has forgiven you" (Ephesians 4:32).

REJOICE

Great God of wonders! All Thy ways
    Are matchless, Godlike and divine;
But the fair glories of Thy grace
    More Godlike and unrivalled shine.

    Who is a pardoning God like Thee?
      Or who has grace so rich and free?

Angels and men, resign your claim
    To pity, mercy, love and grace:
These glories crown Jehovah's Name
    With an incomparable glaze.

O may this strange, this matchless grace,
    This Godlike miracle of love,
Fill the whole earth with grateful praise,
    And all th'angelic choirs above.
—*Samuel Davies (1723–1761)*

PART 2: KEY CREEDS AND CONFESSIONS

A. THE EARLY CREEDS

The *Apostles' Creed*[6] and the *Nicene Creed*[7] begin in a similar way. They speak of God as the Father, the Almighty, and the Creator. The *Nicene Creed* also adds the word "one." Its opening words are, "I believe in one God."

1. God as Father

J.N.D. Kelly argues that *Father* and *Almighty* are two distinct statements about God. It is not simply that the Father is almighty, but that first God is Father, then he is Almighty. Kelly finds it significant that God's fatherhood is mentioned first.[8] Early Christian writers often associated God's fatherhood with his goodness and love. For example, Clement of Rome, writing in the second century, speaks of "our gentle and compassionate Father."[9] The fatherhood of God was a special theme in Jesus' teaching. However, it was not new. The Old Testament speaks of God as Father 15 times. It is striking how closely this title for God links with his mercy. This is clearest in the covenant with David. God promises to be the Father of the son of David who will sit on his throne. To be Father means to maintain steadfast love and mercy. This is clear from the following verses in which the LORD makes his covenant commitment:

> I will be to him a Father, and he shall be to me a son. When he commits iniquity, I will discipline him with the rod of men, with the stripes of the sons of men, but my steadfast love (*hesed*) will not depart from him (2 Samuel 7:14-15).

---

6   See Appendix 1.
7   See Appendix 2.
8   J.N.D. Kelly, *Early Christian Creeds* (Harlow: Longman, 1972), 132f.
9   Clement of Rome, *Epistle to the Corinthians*, 11.9.

I will be to him a Father, and he shall be to me a son. I will not take my steadfast love (*hesed*) from him (1 Chronicles 17:13).

Psalm 89 is a celebration of the Davidic covenant. Here are verses 24-28:

24 My faithfulness (*'emunah*) and my steadfast love (*hesed*) shall be with him, and in my name shall his horn be exalted.
25 I will set his hand on the sea and his right hand on the rivers.
26 He shall cry to me, "You are my Father, my God, and the Rock of my salvation."
27 And I will make him the firstborn, the highest of the kings of the earth.
28 My steadfast love (*hesed*) I will keep for him forever, and my covenant will stand firm for him.

In stating first that God is Father, the early Creeds demonstrated their sensitivity to the major Scriptural emphasis.

2. God as Almighty

In the original Greek form of the creeds, the word translated *almighty* is *pantokrator*. This really means all-ruling. It does not refer to God's unlimited ability. It emphasizes the fact that the Lord governs absolutely everything. The word occurs many times in the Bible.[10] Revelation 19:6 says, "Hallelujah! For the Lord our God the Almighty reigns." The Lord God is Almighty in the sense that he reigns over all.

A second-century writer, Theophilos of Antioch, explained the almightiness of God like this: "The heights of the heavens, and the depths of the abysses, and the limits of the world are in his hand."[11] This all-ruling sovereignty enables God to carry through his great purpose of disseminating his mercy in Christ.

---

10 2 Cor. 6:18; Rev. 1:8; 4:8; 11:17; 15:3; 16:7,14; 19:6,15; 21:22; and in the Greek translation of the OT *kurios pantokrator* is the normal rendering of the phrase "LORD of hosts."

11 Theophilos, *To Autolycus*, 1.4.

3. God as Creator

The creeds describe God as "Creator of heaven and earth." This stresses the complete distinction between God and everything else. The universe is not an emanation of God. It is not as if the universe is the body, of which God is the Spirit. God and his creation are completely different realities.

Equally, the creation is not the work of some other being than the God who is the Father Almighty. He alone is the source of absolutely everything existing outside him. We are not pawns in some inconclusive cosmic battle between rival gods. There are only two realities— God and his creation. It is just because the creation is God's work that he rules over it. He fulfils his purpose of enacting his mercy in Christ on the stage of creation.

The *Nicene Creed* expands on the basic statement that God is the Creator of heaven and earth by adding the phrase, "of all things, visible and invisible." This addition serves to emphasize the fact that there are some things which we are unable to see—angels and the spiritual heaven as distinct from the visible heavens, for example. However, these too have no existence apart from the fact that God brought them into being.

4. God as One

This means that he is the only God. This was an important statement in the polytheistic context of Roman religion. R.M. Grant has noted the encounters in the Book of Acts between the early Christian mission and polytheism. Three are particularly significant.[12]

First, in Acts 14:8-18 we read of Paul and Barnabas at Lystra. In response to the healing of a crippled man, the crowds assumed that the missionaries were human likenesses of Zeus and Hermes. These were the chief gods of their region.

Second, in Acts 17:16-34 we find Paul in Athens. We learn that "the city was full of idols" (verse 16). There was even an altar "to the unknown god" (verse 23). This was an insurance policy. This extra altar was there just in case they had missed some god by mistake.

---

12 R.M. Grant, *Gods and the One God* (London: SPCK, 1986), 25-28.

Third, in Acts 19:23-41 we hear of the riot in Ephesus. It was caused by the drop in income the image-makers were suffering because of the success of the apostles' evangelism. Ephesus housed "the temple of the great goddess Artemis" (verse 27). Her temple had brought fame to Ephesus and it was the first of the seven wonders of the ancient world.

Grant also notes how Paul opposed idolatry.[13] He cites Paul's words in 1 Thessalonians 1:9: "you turned to God from idols to serve the living and true God." The implication of these words is that idols are lifeless and false. Grant refers also to 1 Corinthians 12:2-3, where he contrasts "the creative speech of the divine Spirit" with "mute idols." Paul's clearest statement against the polytheism of paganism comes in 1 Corinthians 8:4-6:

> we know that an idol has no real existence, and that there is no God but one. For although there may be so-called gods in heaven or on earth—as indeed there are many "gods" and many "lords"— yet for us there is one God, the Father, from whom are all things and for whom we exist, and one Lord, Jesus Christ, through whom are all things and through whom we exist.

Therefore, there is only one God. Idols are non-existent, imaginary gods. Grant says, "the model for the New Testament view of idols was set in the Old Testament."[14] The truth that the LORD of mercy is the only real God is stressed repeatedly in the Old Testament. For example, in Isaiah 49:9 we read, "I am God, and there is no other; I am God, and there is none like me."[15]

The nearest thing to a statement of faith in the Old Testament is the *shema* in Deuteronomy 6:4: "Hear, O Israel: The LORD our God, the LORD is one." *Shema* is the Hebrew word translated *hear* at the beginning of the verse. In Jewish understanding, hearing includes taking what you hear seriously. Therefore, this solemn declaration that the LORD is the only God is a challenge to remain true to him. That is why the next verse

---

13 Grant, *Gods and the One God*, 46-49.

14 Grant, *Gods and the One God*, 45.

15 See also Deut. 4:35,39; 32:39; 1 Sam. 2:2; 2 Sam. 22:32; 1 Kgs. 8:60; 2 Kgs. 19:19; Isa. 37:16,20; 43:10; 44:6,8; 45:5,6,14,18,21,22; Joel 2:27.

reads: "You shall love the LORD your God with all your heart and with all your soul and with all your might" (Deuteronomy 6:5).

In Mark 12:29-30, Jesus quotes Deuteronomy 6:4-5. He calls it "the most important" of all the commandments. All-embracing love for the Lord is the consequence of believing in his uniqueness. Because he is the only God, he has a claim on every aspect of our lives.

B. THE REFORMATION CONFESSIONS

Seven common themes summarize the teaching of the confessions:

1. There is only one living and true God

This recognizes that other religions claim to have their gods. However, they have no life. They are false. The real God is unique. The *Second Helvetic Confession* (1562, revised in 1564) backs this up with several Scriptures, including these: "Hear, O Israel: The LORD our God, the LORD is one" (Deuteronomy 6:4) and "I am the LORD, and there is no other, besides me there is no God"(Isaiah 45:5).

In the light of these texts, this confession describes the idea of a plurality of gods as an abomination. Some of the confessions stress that the source of God's life is in and of himself. He is not dependent on something else. The existence of God is a matter of necessity.

2. This one living and true God is Spirit

Having said that God is Spirit, the *Westminster Confession* (1646) immediately explains what this means: he is "invisible, without body, parts, or passions." The first three of these descriptions belong together. It is because he has no physical body that we cannot see God. As John 1:18 says, "No one has ever seen God." Having no body, God cannot be divided up into constituent parts. His essence is a unity. Everything that God does, he does with complete integrity. He has no conflicting intentions. Paul summarizes the distress of the person who desires to obey God's law but finds that his personality is divided: "I do not do what I want, but I do the very thing I hate" (Romans 7:15). However, it is never like that with God. A body is always vulnerable. A limb can be amputated because of a serious illness. The person is still alive, but now he is severely handicapped. God has no handicaps. A high-speed car crash may result in the body being crushed. We can be killed. God's life is never in danger.

The confession also says that God is "without passions." At this point, the Reformers are taking up a doctrine much loved by early Christian thinkers. However, such a description of God has been criticized in recent years. A God without passions sounds cold and remote. Yet the Scriptures portray God as passionate in his love. He is a God who burns with anger, who is excited to show mercy, who finds great joy in blessing his people. He is a God grieved by sin and thrilled to save. How, then, can God be "without passions"? One way of explaining it is given by an Anglican writer, Bishop Burnet:

> Passion produces a vehemence of action; so when there is, in the providences of God, such a vehemence as, according to the manner of men, would import a passion, then that passion is ascribed to God. When he punishes men for sin, he is said to be angry; when he does that by severe and redoubled strokes, he is said to be full of fury and revenge; when he punishes for idolatry, or any dishonour done to himself, he is said to be jealous; when he changes the course of his proceedings, he is said to repent.[16]

It is striking how many times Burnet uses the words "said to." God is said to be angry, to be full of fury and revenge, to be jealous, to repent. By implication, Burnet is saying, "But of course he is not really like that." However, in my view, this leads to a rather unsatisfactory doctrine of God. Is God's anger just some automatic reaction without a surge of feeling? Does the idea of passionless love and mercy even make sense? Is it possible to grieve without feeling grief? What is more, if the biblical language about God's anger, jealousy, mercy, love, and grief is not the language of reality, then the Bible is no longer a genuine revelation of God. It is more like a cartoon comic that actually tells us nothing about God.

We need to understand what the early Christian writers meant when they spoke of God as being without passions. Many of the early fathers were careful to define this doctrine very precisely. They did

---

16 Quoted by R. Shaw, *An Exposition of the Confession of Faith* (1845), 26f.

not mean that God has no feelings or that he is unable to suffer. What they meant was that if God suffers, he does so voluntarily. He is never out of control. He is never at the mercy of circumstances that defeat him. He is always in charge, never the victim. Even when he reacts passionately, he remains in sovereign control. He never flares up and loses his temper. When he is angry, his anger burns passionately. His love is not an expression of mere sentimentality, but he does love with feeling. Otherwise, he would be a God who does not care.

A modern writer who develops these early Christian nuances is the Japanese theologian, Kazoh Kitamori. He speaks of "the pain of God," but is still prepared to say that God is without passions, in that his pain derives from his will to embrace the unlovely, not from external circumstances.

3. This one living and true Spirit is sovereign

The confessions use many terms gathered under the heading of God's sovereignty. For example, they speak of his greatness, his blessedness, his infinity, and his all-sufficiency. God is not dependent on other things. He has no needs. He is the fount from which everything has come, and every day he is still guiding all things according to his own will and for his own glory.

In 1993, a commemoration of the 350th anniversary of the Westminster Assembly was held in London. James Montgomery Boice preached the opening sermon. His theme was the sovereignty of God. His text was Daniel 4, which includes these words in verses 34-35:

> his dominion is an everlasting dominion, and his kingdom endures from generation to generation; all the inhabitants of the earth are accounted as nothing, and he does according to his will among the host of heaven and among the inhabitants of the earth; and none can stay his hand or say to him, "What have you done?"

Boice highlighted three blessings we receive in recognizing God's sovereignty: (1) it deepens our worship of God; (2) it brings comfort in the midst of trials, temptation and sorrow; and (3) it provides encouragement for evangelism.[17]

---

17 J.M. Boice, "The Sovereignty of God," in J.L. Carson and D.W. Hall, ed., *To Glorify and Enjoy God* (Edinburgh: The Banner of Truth Trust, 1994), 197-209.

4. This sovereign God has all the equipment he needs for the exercise of his sovereignty

The confessions taught God's *wisdom* and *total knowledge*. There is never any risk that he might make a mistake in exercising his sovereignty. The confessions speak of God's *almighty power*. Robert Reymond notes that God's *omnipotence* does not mean that he can do absolutely anything. The Scriptures tell us of four things which God cannot do: (1) he cannot lie (Hebrews 6:17-18; Titus 1:2); (2) he cannot break his promise (2 Corinthians 1:20); (3) he cannot disown himself (2 Timothy 2:13); and (4) he cannot change (Number 23:19; 1 Samuel 15:29). These impossibilities are vital to God's perfection.[18] God's almighty power is his ability to carry out his will unfailingly as he rules over everything. The confessions also speak of God's *eternity*. This extends in both directions. He never began to be. He will never cease to be. He endures throughout all time—and beyond—and yet is never vulnerable to the aging process. As Psalm 90:2 puts it, "Before the mountains were brought forth, or ever you had formed the earth and the world, from everlasting to everlasting you are God." This is vital to God's sovereignty. If anything had come before God, it might compromise his unrivalled supremacy. This is not so!

The confessions also teach God's *omnipresence*: everything and everyone exists every moment in the inescapable presence of God. David asks the question, "Where shall I go from your Spirit? Or where shall I flee from your presence?" (Psalm 139:7). The answer is, "Nowhere!" Consequently, everything and everyone is permanently under God's sovereignty.

The confessions mention God's *glory*. The Hebrew word normally rendered *glory* is *kabod*. It has to do with a heavy weight. The Greek word is *doxa*: it can be translated *opinion*. Putting the two together, we may say that God is of weighty importance, and that our opinion ought to be that he is of all-surpassing significance. A heavyweight God must leave his mark as he exercises his sovereignty.

5. This sovereign God is the God of mercy

In addition to mercy itself, the confessions mention thirteen more

---

18 R. Reymond, *A New Systematic Theology of the Christian Faith* (Nashville: Nelson, 1998), 192.

divine attributes relating to the Lord's exercise of mercy. Five of them form the dark background against which God's mercy stands out in all its brilliance: God is holy; he hates sin; he is just; he inflicts terrible judgments upon sin; he is unable simply to ignore guilt. God's holiness makes his mercy so amazing.

The other eight attributes are aspects or expressions of mercy: God is immutable, loving, gracious, long-suffering, abundant in goodness, abundant in truth, forgiving, and the "rewarder" of those who seek him. The echoes of the Old Testament revelation of God flowing from Exodus 34:6-7 are obvious here.

6. All this does not mean that we know everything about the true and living God

Some of the confessions include the word *incomprehensible* in their description of God. We understand some things about God. We understand especially that he is merciful, because he has told us so. But there are depths in the being of God that he has seen fit to conceal. Even in those areas where we do know about God, we must never assume that we know all that there is to know. We must always retain humility, admitting the possibility that we have misunderstood. Even where the Bible has clearly revealed truth about God, our finite minds, further limited by sin, may have misread what God has said. So please do not just assume that what I have written in this book is right. Go to the Scriptures yourself and read them prayerfully. Be like the Bereans. Examine the Scriptures daily to find out whether these things are so. God describes such an approach as "noble" (Acts 17:11).

7. The confessions emphasize the practical consequences of confessing faith in this God

One of the earliest of the Reformed confessions was the *Geneva Confession* of 1536. It says this: "We acknowledge that there is only one God, whom we are both to worship and serve, and in whom we are to put all our confidence and hope."[19]

---

19 *Genevan Confession*, 2.

C. MODERN CONFESSIONS OF FAITH

1. Confession of Faith of the United Church of Northern India

This confession locates itself firmly in the Reformed tradition. In its preamble, it commends the following doctrinal standards: the *Westminster Confession* (1646), the *Canons of Dort* (1618–1619), the *Heidelberg Catechism* (1563), and the *Augsburg Confession* (1530).

The article on God centres on the fact that God is a Spirit who is distinct not only from material things, but also from all other spirits. A list of divine attributes builds up to a climax in the word *love*. This appears to be a significant and deliberate emphasis. The confession closely echoes the *Westminster Shorter Catechism* at this point. The catechism describes God as "unchangeable in his being, wisdom, power, holiness, justice, goodness, and truth," while the Indian Confession says that God is "unchangeable in his being, wisdom, power, holiness, justice, goodness, truth and love." Evidently, the theologians of Northern India saw that the British document had stopped short by failing to mention God's chief, defining attribute. They recognized that this attribute must be included if their confession was to be in tune with the biblical emphasis on the divine mercy. The confession stresses the fact that God *must* be worshipped, and that he is the only legitimate object of worship.

2. Confession of Faith of the Huria Batak Protestant

This confession defines itself as "the continuation" of the three ancient creeds, the *Apostles'*, the *Nicene* and the *Athanasian*.[20] It contains many echoes of those documents. It begins with a list of divine attributes. It proclaims that God is one, eternal, almighty, unchanging, faithful, all-knowing, inscrutable, a righteous Judge, gracious, and all-bountiful. This final attribute brings the list to a climax in a way according with the biblical emphasis on God's mercy. The next sentence, likewise, builds up to a climax with the statement that God is "full of love." His omnipresence, truth, and holiness have been mentioned, but his love completes the list. Having said that, the confession is careful to emphasize that God's character is not only gracious. He is also a God

---

20 Leith, ed., *Creeds of the Churches*, 556.

of holiness and justice. To deny this would lead to an unbiblical distortion of the truth about God.

3. Confession of Faith of House Churches in China

This confession has been called "a classic restatement of Protestant Christian theology."[21] The aptness of this description is clear from its doctrine of God. The confession proclaims that there is "only one true God," and that he is eternal and self-existent. He "created all things," and "is the Lord of human history." It is in the course of history that God "manifests his sovereignty." The confession insists that this is true "in all of human history." Nothing at all lies outside the sphere of the divine lordship. The confession offers the following list of divine attributes: "The almighty God is just, holy, faithful, and merciful. He is omniscient, omnipresent, and omnipotent." However, primacy of place is given, at least by implication, to God's mercy. Referring to the three Persons of the Trinity, the confession speaks of the different role of each "in the work of redemption." Each makes his distinctive contribution to human salvation. This stress suggests that the confession regards human redemption and salvation as the chief of the works of God—so all of his various attributes combine to further his work of mercy.

Section summary and personal application

REMEMBER

I believe in God the Father Almighty, maker of heaven and earth: And in Jesus Christ His only Son, our Lord.... I believe in the Holy Spirit, the holy Christian church, the communion of saints, the forgiveness of sins, the resurrection of the body, and the life everlasting. Amen.
—*The Apostles' Creed*

---

21 Aikman, *The Beijing Factor*, 93.

REFLECT

Creeds and confessions systematize our faith. We have examined the doctrine of God and discovered many glorious truths. However, none will benefit us *personally* unless we live in the light of these glorious truths. How should the following truths about God influence your life?

1. God is your Father—how does this affect your relationship with him?
2. God is Almighty—how does this truth affect your perception of problems?
3. God is your Creator—how does this affect your sense of accountability?
4. God is God—what idols do you need to de-throne in your heart and life?

Let us live as *worshippers*, delighting ourselves in the glory of God.

REJOICE

All the way my Saviour leads me;
  What have I to ask beside?
Can I doubt His tender mercy,
  Who through life has been my Guide?
Heav'nly peace, divinest comfort,
  Here by faith in Him to dwell!
For I know, whate'er befall me,
  Jesus doeth all things well.

All the way my Saviour leads me
  O the fullness of His love!
Perfect rest to me is promised
  In my Father's house above.
When my spirit, clothed immortal,
  Wings its flight to realms of day
This my song through endless ages—
  Jesus led me all the way.
—*Fanny Crosby (1820–1915)*

PART 3: KEY HISTORICAL DEVELOPMENTS

In this section, I shall first outline the teaching of two representative theologians from different periods of Christian history, both of whom celebrate the divine mercy. Second, I shall consider the distinction often made between God's *communicable* and *incommunicable* attributes.

A. TWO REPRESENTATIVE THEOLOGIANS

1. Cyprian of Carthage

Cyprian was born around A.D. 200 somewhere in Africa. His family were wealthy pagans, and he was not converted until he was in his forties, by which time he was living in Carthage, on the North African coast. Within three years of his conversion, he had become the senior pastor in the Carthage area. A year later, he had to flee for his life to escape the persecution initiated by the Emperor Decius. The following year, when the persecution had subsided, he returned. Six years later, he was arrested during persecution initiated by Emperor Valerian. After a year in captivity, he was executed on September 14, 258. He was the first African pastor martyred for the faith.

About a year before his arrest, Cyprian wrote a treatise entitled, *On the Advantage of Patience*. At the time, the African church was embroiled in a controversy about the rebaptism of converts from heretical churches. While Cyprian was very clear where he stood on that matter, he was also concerned to maintain Christian unity in a spirit of patience. This work was designed to promote patient acceptance of one another on the part of all true Christians.

Cyprian points out early on in the treatise that we can only achieve patience ourselves if we have known the patience of God.[22] This leads him into an exposition of God's patience. He starts by pointing to the evidence that God is patient. He notes that the earth is full of profane temples, images and idolatrous worship. He observes that people in

---

22 Cyprian, *On the Advantage of Patience*, 2.

general treat God's majesty and honour with contempt. In spite of these things, God makes the sun rise daily and shine on all people. He makes the rain fall, and excludes no one from its benefits. God patiently sends the seasons, and provides food for all people. Cyprian continues like this:

> while God is provoked with frequent, yes, continual offenses, he tempers his anger, and waits patiently for the day of retribution, which he has pre-determined. And even though he has revenge in his power, he prefers to be long-suffering in his patience. He prefers to wait, to bear with us in his mercy, to delay judgment, so that, if at all possible, the long career of evil might at some time be changed; so that man, however deeply he is involved in the contagion of error and crime, may be converted to God, even at a late hour. God himself warns us: he says, "I have no pleasure in the death of the wicked, but that the wicked turn from his way and live" (Ezekiel 33:11). And again, "'Yet even now,' declares the LORD, "return to me'" (Joel 2:12). And again: "Return to the LORD, your God, for he is gracious and merciful, slow to anger, and abounding in steadfast love; and he relents over disaster" (Joel 2:13).

Cyprian quotes Paul's words in Romans 2:4: "God's kindness is meant to lead you to repentance." Cyprian continues:

> God's judgment is just, because it is delayed, because it is repeatedly deferred, and for a long time, so that by God's long-enduring patience, man may be benefited for life eternal.[23]

2. John Calvin

John Calvin was a Frenchman, although for most of his ministry he lived in Geneva, Switzerland. He lived from 1509 to 1564 and was the leading Reformed theologian of his day. John Hesselink finds "the key concepts in Calvin's portrayal of God" to be free mercy, goodness, and love.[24]

---

23 Cyprian, *On the Advantage of Patience*, 4.

24 I.J. Hesselink, *Calvin's First Catechism: A Commentary* (Louisville: Westminster John Knox Press, 1997), 116.

In the opening chapters of his *Institutes of the Christian Religion*, Calvin addresses the issue of our knowledge of God. In the course of this discussion, it becomes obvious how he perceives the character of God. He rejects mere speculation about God's *essence*. What matters is "what kind of *being* God is," by which Calvin means, "what things are agreeable to his nature." However, we may not devise for ourselves a God of any character we please. We must "have him in the character in which he manifests himself." Calvin notes that we do not have a clear understanding of God's nature unless we see him as "the origin and fountain of all goodness."[25]

In his very first paragraph, Calvin describes the "blessings which unceasingly distil to us from heaven," as evidence of "the infinitude of good which resides in God." A little later, he writes, "in the Lord, and none but he, dwell the true light of wisdom, solid virtue, exuberant goodness."[26]

In the following chapter, Calvin says that we worship God because we recognize him to be "the fountain of all goodness." We perceive "that God our Maker supports us by his power, rules us by his providence, fosters us by his goodness, and visits us with all kinds of blessings." Calvin then sums up his understanding of God in these words:

> we must be persuaded not only that as he once formed the world, so he sustains it by his boundless power, governs it by his wisdom, preserves it by his goodness, in particular, rules the human race with justice and judgment, bears with them in mercy, shields them by his protection; but also that not a particle of light, or wisdom, or justice, or power, or rectitude, or genuine truth, will anywhere be found, which does not flow from him, and of which he is not the cause; in this way we must learn to expect and ask all things from him, and thankfully ascribe to him whatever we receive.[27]

These words confirm the truth of Hesselink's observation: Calvin does indeed give generous mercy first place in his portrait of God. He sums

---

25 J. Calvin, *Institutes of the Christian Religion*, 2.2.

26 Calvin, *Institutes*, 1.1.

27 Calvin, *Institutes*, 2.1.

up his doctrine of God in five phrases: he governs all things, he is the source of every blessing, he is good and merciful, he is our Father and Lord, and he is a just judge. Such a God is characterized by faithfulness and clemency. He is a God in whom we may contentedly confide.[28]

B. COMMUNICABLE AND INCOMMUNICABLE ATTRIBUTES

By the beginning of the seventeenth century, it had become customary for the attributes of God to be divided between *incommunicable* and *communicable* attributes. Incommunicable attributes are those having no counterpart in human life, such as God's self-sufficiency or his infinity. Communicable attributes are those reflected, at least to some extent, in human nature. These in turn are often subdivided into mental attributes, such as knowledge or wisdom, and moral attributes, such as patience or mercy.

Not everyone has been happy with this scheme. Both A.A. Hodge in the nineteenth century, and Donald Macleod in the twentieth century, have pointed out that even God's so-called communicable attributes have incommunicable properties.[29] For example, God's patience is infinite, while we cannot claim the same for our own patience. Consequently, Macleod finds these classifications "artificial and misleading." What interests me is that even those theologians who use this scheme tend to give prominence to the moral branch of the communicable attributes. Therefore, Louis Berkhof writes, "The moral attributes of God are generally regarded as the most glorious of the divine perfections."[30]

Robert Lewis Dabney begins his consideration of God's moral attributes with these words: "We have now reached that which is the most glorious, and at the same time, the most important class of God's attributes; those which qualify him as an infinitely perfect moral Being." A few lines later Dabney continues:

---

28 Calvin, *Institutes*, 2.2.

29 A.A. Hodge, *Outlines of Theology* (1879; reprint, Edinburgh: The Banner of Truth Trust, 1972), 137; D. Macleod, *Behold Your God* (Fearn: Christian Focus, 1990), 20.

30 L. Berkhof, *Systematic Theology* (1941; reprint, Edinburgh: The Banner of Truth Trust, 1958), 70.

Blessed be his name, he is declared, by his works and Word, to be a God of complete moral perfections. And this is the ground on which the Scriptures base their most frequent and strongest claims to the praise and love of his creatures. His power, his knowledge, his wisdom, his immutability are glorious; but the glory and loveliness of his moral attributes excels.[31]

It is my contention that to give this prominence to God's moral attributes is to be in line with the Bible's main emphasis on God's mercy. Herman Bavinck goes further, and comes even closer to the biblical priority, when he says, "Among the ethical attributes first place should be assigned to God's goodness."[32] Bavinck proceeds to analyze God's goodness into its component parts. These include loving-kindness, compassion, patience, grace, and love.[33]

PART 4: KEY POINTS OF PRACTICAL APPLICATION

1. *Since God has revealed himself as a God of mercy, our first response can only be casting ourselves upon that mercy.*
Apart from the mercy of God, we are hopelessly lost, forever condemned to hell. Only his mercy can save us from that—and he is a God of mercy. David celebrates God's steadfast love (*hesed*) and draws out its practical relevance in Psalm 36:7: "How precious is your steadfast love, O God! The children of mankind take refuge in the shadow of your wings."

God's mercy is a refuge for us from the judgment our sins deserve. That mercy is located in Jesus Christ. To him we must come. Having come, we discover that God's mercy is the ultimate source of true

---

31 R.L. Dabney, *Systematic Theology* (1871; reprint, Edinburgh: The Banner of Truth Trust, 1985), 165.

32 H. Bavinck, *The Doctrine of God* (1951; reprint, Edinburgh: The Banner of Truth Trust, 1977), 203.

33 Bavinck, *The Doctrine of God*, 206-209.

joy: "But I have trusted in your steadfast love (*hesed*); my heart shall rejoice in your salvation" (Psalm 13:5).

2. Once we have come to know God's mercy in Christ, we must praise him for that mercy.
The apostle Paul sees it as a major outcome of the gospel that "the Gentiles might glorify God for his mercy" (Romans 15:9). The Old Testament refrain exhorts us, "Oh give thanks to the LORD, for he is good! For his steadfast love (*hesed*) endures forever" (1 Chronicles 16:34). Our response should match David's: "I will sing aloud of your steadfast love (*hesed*) in the morning" (Psalm 59:16).

3. As God's people, we need his mercy every day.
We find constant challenge in the circumstances surrounding us. We face many temptations and trials. We are dragged down by our own sins and weaknesses. We need, then, to heed the summons of Hebrews 4:16 every day, taking comfort from the implied promise: "Let us then with confidence draw near to the throne of grace, that we may receive mercy and find grace to help in time of need."

Our prayer must always be the same as David's prayer: "Have mercy on me, O God, according to your steadfast love; according to your abundant mercy, blot out my transgressions" (Psalm 51:1).

4. As those who have experienced the mercy of God, it is our privilege and our duty to proclaim that mercy to fellow sinners.
Because of his mercy, the LORD says, "I have no pleasure in the death of anyone." He appeals to sinners, "turn and live" (Ezekiel 18:32). Our joy as preachers of the gospel is to pass on that invitation. God's mercy makes the Christian proclamation good news. It is an exciting message to preach. Preach it with the thrill of joy in your heart!

REFLECT

1. Are you resting and rejoicing in the mercy of God? List times when you have experienced God's mercy. How has God's mercy reassured you of his love and comforted you in life?
2. Is there a danger in taking God's daily mercy for granted? List ways in which you can safeguard yourself from doing so.

3. Are there any hindrances in your life that prevent you from turning to God's mercy? Examine yourself, confess your sin and receive his mercy.
4. List ways in which you can show and proclaim God's mercy to others.

REJOICE

Surely goodness and mercy shall follow me
    All the days, all the days of my life.
Surely goodness and mercy shall follow me
    All the days, all the days of my life.
And I shall dwell in the House of the Lord forever;
    And I'll feast at the table spread for me.
Surely goodness and mercy shall follow me
    All the days, all the days of my life.
—*John W. Peterson & Alfred B. Smith*

2

What is the glory of
God's mysterious
being?

In Titus 2:13, Paul speaks of Jesus Christ as "our great God and Saviour." Yet we hear Jesus Christ addressing his Father in heaven as God, as he does in John 17:3: "this is eternal life, that they know you the only true God." How can we hold these two facts together? The doctrine of the Trinity answers that question.

The first Christians became convinced that the man they had known as Jesus of Nazareth was nothing less than divine. The formulation of the doctrine of the Trinity was an offshoot of that conviction. The truth of the Trinity in itself, of course, was not the result of that conviction. It is an eternal reality. Only in the light of Christ could it become clear. The Christological conclusions came first. It was then necessary to relate those conclusions back to the doctrine of the one God. With the benefit of that hindsight, we can now put the doctrine of God as Trinity nearer to the front of our systematic theology. We now learn that the God who is sovereign and merciful exists in three "Persons." That sublime character of mercy is at the heart of all three. We must be careful not to think that God the Father is merciful, but that the Son and the Holy Spirit have different characters. The three Persons are one God. They all share the same heart.

Strictly speaking, the doctrine of God is the doctrine of the Trinity. The distinction between the first two parts of these studies is as follows. The doctrine of God concerns the attributes, qualities, and character of the one God. The doctrine of the Trinity tells us of the nature of God's being—it has a threefold aspect.

Some say that Scripture does not teach the doctrine of the Trinity. That is true in the sense that the Bible does not contain a fully formulated declaration that the only God exists in three Persons. However, the raw materials for the doctrine are present. They are so obviously present that, once we start to ponder the hints and clues, no other conclusion becomes possible than that God is triune. We must now trace some of the clues.

PART 1: KEY TEXTS

A. NEW TESTAMENT

We shall start with the New Testament, because it was in the light of the historical manifestation of the Son of God in Jesus of Nazareth that the trinitarian nature of God became clear. As Warfield says,

> The revelation itself was not made in word but in deed. It was made in the incarnation of God the Son and the outpouring of God the Holy Spirit.[1]

So Robert Reymond can say, "When we turn to the pages of the New Testament we find the doctrine of the Triune character of God everywhere *assumed*."[2]

We might list the following passages as New Testament evidence for the doctrine of the Trinity.

MATTHEW 3:16-17 (CF. MARK 1:9-11; LUKE 3:21F)

> And when Jesus was baptized, immediately he went up from the water, and behold, the heavens were opened to him, and he saw the Spirit of God descending like a dove and coming to rest on him; and behold, a voice from heaven said, "This is my beloved Son, with whom I am well pleased."

Here the Father speaks from heaven, claiming Jesus as his Son, while the Spirit descends to authenticate the claim. Albert Barnes writes:

> It is impossible to explain this transaction consistently in any other way than by supposing that there are three equal Persons in the Divine Nature or Essence, and that each of these sustains important parts in the work of redeeming men.[3]

---

1 B.B. Warfield, "The Biblical Doctrine of the Trinity," in *Biblical and Theological Studies* (Philadelphia: Presbyterian and Reformed, 1952), 33.

2 Reymond, *A New Systematic Theology*, 209.

3 A. Barnes, *Matthew and Mark*, vol. 1, *A Popular Family Commentary on the New*

MATTHEW 28:19

"Go therefore and make disciples of all nations, baptizing them
in the name of the Father and of the Son and of the Holy Spirit."

Notice here the use of the singular word *name* followed by the three
epithets, Father, Son and Holy Spirit. "Father, Son and Holy Spirit"
form one name. They are not three names. John Gill says: "Hence a
confirmation of the doctrine of the Trinity, there are three persons,
but one name, but one God."[4]

In the Old Testament God's name is "I AM" or Jehovah. In the New
Testament Jehovah is spelled out as Father, Son and Holy Spirit.

JOHN 14-16

This is what Charles Hodge says about these chapters:

In the discourse of Christ, recorded in the 14th, 15th, and 16th
chapters of John's Gospel, our Lord speaks to and of the Father,
and promises to send the Spirit to teach, guide, and comfort his
disciples. In that discourse the personality and divinity of the
Father, Son and Spirit are recognized with equal clearness.[5]

There are five points in this passage where it mentions the three
persons of the Trinity together.

1. *John 14:16-18*

16 And I will ask the Father, and he will give you another Helper,
to be with you forever,
17 even the Spirit of truth, whom the world cannot receive,
because it neither sees him nor knows him. You know him, for
he dwells with you and will be in you.

Testament (London: Blackie, 1886), 31.

   4   J. Gill, *An Exposition of the Old and New Testament* (London: Mathews and Leigh,
1809), on Matthew 28:19.

   5   C. Hodge, *Systematic Theology*, vol. 1 (London: Nelson, 1880), 448.

18 I will not leave you as orphans; I will come to you.

Jesus, who is speaking, the Father, and the Helper, soon identified as
the Spirit, are mentioned together in verse 16. Verses 17 and 18 indicate that, in the coming of the Spirit, Jesus himself is present with
his disciples.

2. John 14:23-26

23 Jesus answered him, "If anyone loves me, he will keep my
word, and my Father will love him, and we will come to him and
make our home with him.
24 Whoever does not love me does not keep my words. And the
word that you hear is not mine but the Father's who sent me.
25 These things I have spoken to you while I am still with you.
26 But the Helper, the Holy Spirit, whom the Father will send in
my name, he will teach you all things and bring to your remembrance all that I have said to you."

We have heard already that Jesus comes in the Spirit. That is why
verse 26 can say that the voice of Jesus is heard in the teaching of the
Spirit. From verse 23, we learn further that in this coming of Jesus, the
Father also comes to live with his people.

3. John 15:26

But when the Helper comes, whom I will send to you from the
Father, the Spirit of truth, who proceeds from the Father, he will
bear witness about me.

In 14:16, Jesus asks the Father to send the Spirit. In 14:26, the Father
sends the Spirit in the name of the Son. Here Jesus sends the Spirit
from the Father. These parallel forms of description emphasize the
oneness of the Father and the Son. The Spirit proceeds from the
Father. This underlines that his essential nature is identical with that
of the Father.

4. John 16:5-7

> 5 But now I am going to him who sent me, and none of you asks me, 'Where are you going?'
> 6 But because I have said these things to you, sorrow has filled your heart.
> 7 Nevertheless, I tell you the truth: it is to your advantage that I go away, for if I do not go away, the Helper will not come to you. But if I go, I will send him to you.

Here again, in verse 7, Jesus sends the Spirit. The occasion when he does this is indicated by verse 5: it is when the Son returns to the Father.

5. John 16:13-15

> 13 When the Spirit of truth comes, he will guide you into all the truth, for he will not speak on his own authority, but whatever he hears he will speak, and he will declare to you the things that are to come.
> 14 He will glorify me, for he will take what is mine and declare it to you.
> 15 All that the Father has is mine; therefore I said that he will take what is mine and declare it to you.

Verse 13 shows us that the Spirit is not a lone agent. He speaks under the authority of the whole triune Godhead. According to verse 14, his task is to glorify Christ by conferring what is Christ's upon his disciples. As verse 15 says, Jesus possesses everything that the Father has: they share the same essential divine nature.

1 CORINTHIANS 12:4-6

> 3 Therefore I want you to understand that no one speaking in the Spirit of God ever says "Jesus is accursed!" and no one can say "Jesus is Lord" except in the Holy Spirit.
> 4 Now there are varieties of gifts, but the same Spirit;
> 5 and there are varieties of service, but the same Lord;

6 and there are varieties of activities, but it is the same God who empowers them all in everyone.

In this poetically repetitive passage, we have the three parallel terms, Spirit, Lord, and God in verses 4-6. The word *Spirit* is defined by verse 3. It refers to the Holy Spirit, the Spirit of God. This phrase indicates that there is a distinction, in some sense, between God and his Spirit. *Lord* is the New Testament's favourite title for Jesus Christ. Verse 3, indeed, identifies him as the person in view in the use of this title here. In the providence of God it is significant that in the Hebrew Old Testament the divine name, *Jehovah*, was replaced out of deference and respect by the title "LORD." Therefore, when the New Testament takes up that title and applies it to Jesus, there lies behind it the divine name. Jesus is Jehovah. In the move from Old Testament to New, the way has been prepared for the recognition of the triune nature of the Godhead. The word *God* is often used in the New Testament of the Father specifically, though in a way which by no means reduces the divinity of the Son and the Spirit. Although, in verse 3, the Spirit is distinguished from God in one sense, the parallelism between verses 4 and 6 equates them in another sense. Verse 5 locates Jesus as Lord with the Father and the Spirit in the unity of the triune God.

2 CORINTHIANS 13:14

The grace of the Lord Jesus Christ and the love of God and the fellowship of the Holy Spirit be with you all.

Murray Harris describes this verse as an "embryonic Trinitarian formula."[6] It has often been pointed out that to see Jesus Christ and the Holy Spirit as anything less than fully and truly divine would render this blessing absurd. Charles Hodge suggests that this apostolic benediction, along with the baptismal formula of Matthew 28:19, has a vital role to play in connection with the doctrine of the Trinity. In

---

6 M. Harris, "Commentary on 2 Corinthians," in F.E. Gaebelein, ed., *Expositor's Bible Commentary, New Testament* (Grand Rapids: Zondervan, 1976–1992), on 2 Corinthians 13:13.

these liturgical forms, he writes, "provision was made to keep this doctrine constantly before the minds of the people, as a cardinal article of the Christian faith."[7]

GALATIANS 4:4-6

> 4 But when the fullness of time had come, God sent forth his Son, born of woman, born under the law,
> 5 to redeem those who were under the law, so that we might receive adoption as sons.
> 6 And because you are sons, God has sent the Spirit of his Son into our hearts, crying, "Abba! Father!"

Verse 4 designates Jesus as the Son of God sent forth. The fact that he was sent forth proves that he had an eternal existence as the second Person of the Trinity before his incarnation. Verse 6 identifies the indwelling Spirit as the Spirit of God's Son. The Father also sent the Spirit.

EPHESIANS 2:18

> For through him we both have access in one Spirit to the Father.

The trinitarian implications of this verse are, as Skevington Wood says, obvious.[8] If access to God the Father is through Christ and in the Spirit, then both Christ and the Spirit must be equal with the Father, but the three are clearly distinguishable from one another.

TITUS 3:4-6

> 4 But when the goodness and loving kindness of God our Saviour appeared,
> 5 he saved us, not because of works done by us in righteousness,

7   C. Hodge, *Systematic Theology*, vol. 1, 447.

8   A. Skevington Wood, "Commentary on Ephesians," in Gaebelein, ed., *Expositor's Bible Commentary, New Testament*, on Ephesians 2:18.

but according to his own mercy, by the washing of regeneration and renewal of the Holy Spirit,

6 whom he poured out on us richly through Jesus Christ our Saviour.

Verse 4 describes God as "our Saviour." In verse 6, the same title is applied to Jesus Christ. This confirms the identity of Jesus Christ with God. Yet, at the same time, God has poured out the Holy Spirit through Christ. This affirms that the two are distinct from each other in some sense. The fact that the Holy Spirit is poured out by God through Christ also indicates that he is to be understood as a third Person in union with them.

1 PETER 1:1-2

Peter, an apostle of Jesus Christ, to those who are elect exiles of the dispersion in Pontus, Galatia, Cappadocia, Asia, and Bithynia, according to the foreknowledge of God the Father, in the sanctification of the Spirit, for obedience to Jesus Christ and for sprinkling with his blood.

Edwin Blum comments that here Peter

reminds his readers of their Triune faith and of the Triune work of God. While Peter does not go into the developed theological form of the Trinitarian faith, the triadic pattern of the Christian faith is already evident in his words.[9]

REVELATION 1:4-5

4 Grace to you and peace from him who is and who was and who is to come, and from the seven spirits who are before his throne, 5 and from Jesus Christ the faithful witness, the firstborn of the dead, and the ruler of kings on earth.

---

9 E.A. Blum, "Commentary on 1 & 2 Peter and Jude," in Gaebelein, ed., *Expositor's Bible Commentary, New Testament*, on 1 Peter 1:2.

The phrase in verse 4, "him who is and who was and who is to come," clearly refers to God. The "seven spirits" is a description of the Holy Spirit. The number seven symbolizes perfection and completeness. It is a way of saying that the Holy Spirit is flawless. Verse 5 speaks of Jesus Christ. Grace and peace flow from the three Persons together. That is possible only if the Holy Spirit and Jesus Christ are also divine beings.

1 JOHN 5:7-8

7 There are three that bear witness in heaven: the Father, the Word, and the Holy Spirit; and these three are one.
8 And there are three that bear witness on earth: the Spirit, the water, and the blood; and these three agree as one.

I have kept this passage until last because there are those who would question whether it does refer to the Trinity. The translation above is taken from the New King James Version. The English Standard Version translates like this:

7 There are three that testify:
8 the Spirit and the water and the blood; and these three agree.

The difference results from a discrepancy between different ancient Greek manuscripts. The majority of manuscripts do not have the words forming the second part of verse 7 and the first part of verse 8 in the NKJV translation. Beza's edition of the New Testament, known as the *Textus Receptus* (Received Text), includes them. Whether we include this passage amongst the raw materials for the doctrine of the Trinity depends, therefore, on the conclusion we reach on the issue of the correct text. That discussion is beyond the scope of these studies.

B. OLD TESTAMENT

If we read the Old Testament without the light of New Testament fullness, we are bound to miss the clues to the trinitarian nature of God. As Augustine points out, "The Old is in the New revealed, the

New is in the Old concealed."[10] With that light shining on it, we find that the Old Testament contains numerous hints that the one God exists in three Persons. Why this truth was largely concealed as long as the Old Testament age continued is the question we must ask. One reason must have been that it was God's intention first to establish the truth of the oneness of God in the face of the polytheistic religions of the time. Louis Berkhof suggests another reason: "The Bible never deals with the doctrine of the Trinity as an abstract truth, but reveals the Trinitarian life in its various relations as a living reality."[11]

Therefore, it is in relation to the work of redemption, as that work reached its climax in the coming of Jesus Christ, and the outpouring of the Holy Spirit, that the doctrine burst forth into clarity. The doctrine of the Trinity was made manifest in connection with the work of the Godhead for human salvation. However, there are pointers to this doctrine even prior to the coming of Christ. Reymond lists eight categories of Old Testament evidence for the Trinity. I shall cite one example of each.

1. The use of plural pronouns for God

We find an example of this in the very first chapter of the Bible, where God says, 'Let us make man in our image' (Genesis 1:26). Gordon Wenham writes: "It is now universally admitted that this was not what the plural meant to the original author."[12] This may be true, but we must not overlook the intention of the Divine Author. He could have inspired the original human author to give a hint of something beyond his own awareness.

2. God in one sense distinguished from God in another sense

Our example comes from Psalm 45:6-7:

> 6 Your throne, O God, is forever and ever. The sceptre of your kingdom is a sceptre of uprightness;
> 7 you have loved righteousness and hated wickedness. Therefore

---

10 Augustine, adapted from *Quaestiones in Heptateuchum*, 2.73.
11 Berkhof, *Systematic Theology*, 85.
12 G.J. Wenham, *Genesis 1-15* (Dallas: Word, 1987), on Genesis 1:26.

God, your God, has anointed you with the oil of gladness beyond
your companions.

From verse 6 we see that these verses are addressed to a being called
God. Verse 7 speaks of the one whom this being knows as God. Moreover, the one referred to in verse 7 is God absolutely—the only God.
In the light of the New Testament, we understand these verses to be
addressed to God the Son and to speak about God the Father.

3. The "angel of the Lord" identified as God and yet distinguished from God
In Genesis 16:7, "the angel of the Lord" finds Hagar. In verses 8-12,
"the angel of the Lord" speaks to her. In the course of his speech, he
refers to the Lord, who has listened to Hagar in her affliction. Then,
in verse 13, Hagar's words show that she has recognized in the angel
of the Lord none other than the Lord himself: "So she called the
name of the Lord who spoke to her, 'You are a God of seeing,' for she
said, 'Truly here I have seen him who looks after me.'" "The angel of
the Lord" is the Son of God taking human appearance. The Lord to
whom he refers is the Father.

4. The Word and the Spirit depicted as co-workers with God
Psalm 33:6 says: "By the word of the Lord the heavens were made,
and by the breath of his mouth all their host." The Hebrew word
translated *breath* is *ruah*. It is often translated *spirit*. In the light of
John 1:1-14 we know that the Word of God has a personal existence
which became human in Jesus. We may therefore read this verse in
the light of that fuller truth.

5. God's Word or God's Spirit personalized
In fact, we do not have to wait for the New Testament revelation to
realize that God's Word can be spoken of in personal terms. Psalm
107:20 says, "God sent out his word and healed them." A word with
healing powers—which is not merely spoken, but sent—is a being
with personal properties.

God's Spirit too is personal. That is clear from Isaiah 63:10: "they
rebelled and grieved his Holy Spirit." Only a personal being can experience grief.

6. The Messiah, as a divine speaker, referring to the LORD *who sent him*
Zechariah 2:10-11 is a remarkable passage in this respect:

> 10 Sing and rejoice, O daughter of Zion, for behold, I come and
> I will dwell in your midst, declares the LORD.
> 11 And many nations shall join themselves to the LORD in that
> day, and shall be my people. And I will dwell in your midst, and
> you shall know that the LORD of hosts has sent me to you.

In verse 10 the LORD is speaking, and promises to come. In verse 11,
the same speaker refers to the LORD as a distinct being, and says that
he has sent him. Clearly, in the light of the completed revelation of
the New Testament, God the Son is the speaker, and God the Father
the sender.

7. The LORD, *the angel, and the Holy Spirit depicted as distinct Persons*
In Isaiah 63:7-10, the pronouns *he* and *his* refer to the LORD who has
been mentioned by name three times. He is Israel's Saviour, but we
hear that his angel also saved them. He became their enemy, but we
learn that his Spirit was grieved:

> 7 I will recount the steadfast love of the LORD, the praises of the
> LORD, according to all that the LORD has granted us, and the
> great goodness to the house of Israel that he has granted them
> according to his compassion, according to the abundance of his
> steadfast love.
> 8 For he said, "Surely they are my people, children who will not
> deal falsely." And he became their Saviour.
> 9 In all their affliction he was afflicted, and the angel of his pres-
> ence saved them; in his love and in his pity he redeemed them;
> he lifted them up and carried them all the days of old.
> 10 But they rebelled and grieved his Holy Spirit; therefore he
> turned to be their enemy, and himself fought against them.

8. The use of a plural noun to refer to God
Isaiah 54:5 says: "For your maker is your husband, the LORD of hosts
is his name." Both the words *maker* and *husband* are plural in Hebrew.

This may be a hint of the plurality present in the Godhead.

In addition to these eight categories, we might add two more passages as Old Testament evidence for the Trinity.

First, Berkhof refers to the personification of divine wisdom in Proverbs 8:12-31.[13] This personalization of wisdom is seen especially in verses 12, 22-27, and 30-31:

> 12 I, wisdom, dwell with prudence, and I find knowledge and discretion....
>
> 22 The LORD possessed me at the beginning of his work, the first of his acts of old.
>
> 23 Ages ago I was set up, at the first, before the beginning of the earth.
>
> 24 When there were no depths I was brought forth, when there were no springs abounding with water.
>
> 25 Before the mountains had been shaped, before the hills, I was brought forth,
>
> 26 before he had made the earth with its fields, or the first of the dust of the world.
>
> 27 When he established the heavens, I was there; when he drew a circle on the face of the deep....
>
> 30 Then I was beside him, like a master workman, and I was daily his delight, rejoicing before him always,
>
> 31 rejoicing in his inhabited world and delighting in the children of man.

Second, Hodge sees trinitarian significance in the threefold form of the priestly blessing in Numbers 6:24-26:[14]

> 24 The LORD bless you and keep you;
>
> 25 the LORD make his face to shine upon you and be gracious to you;
>
> 26 the LORD lift up his countenance upon you and give you peace.

---

13 Berkhof, *Systematic Theology*, 86.

14 Hodge, *Systematic Theology*, vol. 1, 446.

Section summary and personal application

REMEMBER

God the Father is the Fountain of grace, God the Son is the Channel of grace, and God the Holy Spirit is the Cup from which we drink of the flowing stream.[15]

—*C.H. Spurgeon (1834–1892)*

May the grace of the Lord Jesus Christ, and the love of God, and the fellowship of the Holy Spirit be with you all.

—*2 Corinthians 13:14*

REFLECT

1. Has the doctrine of the Trinity always been obvious to you? If not, why not? How did you come to believe this glorious truth?
2. How does the characteristic of mercy evidence itself in each Person of the sacred Trinity?
3. How does the doctrine of the Trinity influence your life in grief, guilt and grim circumstance?

REJOICE

The Father, Son, and Spirit, Thou,
　　The triune God, my life fore'er;
In me Thou art the full supply
　　That I Thy holy nature share.

The triune God the Spirit is,
　　And comes as breath and wind to me;
'Tis thus I may experience
　　The Godhead's wondrous mystery.

---

15 C.H. Spurgeon, *Metropolitan Tabernacle Pulpit*, 58:184.

All that the Father is and has
  In His beloved Son doth rest,
And all the riches of the Son
  Are by the Spirit now possessed.
—*Ralph Harrison (1748–1810)*

PART 2: KEY CREEDS AND CONFESSIONS

A. THE EARLY CREEDS

The fullest statement of the doctrine of the Trinity from the early centuries is in the so-called *Athanasian Creed*. Athanasius (c. A.D. 296-373) energetically defended the trinitarian doctrine against the Arians, who claimed that the Son of God was not fully divine, but the first created being. Athanasius did not write this creed, but it was named after him. It sums up the theology for which he fought. It was written in Latin sometime between the fifth and eighth centuries. The relevant section reads as follows:

> We worship one God in Trinity, and Trinity in Unity; neither confounding the persons nor dividing the substance. For there is one person of the Father, another of the Son, and another of the Holy Spirit. But the Godhead of the Father, of the Son, and of the Holy Spirit is all one, the glory equal, the majesty coeternal. Such as the Father is, such is the Son, and such is the Holy Spirit; the Father uncreated, the Son uncreated, and the Holy Spirit uncreated; the Father incomprehensible, the Son incomprehensible, and the Holy Spirit incomprehensible; the Father eternal, the Son eternal, and the Holy Spirit eternal. And yet they are not three eternals but one eternal; as also there are not three uncreated nor three incomprehensible, but one uncreated and one incomprehensible. So likewise the Father is almighty, the Son almighty, and the Holy Spirit almighty; and yet they are not three almighties, but one almighty. So the Father is God, the Son is

God, and the Holy Spirit is God; and yet they are not three Gods,
but one God. So likewise the Father is Lord, the Son Lord, and
the Holy Spirit Lord; and yet they are not three Lords but one
Lord. For just as we are compelled by Christian truth to acknowledge every Person by himself to be God and Lord; so are we
forbidden by the catholic faith to say that there are three Gods
or three Lords. The Father is made of none, neither created nor
begotten. The Son is of the Father alone, not made nor created,
but begotten. The Holy Spirit is of the Father and of the Son,
neither made, nor created, nor begotten, but proceeding. So
there is one Father, not three Fathers, one Son, not three Sons,
one Holy Spirit, not three Holy Spirits. And in this Trinity none
is before or after another, none is greater or less than another,
but the whole three persons are coeternal, and coequal. So that
in all things, as aforesaid, the Trinity in Unity and the Unity in
Trinity is to be worshipped.[16]

We may summarize the teaching of the creed in eight statements:

1. There is only one undivided divine substance
The Latin word *substantia* means the fundamental, underlying
essence of something. It does not have the material connotations that
the English word *substance* might imply. Here it refers to the fundamental *Godness* of God which can never be modified. There is only
one such reality.

2. A number of attributes characterize this divine substance
This creed mentions seven attributes in particular: eternity, glory,
majesty, infinity, omnipotence, sovereignty, and uncreatedness. No
doubt, these are intended only as representative examples.

3. Within this single divine substance, there are three distinct Persons, who are not to be confused with one another
The word *Person* emphasizes the fact that the Father, the Son, and the
Holy Spirit each have an individual personality. Each has a specific

---

16 *Athanasian Creed*, 3–27. See also Appendix 4.

function within the total work of the Godhead. The Latin word *persona* comes from the verb *persono*, which means "to sound through" or "to resound." The divine reality sounds through all three Persons. Each of them resounds with divine glory. Each person sings his own part in the harmony of the single divine music.

4. All three Persons share all the divine attributes

The divine attributes are not shared out between the three Persons. It is not that the Father has some of the attributes, the Son some others and the Spirit a different set again. All three fully possess every attribute.

5. Each Person shares fully in divinity in his individual Personhood

To take omnipotence as an example, God's omnipotence is not divided into three, so that the Father has one-third, the Son another third, and the Spirit the remaining third of the total omnipotence of God. Rather, the totality of the divine omnipotence is present in the Father, and in the Son, and in the Spirit.

6. There are certain individual properties, which make the three Persons truly distinct from one another

It is not just that there are three ways for God to be God. It is not that there are three choices God faces, from which he must choose how to reveal himself at any given moment. Rather, there are unique characteristics marking the Father, but not the Son or the Spirit. There are unique characteristics marking the Son. There are characteristics belonging exclusively to the Spirit. The creed explains this in these terms. The Father was not made by anyone. He is neither created nor begotten. The Father has independent existence. He is not dependent on another being either to make him out of nothing or to give him birth from some pre-existing reality. The Son is begotten. He was not made. He is not a creature. He is on the divine side of the absolute divide between God and creation. He is brought forth from the Father alone. He is the Father's offspring. Other creeds stress this generation of the Son as an eternal fact. There was never a moment when the Father existed alone without his Son. Nevertheless, the *Athanasian Creed* sees the Son's life as derived from the Father. This was an aspect

of the early creeds Calvin questioned, as we shall see later. The Spirit
was not made or created. He is genuinely God, and eternally so. He
was not begotten like the Son. He proceeds, again as an eternal reality.

There is an interesting difference in tense in the way in which the
Athanasian Creed speaks of the Son and the Spirit. The Son was begot-
ten. The Latin word *genitus* is in the past tense. The begetting of the
Son was a unique event. It cannot be dated. It happened in eternity,
not in time. It is unrepeatable. On the other hand, the creed uses the
present tense, *procedens*, when it speaks of the procession of the Spirit.
The Holy Spirit is every moment going forth from the Father and the
Son. This procession is a permanent reality.

The vocabulary chosen for the creed here was influenced by the
Latin Bible, which uses the word *unigenitus* of the Son on five occasions in the writings of John. For example, in John 3:16: "For God so
loved the world, that he gave his only [*unigenitus*] Son, that whoever
believes in him should not perish but have eternal life."[17]

The Spirit proceeds from the Father in John 15:26. There has been
disagreement over whether the Spirit proceeds from the Father alone,
or from the Father and the Son. In its original form, the *Nicene Creed*
said that the Holy Spirit proceeds from the Father. The words 'and the
Son' were added in the ninth century, and adopted by the churches of
Western Europe. However, the churches of the Middle East did not
accept the addition. Ted Campbell explains the issue at stake:

> Western theologians argued that adding the words "and the Son"
> was a more appropriate expression of the equality of the Persons.
> Without these words, they argued, God the Father would appear
> to be the only source of the Godhead, and so could be seen as
> having priority over the Son and the Holy Spirit. Eastern theolo-
> gians reasoned differently. The expression "from the Father"
> (without "and the Son") expressed better the equality of the
> Persons, as they saw it, since it would be unbalanced to have the
> Son originating from the Father only, and the Spirit originating
> from the Father and the Son.[18]

---

17 The other references are Jn. 1:14,18; 3:18; 1 Jn. 4:9.
18 T.A. Campbell, *Christian Confessions* (Louisville: Westminster John Knox, 1996), 85.

7. The three Persons are equal

This is true in two ways. First, they are equal in time. None of the Persons comes before or after another. The generation of the Son and the procession of the Spirit did not take place later than the origin of the divinity itself. God is eternally trinitarian. He was not a monad to start with, who at some point gave birth to his Son and put forth his Spirit. To be Father, Son, and Holy Spirit is the eternal nature of God. Second, they are equal in status. The Son and the Spirit are not lesser deities than the Father. All three together are the one God. Without the Son and the Spirit, God would not exist. To be Father, Son and Holy Spirit is what it is for the true God to exist at all.

8. This triune God is to be worshipped

The section of the *Athanasian Creed* quoted above begins and ends with a mention of the duty we have not just to think correctly about God, but also to worship him. The creed is not mere, bare, dry theology. It is an expression of faith and devotion. The very mystery of which it speaks should drive us to our knees in adoration. The arithmetical impossibility of working God out should prompt us to praise the Father, Son and Holy Spirit, the only true God.

B. THE REFORMATION CONFESSIONS

The doctrine of the Trinity was not a matter of dispute during the Reformation. Therefore, the confessions did not make an elaborate declaration of this doctrine. A brief statement to the effect that there is one God in three Persons was usually considered sufficient. Those confessions that did have more detail simply reproduced the language of the early centuries. Some of them included some selected quotations from the *Athanasian Creed*.

C. MODERN CONFESSIONS OF FAITH

1. Confession of Faith of the United Church of Northern India

The article on the Trinity in this Indian Confession is brief. It is content to affirm the unity of God and his tri-personality. It insists on the equality of the three Persons.

2. Confession of Faith of the Huria Batak Protestant

This Indonesian Confession reflects the ancient Creeds. It clarifies the
doctrine of the eternal generation of the Son in these words: "just as
the Father is without beginning and without end, so also is the Son."
The confession goes on to reject two errors in connection with the
Trinity: the idea that the Son and the Spirit are subordinate deities, and
the idea that the Holy Spirit is God the Mother in relation to the Son.

3. Confession of Faith of House Churches in China

The Chinese Confession also reproduces the traditional wording. Like
the *Athanasian Creed*, it emphasizes the worship due to the triune God,
and to no other. The section of this confession dealing with the Trinity
finishes like this:

> We refute all mistaken explanations of the Trinity, such as one
> entity with three modes of expression (such as water, ice, and
> steam); or one entity with three identities (such as a person can
> be son, a husband, and a father, or as the sun, its light and heat).[19]

Perhaps its intent is a rejection of all attempts to find illustrations of
the Trinity in the world of nature or in human experience. The confession recognizes that the mystery of the Trinity is so unique that any
analogy is bound to be misleading. Perhaps the Chinese House Church
leaders had in mind the words of Isaiah 40:18, which says, "To whom
then will you liken God, or what likeness compare with him?"

Section summary and personal application

REMEMBER

We believe, we maintain, we faithfully preach, that the Father
begat the Word, that is, Wisdom, by which all things were made,
the only-begotten Son, one as the Father is one, eternal as the

---

19 Confession of Faith of House Churches in China, 2.

Father is eternal, and, equally with the Father, supremely good; and that the Holy Spirit is the Spirit alike of Father and of Son, and is Himself consubstantial and co-eternal with both; and that this whole is a Trinity by reason of the individuality of the persons, and one God by reason of the indivisible divine substance, as also one Almighty by reason of the indivisible omnipotence; yet so that, when we inquire regarding each singly, it is said that each is God and Almighty; and, when we speak of all together, it is said that there are not three Gods, nor three Almighties, but one God Almighty; so great is the indivisible unity of these Three, which requires that it be so stated.[20]

—*Augustine (A.D. 354–430)*

REFLECT

1. How does the doctrine of the Trinity influence your presentation of the gospel?
2. Would confusing the Persons of the sacred Trinity affect the gospel message? If so, in what way?
3. List some inherent dangers in illustrating the reality of the sacred Trinity by the world of nature and human experience.
4. How does the doctrine of the Trinity influence your praise and prayers?

REJOICE

O Trinity of blessed light,
  O Unity of princely might,
The fiery sun now goes his way;
  Shed Thou within our hearts a ray.

To Thee our morning song of praise,
  To Thee our evening prayer we raise;
O grant us with Thy saints on high
  To praise Thee through eternity.

---

20 Augustine, *City of God*, 11.24.

All laud to God the Father be,
   All praise, eternal Son, to Thee,
All glory, as is ever meet,
   To God the holy Paraclete.
—*Ambrose of Milan (c. 337–397), trans. John M. Neale (1818–1866)*

PART 3: KEY HISTORICAL DEVELOPMENTS

In this section, I want to do two things. First, we shall trace the route the early church travelled in coming to a worked out understanding of the truth of the Trinity. Then we shall look at the trinitarian theology of Augustine and Calvin.

A. THE ROUTE TO A FULL TRINITARIAN UNDERSTANDING

In the early centuries, various explanations of how God could be both one and three were put forward, which the church then rejected. They became classed as 'heresies.' This does not mean that the men who put them forward were necessarily heretical unbelievers. They may have been sincere Christians trying their best to delve as deeply as they could into the mystery of the Trinity. The church was thrashing this doctrine out for several centuries. Along the way, they came to see that some attempts to explain the doctrine had been inadequate. To teach them later would be brazen heresy. At the time, they were well meaning though misguided attempts to make progress towards a better understanding. The faulty attempts helped in that process. It was often against the background of what became recognized as unacceptable ways of describing the Trinity that genuine progress was made towards a correct understanding.

We can see the Holy Spirit at work in all the deliberations of the early Christians. He was leading them, slowly but surely, to the richest possible interpretation of the biblical data gathered together into the doctrine of the Trinity. We can indentify five inadequate explanations of the Trinity that appeared before the Council of Nicaea in A.D. 325.

The motivation for all of them was the concern to safeguard monotheism and to avoid any hint that Christians believed in three separate gods.

The first became known as *Economic Trinitarianism*. It dominated theological reflection during the second century. This view taught that the Father is eternal God, and that he became a Trinity in order to conduct the divine economy, that is, to create, govern, and redeem the world. God's eternal nature is not triune. God's triune nature is a functional thing.

The next approach emerged in the third century. This was *Adoptionism*. This taught that Jesus was an ordinary man until his baptism, at which point he was adopted as the divine Son. The essential nature of God, however, remains Unitarian.

Modalism, which also developed in the third century, taught that God is a unity, but he that he has three different ways of being God for different purposes and at different times. Modalism held that the Father became the Son for a time, and later became the Spirit. This view is also known as *Patripassianism*, because it implied that it was the Person of the Father who suffered and died on the cross. Its most famous representative was Sabellius, so it is also known as *Sabellianism*.

The fourth approach, also dating from the third century, was *Subordinationism*. This taught that the transcendent divine essence is a unity, and is found in God the Father. The Son and the Spirit are both eternal beings, but they derive their deity from the fullness of Godhead concentrated in the Father. That means that they are secondary gods, subordinate to the Father.

In the early fourth century, Arius, an Egyptian pastor, pushed Subordinationism a step further away from an acceptable trinitarian understanding. The fundamental premise of *Arianism* was the unity of God. Arius taught that the Son is not a truly divine Person. He is a creature of the Father. He is the first of God's creatures, and he was created prior to the creation of the world, but still he had a definite beginning and is not eternal.

The Council of Nicaea condemned Arianism. It used the Greek word *homoousios*, meaning "the same essence." The *Nicene Creed* affirmed that the Son is of identical nature to the Father. The same word came to be used of the Holy Spirit. For the rest of the fourth century the appropriateness of the term *homoousios* was much debated. Some wanted a compromise term, *homoiousios*. This meant that the Son is of a similar essence to the Father, but not identical. The chief champion of Nicene orthodoxy was Athanasius. He insisted that the Father eternally begets the Son. His generation was not a specific act, but is an eternal process. He taught that the generation of the Son is not an act of the Father's will, but something intrinsic to the divine nature.

Up until now, the main concern had been with the divine status of Jesus Christ. Once his full deity had been settled, the church turned its attention to the Holy Spirit. The word *homoousios* was used of the Spirit too. Some people said this implied that the Father had two Sons, so the Cappadocian Fathers—Basil, Gregory of Nyssa and Gregory of Nazianzen—thought through the different modes of origin of the Son and the Spirit.

In A.D. 381, the Council of Constantinople ratified the Nicene teaching. There is one God existing eternally in three Persons. The Son and the Spirit are *homoousios* with the Father. The Son is begotten by the Father, from whom the Spirit proceeds.

B. THE TRINITARIAN THEOLOGY OF AUGUSTINE AND CALVIN

Robert Reymond argues that there is one great weakness in the trinitarian theology of the *Nicene* and the *Athanasian Creeds*. There is an implicit tendency to subordinate the deity of the Son and the Spirit to that of the Father. The Father is seen as the fount and source of the Godhead, and deity passed from him to the Son by eternal generation and to the Spirit by eternal procession. The result of this way of putting it is that the Son and the Spirit derive their deity from the Father. They are not self-existent as divine Persons. Yet, as Reymond points out, part of the essence of true and full deity is self-existence. Reymond refers also to paragraph 9 of the *Irish Articles*, a statement of faith prepared by James Ussher of Dublin in 1615. It makes this comment on the doctrine of the Trinity:

> The essence of the Father did not beget the essence of the Son; but the Person of the Father begets the Person of the Son by communicating his whole essence to the Person begotten from eternity.[21]

---

21 *Irish Articles*, 9.

Reymond argues that this suggests that the Son has no personal exis-tence apart from the fact that the Father begets him. However, personal existence is essential to the nature of God. Therefore, this wording has the effect of making the deity of the Son secondary. Reymond notes that, "in the sixteenth century, John Calvin contended against the Subordina-tionism implicit in the Nicene language." The *Nicene Creed* said that Jesus Christ was "God from God." This implied that he drew his Godness from somewhere else outside himself. Calvin argued that the Son of God was *autotheos*—God from himself.[22] The relevant passage in Cal-vin's *Institutes* is Book 1, chapter 13. Throughout the chapter, Calvin declares his basic agreement with the traditional doctrine, and his general sympathy with the statements of the orthodox early church fathers. The final couple of sentences relate to the distinction Reymond points out between Calvin and the earlier formulations:

> I have thought it better not to touch on various topics, which could have yielded little profit, while they must have needlessly burdened and fatigued the reader. For instance, what avails it to discuss…whether or not the Father always generates? This idea of continual generation becomes an absurd fiction from the moment it is seen that from eternity there were three Persons in one God.[23]

Calvin's concern always was to stay within the boundaries laid down by Scripture, to go as far as Scripture allows, and then stop. He sought to avoid mere speculation. He was, therefore, happy to speak of Christ as the Word, the Son, as begotten by God (paragraph 8), and begotten by the Father (paragraph 24). He was happy to speak of the Son as being from the Father, and the Spirit as being from the Father and the Son (paragraph 18). He was equally clear that while, in terms of order, the Father is first, then the Son and then the Spirit, as regards the divine essence, there is no distinction (paragraph 24). Therefore, as Son, the second Person of the Trinity is the Son of the Father, but as God, he is the Son from himself (paragraph 19).

---

22 Reymond, *A New Systematic Theology*, 317-341.
23 Calvin, *Institutes*, 1.13,29.

Calvin also points out the problems arising from defining the Father as the essence of God, as if he transfused deity into the Son and the Spirit:

> On the supposition that the whole essence is in the Father only, the essence becomes divisible, or is denied to the Son, who, being thus robbed of his essence, will be only a titular God.... In this way, the divinity of the Son will be something abstracted from the essence of God, or the derivation of a part from the whole.[24]

Calvin declares himself content with a sober definition according to the measure of faith set down in the Bible:

> When we profess to believe in one God, by the name 'God' is understood the one simple essence, comprehending three Persons...; and accordingly, whenever the name of God is used indefinitely, the Son and the Spirit, not less than the Father is meant. But when the Son is joined with the Father, relation comes into view, and so we distinguish between the Persons. But as the personal subsistences carry an order with them, the principle and origin being in the Father, whenever mention is made of the Father and the Son, or of the Father and Spirit together, the name of God is specially given to the Father. In this way the unity of essence is retained, and respect is had to the order, which, however, derogates in no way from the divinity of the Son and Spirit.[25]

Calvin seems to be building on the teaching of Augustine. He lived during the fifth century, and made one clarification of the doctrine of the Trinity. Whereas earlier theologians had tended to make the Father the starting point for their thinking, Augustine took the divine nature itself as his starting point. He taught that the divine essence is the Trinity.

---

24 Calvin, *Institutes*, 1.13,23.
25 Calvin, *Institutes*, 1.13,20.

If by now we find this entire matter completely baffling, we may be encouraged by Calvin's final sentence in paragraph 21:

> But if the distinction of Father, Son, and Spirit, subsisting in the one Godhead (certainly a subject of great difficulty), gives more trouble and annoyance to some intellects than is meet, let us remember that the human mind enters a labyrinth whenever it indulges its curiosity, and thus submit to be guided by the divine oracles, how much so ever the mystery may be beyond our reach.[26]

PART 4: KEY POINTS OF PRACTICAL APPLICATION

1. We must believe everything revealed about God, even where we cannot possibly understand it fully.
We must struggle to understand as much as we can. When we reach the limits of our finite ability, our reaction must not be rebellion and unbelief, but humility and worship.

2. We must take care how we word our prayers.
This is especially important for those of us entrusted with the responsibility of leading God's people in prayer. Here are two examples of prayers betraying some confusion about the doctrine of the Trinity.

> Heavenly Father, we praise and worship You. You are the great and glorious God. We thank You for all Your goodness to us. We praise You for Your amazing mercy. We worship You as the God of love. We thank You for coming down from heaven and becoming a human being. We praise You for dying on the cross for our sins. In Jesus' name, Amen.

Perhaps the person who was praying here forgot how he had begun

---

26 Calvin, *Institutes*, 1.13,21.

the prayer by the time he reached the sixth sentence. As a result, he carelessly spoke of the incarnation and crucifixion of the Father instead of the Father's Son. This echoes the ancient heresy of Modalism.

> Dear Lord Jesus Christ, You are worthy of all our love and adoration. We praise You for Your great glory. All honour and blessing belong to You. We thank You for sending Your Son to live in this world and to die for our sins. We thank You for showing us Your love in such an amazing way. In Jesus' name, Amen.

Here is a prayer addressed to God the Son. In principle, there is nothing wrong with that. However, Jesus did not have any children. Some confusion about the respective roles of the Father and the Son has crept into this prayer. Of course, any of us can have a slip of the tongue from time to time. We certainly should not become hypercritical of other people's prayers. Yet if we constantly make mistakes like these, it would suggest that we have not properly understood the truth of the Trinity. In that case, we need to think it through seriously.

3. We must rejoice that there is a trinitarian framework to our salvation.
Father, Son and Holy Spirit are all equally committed to the joyful task of bringing many sons to glory. Jesus says, "No one comes to the Father except through me" (John 14:6). This means that through him there really is a way back to God. Moreover, it means that the Father is one who desires that we should come, and who welcomes us warmly when we do. We may "...testify that the Father has sent his Son to be the Saviour of the world" (1 John 4:14). Since we received that salvation, "God has sent the Spirit of his Son into our hearts, crying, 'Abba! Father!'" (Galatians 4:6).

4. We must preach the gospel of God.
Earlier we saw how Charles Hodge suggested that the design of the apostolic benediction was to keep the truth of the Trinity at the forefront of the Church's consciousness: "The grace of the Lord Jesus Christ and the love of God and the fellowship of the Holy Spirit be with you all" (2 Corinthians 13:14). The three qualities associated with the three Persons of the Trinity here point us to the very heart of the

gospel. Jesus Christ's grace is his willing saving work on behalf of sinners, who deserved nothing from him. God the Father's love is the ultimate motivation of his will to reconcile the world to himself in Christ. The Holy Spirit's fellowship is probably[27] to be understood to mean that the Holy Spirit is the channel through which the desire of the triune God to be restored to relationship with sinners is realized. Matthew Poole says that it is the Holy Spirit "by whom the Father and Son communicate their love and grace to the saints."[28] These three divine attributes—grace, love, and fellowship—are those by which the divine mercy becomes operative in our experience. As Murray Harris says, "It is through the grace shown by Christ in living and dying for men that God demonstrates his love and the Spirit creates fellowship."[29]

Our calling is to proclaim to a sinful world the grace of a triune God of love, who recalls straying sinners into fellowship with himself. To be reconciled to him is to be "filled with all the fullness of God" (Ephesians 3:19) in his triune glory.

REFLECT

1. Evaluate the flaws of the following views of the Trinity:
   (a) Economic Trinitarianism
   (b) Adoptionism
   (c) Modalism
   (d) Subordinationism
2. How does your understanding of the sacred Trinity shape your perception of creation and salvation?

REJOICE:

Holy, holy, holy! Lord God Almighty!
   All thy works shall praise thy name, in earth and sky and sea.
Holy, holy, holy! Merciful and mighty,
   God in three persons, blessed Trinity.
—*Reginald Heber (1783–1826)*

---

27 Several ways of understanding this phrase have been suggested.

28 M. Poole, *Commentary on the Holy Bible* (1685), on 2 Corinthians 13:14.

29 Harris, "Commentary on 2 Corinthians," in Gaebelein, ed., *Expositor's Bible Commentary, New Testament,* on 2 Corinthians 13:13.

3

THE DOCTRINE OF REVELATION IN SCRIPTURE

How does God make his glory known in the Scriptures?

We have been considering the doctrines of God's character of mercy and God's mysterious being as Trinity. How can we know anything about God and his works? It is only possible because God has made them known to us. God is so great and we are so small that it is impossible for us to find out anything about him unless he tells us. More than that, sin has blinded our minds, so that we have to pray, "Open my eyes, that I may behold wondrous things out of your law" (Psalm 119:18).

We also have to remember that God has chosen *not* to reveal everything that he could reveal:

> The secret things belong to the LORD our God, but the things that are revealed belong to us and to our children for ever, that we may do all the words of this law (Deuteronomy 29:29).

This means that in all our attempts to formulate a tidy faith we must proceed with humility. As this text also reminds us, God's purpose in revealing certain things to us is not just to interest us or to amuse us, but so that we can *do what he commands*. Unless our study of systematic theology leads us into deeper obedience, we are just wasting our time with fruitless knowledge.

In Isaiah 40:5, the prophet assures us that "the mouth of the LORD has spoken." Earlier on, the same prophet wrote: "To the teaching and to the testimony! If they will not speak according to this word, it is because they have no dawn" (Isaiah 8:20). These words inform us that God records his speech for us in his Word: the doctrine of revelation focuses as the doctrine of Scripture. In the story of Samuel, we learn that in his early years he "did not yet know the LORD, and the word of the LORD had not yet been revealed to him" (1 Samuel 3:7). By placing these phrases side-by-side, God shows us that it is through his Word that we get to know him, and it is *always* through the Word of God that we get to know him better. We are not to study the Bible just to become experts in theology. In our studies, we are aiming to have a tidy faith so that we may grow in our knowledge of the Lord: "The LORD revealed himself to Samuel…by the word of the LORD" (1 Samuel 3:21). As we proceed with these studies in systematic theology, let us pray that the result will be that we see the Lord himself revealed to us afresh.

On the road to Emmaus, as Jesus spoke with Cleopas and his companion, "he interpreted to them in all the Scriptures the things concerning himself" (Luke 24:27). In the end, all God's revelation leads to Jesus Christ. He is the true focus of all the Scriptures. The whole Bible is Christ-centred. We study it so that we may "grow in the grace and knowledge of our Lord and Saviour Jesus Christ" (2 Peter 3:18). However, the Bible itself speaks of another source of revelation. There is a revelation of God in creation also. We shall therefore divide our study of the doctrine of revelation into two parts. In this chapter we will consider revelation in Scripture, and then, in chapter four, revelation in creation.

PART 1: KEY TEXTS

A. OLD TESTAMENT

PSALM 19:7-11

> 7 The law of the LORD is perfect, reviving the soul; the testimony of the LORD is sure, making wise the simple;
> 8 the precepts of the LORD are right, rejoicing the heart; the commandment of the LORD is pure, enlightening the eyes;
> 9 the fear of the LORD is clean, enduring forever; the rules of the LORD are true, and righteous altogether.
> 10 More to be desired are they than gold, even much fine gold; sweeter also than honey and drippings of the honeycomb.
> 11 Moreover, by them is your servant warned; in keeping them there is great reward.

Notice three things from this passage:

1. The terms used to refer to God's Word

Six different terms are used. Taken together they refer to Scripture as a whole. Each term brings out a different aspect of God's Word.

(1) The word *law* (verse 7) translates the Hebrew word *torah*. This does not only mean law in the sense of commandments. It means

instruction. It derives from the verb *yarah*, which means "to show" or "to point out." This compares the Bible to a teacher. Just as a teacher points out to his students the truths that they would not and could not otherwise know, so Scripture shows us truth that we would otherwise be ignorant of, and so it instructs us. *Torah* can also mean "direction," and *yarah* can mean, specifically, "to show the way." The Bible is like a signpost. God's Word shows us the way that we should go. It points us to Jesus, who said, "I am the way" (John 14:6).

(2) The word *testimony* (verse 7) translates *'edut*. It refers to the testimony of a witness, to the evidence the witness presents. When a witness gives evidence in a court case, his testimony should be reliable. He is under a solemn charge to speak truthfully, so that his testimony is irrefutable. The evidence he presents should be conclusive so that the case is clearly settled. The Bible certainly is reliable: nothing it says can be refuted, because everything it says is true. The Scriptures are not to be taken lightly. They proclaim a serious message about serious issues. The word *'edut* is connected with the verb *'ed*, meaning, "to say something again and again." The thing about committing something to writing is that every time you read it you read the same words. Every person who comes to a written document reads the same thing. Repeatedly, always, the Bible is saying the same thing. Subjectively, there is such a wealth of truth in the Scriptures that we may go on discovering new things even while reading the same words. However, what we discover is truth that has always been there. Only now, our eyes are open to perceive it. Therefore, *the change is in us, not the Scriptures.* The Bible is God's unchanging Word. It does not alter with changes of culture or fashion.

(3) The word *precepts* (verse 8) speaks of the requirements of a properly appointed authority, the legislation passed by a properly constituted government. When an election takes place, we may or may not like the outcome. Provided the result has not been rigged, provided there have been no threats or bribes, the outcome is constitutionally valid, and we have to accept it. We have to respect the decisions of the duly appointed authority. The God who is the properly constituted king over all has appointed everything in the Bible. Our duty is to accept it.

(4) The word *commandment* (verse 8) translates *mitswah*. It is derived from *sawah*, which means "to give orders." So this word draws

attention to those aspects of the Bible which are more specifically directive. Scripture tells us what we ought to do, how we should behave. It reveals to us what sort of life God orders.

(5) The word *fear* is used (verse 9). Normally we think of fear as an emotion inside us. Psalm 2:11 exhorts us to "serve the LORD with fear." We read in Proverbs 1:7: "The fear of the LORD is the beginning of knowledge." True knowledge starts with that subjective fear. How do we obtain it? Here in Psalm 19:8 the Bible is called "the fear of the LORD," because it is through God's Word that we learn to fear him, and so get to know him.

(6) The word translated *rules* (verse 9) means "decision" or "sentence." It would be used of the sentence passed by a court of law at the conclusion of a case, once the decision has been made that the accused is guilty. The Bible pronounces God's decision about us. It announces his sentence against a world found guilty in sin. It rules that we are under condemnation, and so drives us in desperation to the Saviour.

In the Psalm, all six of these terms are followed by the phrase "of the LORD." The phrase "the LORD" translates God's covenant name, *Jehovah*. This God said to Moses,

> 6 I am the LORD, and I will bring you out from under the burdens of the Egyptians, and I will deliver you from slavery to them, and I will redeem you with an outstretched arm and with great acts of judgment.
> 7 I will take you to be my people, and I will be your God, and you shall know that I am the LORD your God, who has brought you out from under the burdens of the Egyptians (Exodus 6:6-7).

These words explain what God's covenant name implies: it means that he is the God who liberates, rescues, and redeems his people, so that he and they can belong to each other in an unbreakable commitment. God speaks the Word of revelation. His Word is the revelation of his saving grace.

The first of these six words, *torah*, is often used as a summary term for the Word of God as a whole. Although it is translated *law*, we need to be clear that it means the whole of God's message of grace. The Bible recognizes no antithesis between law and gospel. The Dispensationalist tendency to characterize the Old Testament as a word of law and the New Testament as a word of gospel grace is quite false. The Old Testament, just as much as the New, is the proclamation of the grace of God in the gospel. The New Testament continues and brings to its conclusion the gospel message proclaimed in the Old Testament from the very beginning of Genesis onwards.

2. The qualities of God's revelation

Each of these six terms is associated with an adjective describing a *quality* of God's Word. Taken together they add up to the declaration that God's Word is of the highest possible quality.

(1) The word *perfect* (verse 7) translates *tamim*. This same word is used to describe a lamb as being "without blemish." If a lamb was to be good enough for a sacrifice, it had to be sound, healthy, and complete. This emphasizes the truth that God's Word as given to us in the Bible is perfect. There is nothing at all wrong with the Bible. Nothing can be added, and nothing needs to be removed. Of course, when Psalm 19 was first written, God's Word was not yet complete. This statement anticipates the day of full revelation with the coming of Christ. It was also true, concerning the stage of progress in revelation reached up to that point, that there were no deficiencies in God's Word.

(2) The word *sure* (verse 7) translates *'aman*. This word has a range of meanings. Its basic sense is "to be built," but it can also mean "to be supported," or "to be established," and sometimes "to be lasting," and "to be permanent." It would be used of a building made to last, a building standing on a firm foundation, so that it is a safe place to be. The Bible will stand firm forever. Shifting human opinions may come and go, but God's revelation lasts. It is of permanent validity.

(3) The word *right* (verse 8) translates *yashar*. This means straight, whether upright (perfectly vertical), or level (perfectly horizontal). In Ezekiel 1, we have an example of both uses of this word. In verse 7, the four living creatures' legs are said to be "straight"—up and down. In verse 23, their wings are said to be "straight"—from side to side. If a plumb line finds a wall to be vertical, the wall could be described as *yashar*. If a level finds a ledge to be perfectly horizontal, the ledge could be described as *yashar*. From whatever angle you examine the message of the Bible you will find it to be exactly right.

Yashar can also mean "pleasing." Joab used this word when he said that David would have been pleased if Absalom had survived, even though he had become an enemy (2 Samuel 19:6). The perfection of God's revelation is such that it is pleasing to those who receive it with faith and love.

(4) The word *pure* (verse 8) translates *bar*. This term means "clean" or "choice." It comes from the word *barar*, meaning "polished." It is used in Isaiah 49:2: "He made my mouth like a sharp sword; in the shadow of his hand he hid me; he made me a polished arrow; in his quiver he hid me away." It speaks of polishing weapons to make them bright and clean for a parade. In Psalm 19:8, this word points to the dazzling splendour of God's Word. The Bible puts any other message in the shade.

(5) The word *clean* (verse 9) translates *tahor*. It is the word used of the pure gold used in the construction of the tabernacle. For example, Exodus 25:17 says, "You shall make a mercy seat of pure gold." Pure gold is gold without any mixture of inferior contents. The Bible is God's truth, and there is not a scrap of error mixed up with it.

(6) The word *true* (verse 9) translates *'emet*. This term speaks of something stable and firm, something reliable and trustworthy, true and certain. All these descriptions are applicable to God's Word. The Bible is unique, unrivalled, unbeatable, and true. The LORD's revelation is beyond question.

In addition to these six adjectives, two phrases in verse 9 tell us more about the qualities of God's revelation:

(a) It is *enduring forever*. It will never ever be necessary to make any changes to the Bible. It will never become obsolete or out of date. No opponent will ever succeed in destroying it.

(b) It is *righteous altogether*. The word *righteous* translates *tsadaq*. It means "to be in the right." This word teaches us that there is nothing in the Bible that will ever be exposed as a sham, nothing that could ever be found out to be incorrect. The word *altogether* tells us that this is equally true whether you consider God's Word as a unified whole or whether you delve into every particular part. Every detail of God's Word is right and true.

All six of these adjectives and words similar to both these phrases are used in other parts of the Old Testament as descriptions of God himself.[1] God's Word is as it is because God is as he is. The Bible reflects the character of the LORD who gave it. It derives all its qualities from him. By its very nature, it truly is a revelation of him, and we can rely on it.

3. The impact of God's Word

Each clause in verses 7-8 ends with a statement about what God's Word does for those who receive it.

(1) God's Word *revives the soul* (verse 7). The word *revives* translates *shub*. It means "to turn back." The picture is of the sinful soul glibly marching on in wilful unbelief, oblivious of the destruction lurking just ahead. The person who is dead in sin careers towards the edge of a precipice, and yet is completely unaware of the danger. The message of Scripture says, "Wake up! Be alert! Stop! Go into reverse!" The soul is rescued and revived, and the Word of God is responsible for the sinner's new spiritual vitality.

(2) God's Word *makes wise the simple* (verse 7). The word translated *simple* is *peti*. It means "easily enticed" or "deceived." It speaks of the gullible person, who is led astray very easily. It speaks of the foolish person, who can be persuaded to do anything, however disastrous. Here is a sad picture of human life in sin. We are prone to deception. We are hopelessly misled. We are naïvely open to listen to any voice. We are tragically misguided. We are led astray, enticed into wrong ways by the voices of unbelief. Then the Word of God speaks. It brings wisdom. It guides us so that we can begin to live well. It sets us going in the right direction. It enables us to act with shrewd foresight.

(3) God's Word *rejoices the heart* (verse 8). The Hebrew word translated *rejoices* is *samah*. It means "to brighten," and so "to gladden," "to make joyful." The life of sin is a miserable life. When the Bible's message of grace and salvation and hope breaks into the sinner's heart, it brings light, gladness, and true joy.

(4) God's Word *enlightens the eyes* (verse 8). Life in sin is like groping in the dark. When you grope in the dark, you are in danger. You are

---

1   For example: *tamim*—Ps. 18:30; *'aman*—Deut. 7:9; *yashar*—Deut. 32:4; *bar*—Ps. 18:26; *tahor*—Hab. 1:13; *'emet*—Ex. 34:6; *enduring forever*—Ps. 48:14; *tsadaq*—Job 4:17.

exposed to threats you cannot see. The sinner is unaware of temptation or of impending judgment. To receive the message of Scripture
is like having the light turned on. It is like having a torch shining on
your pathway, or like the sunrise ending the night.

Then verses 10-11 underline the power of God's revelation. Here are
three aspects of the response made by those who receive the Word:

(a) *They love it* (verse 10). They find the message of Scripture more
desirable than gold and sweeter than honey to their taste. To the true
believer, the Word of God is worth more than all the riches this
world can offer. In their love for the Bible, believers find it far more
palatable than the richest delicacies the most fashionable restaurant
can serve.

(b) *They are warned by it* (verse 11). The word translated *warned* is
zahar. The same word is used in two passages in Ezekiel. Here is Ezekiel 3:17: "Son of man, I have made you a watchman for the house of
Israel. Whenever you hear a word from my mouth, you shall give them
warning from me."[2] The prophet Ezekiel was appointed "a watchman
for the house of Israel." His task was to "give them warning" of the
judgment of death hanging over the wicked, to turn them from their
wicked ways, so that their life would be spared. The Bible warns us, so
that we constantly turn away from error and sin.

(c) *They are rewarded in keeping it* (verse 11). We keep God's Word
by believing it, by accepting it, by refusing to question it, by obeying
it. This is not saying that salvation is a reward for our obedience. It is
in keeping God's Word that the reward is enjoyed. The reward is not
something received later as payment *for* keeping God's Word.

The word translated *reward* is *'eqeb*. It connects with the word
'aqeb, which means "feet" or "footsteps." This suggests that the reward
consists in following in the footsteps of our Lord. In his footsteps, we
find security and joy. This reward is altogether a kindness of undeserved grace.

---

2   The word *zahar* appears in every verse from Ezekiel 3:17-21; the other passage
is Ezekiel 33:3-9.

B. NEW TESTAMENT

2 TIMOTHY 3:15-17

15 From childhood you have been acquainted with the sacred
writings, which are able to make you wise for salvation through
faith in Christ Jesus.

16 All Scripture is breathed out by God and profitable for teaching,
for reproof, for correction, and for training in righteousness,

17 that the man of God may be competent, equipped for every
good work.

Notice three things from this passage:

1. There are two words for the Bible

The word *writings* (verse 15) translates the Greek word *gramma*, while
the word *Scripture* (verse 16) translates *graphe*. The two words are
related, though slightly different in meaning. *Graphe* emphasizes the
fact of writtenness, and so indicates the method by which God has
chosen to get his Word to us. *Gramma* emphasizes the finished product,
the document resulting from the act of writing. Together they emphasize that God has ensured that his revelation has been written down.
We have his Word in writing.

2. There are two descriptions of the Bible

(1) The word *sacred* (verse 15) translates *hieros*. Only one other place
in the New Testament uses this—1 Corinthians 9:13, where it refers
to the holy things of Old Testament worship, the sacrifices.

In Leviticus 22:3, we read:

If any one of all your offspring throughout your generations
approaches the holy things that the people of Israel dedicate to
the LORD, while he has an uncleanness, that person shall be cut
off from my presence: I am the LORD.

The holy things were so sacred that to handle them while unclean was
to profane the LORD's name, and resulted in banishment from his

presence. The holy Scriptures are just as sacred. We are to handle them with extreme reverence.

In Ezekiel 22:26, the LORD complains that the priests have profaned his holy things in that "they have made no distinction between the holy and the common." To treat the holy things as if they were merely ordinary was one way of profaning them. We need to remember that the Bible is no ordinary book. It is unique and sacred. To read the Bible as if it is just like any other book is an act of profanity. We must read it with reverence, awe, and faith.

(2) The phrase *breathed out by God* (verse 16) translates literally the single Greek word *theopneustos*. When we breathe out, we release air. When words are carried on the air we release, we speak: our breath gives a meaningful sound. This verse is telling us that having the Scriptures is no different from God actually making sounds in the air for us to hear with our ears. If we want to know what God is saying, we must turn to the Bible. The Bible is his speech. *Theopneustos* relates to the word *pneuma*, which means "Spirit." To say that God breathes out the Scriptures is to say that God's Spirit gives them, that God's Spirit imbues them. This applies to "all Scripture." God breathes out the Bible as a whole, and God breathes out every separate bit of the Bible. We cannot say that some parts of the Bible are more inspired and some less. All of it is God's speech.

3. There are two things which the Bible does

(1) It is *able to make you wise for salvation* (verse 15). The Bible has dynamic power. It has the ability to give us a clear understanding of the message of the gospel.

(2) It is *profitable* (verse 16). The Bible brings us countless benefits and huge advantages. It teaches us the truth. It convicts us of sin. It straightens out our distorted lives. It trains us in godly living. In all this, there is one goal in view: that the believer may competently live for God. The words rendered 'competent' and equipped' in verse 17 are related: *competent* translates *artios*, while *equipped* translates *exartizo*. Both link with the word *arti*, meaning 'now.' We are called to live for God appropriately for our own time and place. God has placed each of us where we are. We are to serve him using methods relevant to our own generation, in ways significant for our own context. To achieve that, we need the Word of God.

One question arises from the study of these verses. Since Paul's primary reference here is to the Hebrew Scriptures (the Old Testament), does this passage have anything to tell us about the New Testament? Three other short passages are helpful in answering this question:

1. 2 Peter 3:16

Speaking of Paul's letters, Peter says, "There are some things in them that are hard to understand, which the ignorant and unstable twist to their own destruction, as they do the other Scriptures." Peter puts the writings of his fellow apostle on a par with the accepted canon of the Hebrew Bible. That means that everything 2 Timothy 3:15-17 has said about the Old Testament applies equally to Paul's letters.

2. Ephesians 3:3-5

If Peter is referring only to Paul's writings, is the rest of the New Testament not equal to the Old Testament? Here Paul links himself with all the apostles as those to whom the Holy Spirit gave God's revelation:

> 3 The mystery was made known to me by revelation, as I have written briefly.
> 4 When you read this, you can perceive my insight into the mystery of Christ,
> 5 which was not made known to the sons of men in other generations as it has now been revealed to his holy apostles and prophets by the Spirit.

The phrase "apostles and prophets" is probably to be read as meaning "apostles, who are prophets." Paul informs us that the apostles are a prophetic group. They are described as *holy*. This translates the word *hagios*, which means "set apart." The apostles were specially called to be the official channel of the final chapter in God's revelation. They are the authentic interpreters of Christ and of the salvation given in him. Their writings are as much part of God's Word as the prophetic Scriptures of the Old Testament.

3. 2 Peter 3:2

Here the apostles are distinguished from the prophets: "You should remember the predictions of the holy prophets and the commandment of the Lord and Saviour through your apostles." The prophets predicted the coming of Christ. Peter is talking about the men whose writings form the Old Testament Scriptures. However, he then sets the Lord's commandment through the apostles alongside the prophetic revelation in the Old Testament. The apostolic writings rank equally as Scripture. They are in fact the words of the Lord himself speaking through the men who are his mouthpiece.

These three passages show that everything 2 Timothy 3:15-17 says about the Old Testament applies by extension to the New Testament. The whole Bible is revelation breathed out by God.

2 PETER 1:19-21

> 19 And we have something more sure, the prophetic word, to which you will do well to pay attention as to a lamp shining in a dark place, until the day dawns and the morning star rises in your hearts,
> 20 knowing this first of all, that no prophecy of Scripture comes from someone's own interpretation.
> 21 For no prophecy was ever produced by the will of man, but men spoke from God as they were carried along by the Holy Spirit.

Notice four things from this passage:

1. The terms used for God's Word

(1) The phrase *the prophetic word* (verse 19) translates *ho prophetikos logos*. The "pro-" bit of the word *prophetic* can mean either "before" or "above." Therefore, this whole phrase can mean two things: (i) it can mean that the Bible declares things before they happen; or (ii) it can mean that the Bible is something spoken from above. Both are true. Some parts of the Bible are prophecies foretelling something in the future. Every part of the Bible is God speaking from above, making his revelation known.

(2) The phrase *prophecy of Scripture* (verse 20) translates *propheteia graphes*. *Propheteia* comes from the same root as *prophetikos*. It has the same significance: it refers to a word of truth, spoken from above. The phrase as a whole spells out for us where we find the prophetic word—in the Scripture. The singular is significant. Although Peter uses the word in the plural in 2 Peter 3:16, here the singular emphasizes that there is a unity to the whole of God's revelation. Every part of the Bible is conveying the same message.

2. The "more sure" prophetic word

Verse 19 tells us that once the prophetic word has been committed to writing in the Scriptures, it provides firmer ground, where we can tread with greater sure-footedness. This forces us to ask a question: the Bible is "more sure" *than what?* We find the answer in the previous verses. In verses 17 and 18, Peter describes the awesome moment when he was on the Mount of Transfiguration. He and his companions heard the "very voice borne from heaven," identifying Jesus as the beloved Son of God the Father. Now, thirty years later, Peter looks back to that tremendous experience and says that, for all the majestic glory of that occasion, it was not the greatest example of God speaking that he has ever known. We have the written Word of God in the Scriptures, and that is the more sure prophetic word. The Bible is surer than voices from heaven. It provides a far firmer foundation for our faith. We are on much safer ground when we walk in the light of the written Word. Even today, there is the temptation to look for voices from heaven. We sometimes wish that God would communicate to us directly. We need to remember that even the apostle who heard an audible voice says that that experience was nothing in comparison with the Scriptures. If I claim that the Lord has told me something directly, there is no way of checking whether I am right. If I turn to the Scriptures, it documents everything God has said. The evidence of what he has revealed is there for all to see. It is far surer.

A few years ago, a member of the British government had to resign. She had been accused of breaking the law. For a couple of weeks she kept denying it, both in Parliament and to the press. She clung on to her job. Then one day, a member of the opposition came across an email proving that she was not telling the truth. She resigned the next day.

She had no option. The documentary evidence was out in the open. As long as verbal accusations were made and she was verbally denying them, no one could be sure who was right. The document clinched it. In the Bible, we have documentary proof of everything that God has said. It is far more certain and reliable than any guesses or claims I might make. It is the clinching evidence that we can rely on.

3. What we know as a matter of primary importance

"First of all," says verse 20, we know that God's revelation in Scripture does not come "from someone's own interpretation." It was not some idiosyncratic whim which prompted the prophets to speak. Their message did not find its source within themselves. Verse 21 explains: the Scriptures did not originate in a decision of the human will. The teachings of the Bible are not mere products of the human mind or imagination. Rather, "men spoke as they were carried along by the Holy Spirit." The word translated *carried along* is the root from which we get our English word *ferry*. On two occasions when I have been in the Philippines, I have travelled from Manila to Iloilo by boat. The ferry carried me along and brought me to where I needed to be. As the prophets wrote their words, the Holy Spirit ferried them to the place where God wanted them to arrive. As a result, running through all the human features of the Bible, there is a divine quality. Every word is what God himself has spoken.

4. We must therefore pay attention to the Scriptures

This world is the dark place mentioned in verse 19. Ephesians 6:12 speaks of "this present darkness." Sin has cast a dark shadow across human existence. The Bible is a lamp, and it is an absolute necessity "until the day dawns" with the second coming of Christ. That daybreak will be the time when "the morning star rises in your hearts." This refers to the climax and fullness of divine revelation that will affect the heart of every believer when we finally see the Lord. Until then we shall always need the revelation we have now in the Scriptures. The Scriptures are complete and infallible, but they are only for this life. Once we are in heaven there will be an even better revelation. The Bible will be superfluous then, just as a candle adds nothing to the brilliance of unclouded summer sunshine.

Section summary and personal application

REMEMBER

All Scripture is breathed out by God and profitable for teaching, for reproof, for correction, and for training in righteousness, that the man of God may be complete, equipped for every good work.
—*2 Timothy 3:16-17*

Nobody ever outgrows Scripture; the book widens and deepens with our years.
—*Charles H. Spurgeon*

REFLECT

1. Do you resonate with David's delight in the meditation of God's Word (Psalm 19:7–11)?
2. How have experiences in your life served to make God's Word more precious to you?
3. In what specific ways have you been warned by Scripture?
4. Have you ever "heard the voice of God" outside the Scriptures? Do you believe all such events should be tested by Scripture? If so, how? If not, why not?

REJOICE

How firm a foundation, ye saints of the Lord,
   Is laid for your faith in His excellent Word!
What more can He say than to you He hath said,
   You, who unto Jesus for refuge have fled?

Fear not, I am with thee, O be not dismayed,
   For I am thy God and will still give thee aid;
I'll strengthen and help thee, and cause thee to stand
   Upheld by My righteous, omnipotent hand.

The soul that on Jesus has leaned for repose,
    I will not, I will not desert to its foes;
That soul, though all hell should endeavor to shake,
    I'll never, no never, no never forsake.
—*John Rippon* (1751–1836)

PART 2: KEY CREEDS AND CONFESSIONS

A. THE EARLY CREEDS

The fourth century *Nicene Creed* includes the words, "I believe in the Holy Spirit…, who spoke by the prophets." This statement affirms that the voice of the Spirit of God is heard in the prophetic Scriptures. The reference to 'the prophets' probably includes the writings of both the Old Testament prophets and the apostles whose prophetic calling has given us the New Testament. In the original statement from Nicaea in A.D. 325, the doctrine of the Holy Spirit was confined to the words, "and [I believe] in the Holy Spirit." At Constantinople in 381, this was enlarged to include the phrase, "who spoke by the prophets."

In the early centuries of the Christian era, many local churches prepared their own creedal summaries, just as local churches often do today. The revision of the *Nicene Creed* at Constantinople was based on a local creed used in the church at Salamis, a city on the island of Cyprus. It included this clause in its creed: "We believe in the Holy Spirit, who spoke in the Law, and preached in the prophets, and descended at Jordan, and spoke in the apostles."[3] The briefer addition to the *Nicene Creed* is probably intended as a summary of those words. The Holy Spirit spoke by the prophets in the sense of the Law and the Prophets of the Old Testament and the New Testament apostles. The mention of the descent of the Spirit upon Jesus Christ at Jordan is a reminder that every word he spoke was likewise the genuine voice of the Spirit of God. By setting

---

3 Quoted in P. Schaff, ed., *Nicene and Post Nicene Fathers*, vol. 14 (Albany: Ages, 1997), Second Series, 344.

the teaching of Jesus in the context of the references to the Spirit-inspired writing, speaking and preaching, both before and after his time, this sentence makes a wonderful point. To read the Scriptures is to hear the voice of Christ as authentically, as clearly, as if we had been there in Galilee when he was teaching here on earth.

In the following century the Chalcedonian Definition,[4] having spelled out the truth of the two natures of our Lord Jesus Christ, adds this phrase, "even as the prophets from earliest times spoke of him." Here is recognition that *Christ is the heart, the focus, of all God's revelation.* Everything contained in both the Old and the New Testaments points us to him.

B. THE REFORMATION CONFESSIONS

The confessions typically include a list of the 66 books of the Old and New Testaments, and distinguish them from the Apocrypha. Several of the apocryphal books—Tobit, Judith, the first two books of the Maccabees, the Wisdom of Solomon, Ecclesiasticus, and Baruch, as well as some additional passages in the books of Esther and Daniel—had come into use on a par with the Scriptures in the medieval Catholic Church. The Reformed churches reasserted the clear distinction between the inspired Scriptures and other religious writings, however valuable the latter might be as a source of historical information, or as objects of literary interest. The canonical books alone are the Holy Scriptures, the written Word of God.

The confessions trace the process by which the Scriptures were transmitted to the world in five stages:

1. *Scripture originated with God.* Scripture does not find its source in human will; it comes from God.
2. *God revealed his Word to chosen men.* The Holy Spirit handed down the Scriptures as divine oracles given to the prophets at various times and in various ways.
3. *God published his Word to the world.* Through the preaching of the prophets and apostles, God's revelation was passed on.
4. *God's Word was committed to writing.* This is evidence of God's special care for us. It ensures that the truth is preserved.

---

4   See Appendix 3.

5. *The Bible is the living voice of God.* As he spoke to the prophets, so he still speaks to us through the Scriptures.

The confessions also face another important question: how do we know that this particular set of 66 books is canonical, and on what grounds do we exclude the Apocrypha? The confessions gave three reasons for insisting on the distinctiveness of the books of the Bible.

1. The church's acknowledgement

The earliest Christians adopted the Jewish canon as its first Bible. Over a period of several decades, the 27 books making up our New Testament were added to the canon of Scripture. The church as a whole gave its common consent to the addition of these books. This does not mean that the church created the Bible, or decided which books to accept. It was more a case of the church recognizing those books that had divine authority.

An illustration might help us. A doctor is having difficulty deciding what treatment will be best for his patient. In the end, he gives the patient a huge list of things to try out. "Then come back and tell me what has helped you," the doctor says. The patient returns at the appointed time. He hands the doctor a list, and says, "I've discovered that these 66 things help me." In the same way, the church made a discovery: these 66 books really do help us in our Christian life. They really do have the stamp of divine inspiration.

2. The evidence within the Scriptures themselves

One such evidence is the fulfilment of prophecy. Another is the way in which the Bible's excellent quality reflects its divine origin. This is expressed beautifully in the *Westminster Larger Catechism*:

> The Scriptures manifest themselves to be the Word of God by their majesty and purity, by the consent of all the parts and the scope of the whole, which is to give all glory to God; by their light and power to convince and convert sinners, to comfort and build up believers unto salvation.[5]

---

5 *Westminster Larger Catechism*, Question 4.

3. The witness of the Spirit

The Holy Spirit illumines the believer's heart, so enabling him to discern the supernatural quality of Scripture. This is a work of the Spirit taking place along with the Word itself. As the Word of God is preached or read, the Holy Spirit gives convincing witness of its truth and power. Some claim that this makes the discernment of the divine inspiration of Scripture a subjective or mystical experience, as if understanding comes in a revelatory flash. However, that was not what the Reformers meant. They understood that the Spirit uses the Scriptures themselves, opening a person's spiritual eyes to appreciate the objective marks of truth inescapably present in the Bible.

These, then, are the reasons the Confessions give for accepting the canonical Scriptures as God's inspired Word. Next, they highlight the obvious implication of recognizing the canon of Scripture.

The term *canon* is derived from the Greek word *kanon*, which means a rod. It refers to a straight rod used to measure or test something. The equivalent today would be a ruler. With a ruler, we can draw a straight line, or check that a line is straight. We can measure a line. By using this term, we mean that the Bible is the standard by which we measure everything. Christians find in the Bible the norm for what we must believe, how we ought to behave, how we regulate our worship, and what form our service for Christ should take. The confessions often express this by describing the Bible as a rule. It is the rule of faith, the rule of truth, the rule of knowledge, the rule of obedience. Any merely human authority is rejected.

In putting forward their doctrine of revelation, the confessions emphasize five qualities belonging to Scripture:

(1) *Its sufficiency*

By using this term, the confessions were teaching that we find everything we need to know for Christian life, faith and salvation in the Bible. Nothing needs to be added, subtracted or altered in any way. The Reformers knew that there are things which God has not revealed, things which we shall never be able to discover in this life, or even in all eternity. However, God has left out of the Bible nothing necessary for us to know, so we can approach the Bible with true gratitude.

(2) *Its clarity*

The clarity of Scripture closely relates to its sufficiency. There is an interesting statement in the *Irish Articles* saying that the Holy Scriptures "are able to instruct us sufficiently in all points of faith that we are bound to believe, and all good duties that we are bound to practise."[6] Those are wise words. They acknowledge that there are some things not in the category of "bound to." The confessions note that some parts of Scripture are not crystal clear. They are open to differences in interpretation. However, everything it is vital to believe or to practise is clear and plain. It follows from this that we should never insist on our own interpretation in issues of secondary importance. In such cases, we must show tolerance and mutual respect, but in gospel essentials, absolute unity is required.

(3) *Its infallibility*

This is an obvious consequence of the fact that the God of truth inspires the Bible. Everything Scripture says is beyond question. There are no errors of any sort in the Bible.

(4) *Its translatability*

It is striking that some of the Reformers saw the possibility and the necessity of Bible translation as so important that they included it in their confessions of faith. The *Irish Articles* say this: "The Scriptures ought to be translated out of the original tongues into all languages for the common use of all men."[7] The authors of the confessions rightly saw that God's grace reached out to the world as a whole. They recognized that through translations of the Bible the gospel was to be published to all nations without exception. They saw translation as a necessary means of bringing people of every nation to the true knowledge of God. The Reformation was blessed with a great vision of Christianity as a missionary faith; because it had a vision of a God who is committed to extending salvation in Christ to the very ends of the earth. It is true that the Reformers recognized the special importance of the Hebrew Old Testament and the Greek New Testament. Nevertheless,

---

6   *Irish Articles*, 6.
7   *Irish Articles*, 4.

translations are still the sacred Scriptures. The Scriptures in the common languages of all the world's peoples are still the Word of God. This sets Christianity entirely apart from a religious system like Islam, which claims that the Qur'an can only properly exist in Arabic.

(5) *Its major thrust*
The confessions often speak of the Bible's major thrust. Whatever else it may contain, the main aim of the Bible is to proclaim the message of God's goodwill towards humankind in general. That goodwill is especially declared in his benevolence towards sinners in Christ.

C. MODERN CONFESSIONS OF FAITH

1. Confession of Faith of the United Church of Northern India
The North Indian church explicitly identifies the Old and New Testament Scriptures as the Word of God. They are infallible, and are the only rule of faith and duty. At certain points, it is instructive to compare this confession with the Confession of Faith of the South India United Church. The southern church was founded in 1901. Its confession of faith seems to reflect the influence of western liberal theology. Its doctrine of Scripture is noticeably weaker than that of its northern neighbour. The southern confession defines Scripture as the record of God's revelation, rather than according it revelatory status itself. Moreover, it does not see the content of the Bible itself as the church's ultimate authority, but "the Holy Spirit speaking in the Scriptures." Such wording falls short of a fully biblical theology of the Bible, and risks opening the door to wayward subjective readings of the text. The northern church avoided this deficiency.

2. Confession of Faith of the Huria Batak Protestant
This confession affirms that the words of the Bible "are truly the Word of God." The Confession insists on the sufficiency of Scripture in two respects: to reveal God and his will, and to teach us what we must believe in order to receive eternal life. It rejects all human wisdom differing from God's Word.

3. Confession of Faith of House Churches in China

The Chinese confession teaches that the 66 canonical books are God's inspired Word. Consequently, it is "the complete truth and without error," and no changes to the Bible are permissible. The Bible is the ultimate standard for faith, life, and service. It is never out of date. The Confession emphasizes the Bible's main theme: it "clearly describes God's plan of redemption for man."

There is also a section on the interpretation of the Bible. Any particular Scripture must be interpreted within two contexts: the historical context in which it was first given, and the overall context of Scriptural teachings as a whole. The leading of the Holy Spirit is vital in the interpretation of the Bible. However, this does not mean that a purely individual and subjective interpretation is valid. The confession stresses two things: (1) the traditions of orthodox belief throughout church history must be consulted as we interpret Scripture today; and (2) personal interpretation and subjective spiritualizing of Scripture is ruled out.

Section summary and personal application

REMEMBER

The gospel alone is sufficient to rule the lives of Christians everywhere...any additional rules made to govern men's conduct added nothing to the perfection already found in the Gospel of Jesus Christ.
—*John Wycliffe (1320–1384)*

REFLECT

1. How has Scripture strengthened and encouraged you through the years?
2. All Scripture is divinely inspired. However, within Christendom there are various interpretations of Scripture regarding secondary issues (non-essentials). Our attitude should evidence one of tolerance and mutual respect, rather than culti-

vating a contentious and bitter spirit. List ways in which you can cultivate tolerance and respect for others who may disagree with your viewpoint.

REJOICE

I love the volumes of Thy Word;
    What light and joy those leaves afford
    To souls benighted and distressed!
Thy precepts guide my doubtful way,
    Thy fear forbids my feet to stray,
    Thy promise leads my heart to rest.

From the discoveries of Thy law
    The perfect rules of life I draw;
    These are my study and delight:
Not honey so invites the taste,
    Nor gold that hath the furnace past
    Appears so pleasing to the sight.

Who knows the errors of his thoughts?
    My God, forgive my secret faults,
    And from presumptuous sins restrain:
Accept my poor attempts of praise,
    That I have read Thy book of grace,
    And book of nature, not in vain.
  — Isaac Watts (1674–1748)

PART 3: KEY HISTORICAL DEVELOPMENTS

In this section, we shall do three things. First, it will be useful to look briefly at the process by which the church arrived at the final New Testament canon. Second, we shall read some classic statements on the doctrine of Scripture from different historical periods. Third, we shall consider some inadequate doctrines of Scripture, and seek to respond to them.

A. THE FORMATION OF THE NEW TESTAMENT CANON

Since the church inherited the canon of the Old Testament from its Jewish roots, the main point of interest is the process of New Testament canon formation:

> Christ passed on to his followers, as Holy Scripture, the Bible which he had received, containing the same books as the Hebrew Bible today. The first Christians shared with their Jewish contemporaries a full knowledge of the identity of the canonical books.[8]

However, by the end of the first century various new documents were circulating amongst the churches. As time went by, their number increased. Not every church had access to every document. However, very early on, the thirteen letters of Paul had already been gathered together into a collection, and by the middle of the second century, the four Gospels were also circulating together, indicating that "they were increasingly recognized as normative ecclesiastical documents."[9] However, there were those who questioned whether the emerging consensus was correct. At the end of the second century, Marcion drew up a list of New Testament books including only Luke's Gospel

---

8 R.T. Beckwith, "Canon of the Old Testament," in *The Illustrated Bible Dictionary* (Leicester: IVP, 1980), 1:238.

9 A. du Toit, "Canon: New Testament," in B.M. Metzger and M.D. Coogan, ed., *The Oxford Companion to the Bible* (Oxford: Oxford University Press, 1993), 103.

and ten of Paul's letters. He omitted the Pastoral Epistles. This provided an impetus for the church to think through the question of the canon. In response to Marcion, church leaders such as Irenaeus reaffirmed the position of all four Gospels and all thirteen of Paul's letters. In addition, Irenaeus included in his list of authorized books, Acts, James, 1 Peter, 1 and 2 John, Jude, and Revelation.

On the other hand, there were those who wanted to include additional books in the New Testament. Some churches accepted the remaining books which we now find in the New Testament—Hebrews, 2 Peter, and 3 John, while others were uncertain about their position. For a time, a number of other first- or early second-century writings were accepted as Scripture in some places.

In the middle of the fourth century, Eusebius distinguished four categories of books claiming a place in the New Testament. First, there were the acknowledged books—the four Gospels, the Acts of the Apostles, Paul's thirteen letters, Hebrews, 1 Peter, and 1 John. These were universally accepted as true Scripture. Second, there were the debatable books—James, 2 Peter, 2 and 3 John, and Jude. Most Christians recognized these as canonical, but some disputed them. Third, there were the compromised books—the Acts of Paul, the Shepherd of Hermas, the Revelation of Peter, the Letter of Barnabas, the Didache, and the Gospel according to the Hebrews. Although some earlier writers had included these in their lists of authoritative writings, by Eusebius' time, they were generally recognized not to be inspired Scripture. They were certainly of value for private reading, though they had to be read with discernment, since they were not infallible. Fourth, there were the heretical books— the Gospels of Peter, Thomas, and Matthias, the Acts of Andrew and the Acts of John. Some heretical sects included these in their Bible, but the orthodox Christian community universally dismissed them as fictional writings. The book of Revelation was in a category of its own. It was either fully accepted or completely rejected. Eusebius accepted it as valid Scripture, but he acknowledged that some Christians rejected it outright.[10]

By the later years of the fourth century, the church saw that it was time to settle the issue of the canon. In A.D. 363, a synod meeting at Laodicea decreed that books permitted to be read in the churches were

---

10 Eusebius, *Church History*, 3.25.

"only the Canonical Books of the Old and New Testaments."[11] However, it did not list these books. Such a decree does prove that by then there was general agreement as to the limits of the canon. Four years later Athanasius wrote this in his annual letter to the churches in the area where he served as bishop:

> It is not tedious to speak of the books of the New Testament. These are, the four Gospels, according to Matthew, Mark, Luke, and John. Afterwards, the Acts of the Apostles and Epistles (called Catholic), seven, viz. of James, one; of Peter, two; of John, three; after these, one of Jude. In addition, there are fourteen Epistles of Paul, written in this order. The first, to the Romans; then two to the Corinthians; after these, to the Galatians; next, to the Ephesians; then to the Philippians; then to the Colossians; after these, two to the Thessalonians, and that to the Hebrews; and again, two to Timothy; one to Titus; and lastly, that to Philemon. And besides, the Revelation of John.[12]

Athanasius' list corresponds exactly with the 27 books making up the New Testament which we know today. In A.D. 397, a church council meeting at Carthage published the same list. The canon was now definitively fixed.

However, we must never forget that it would be

> a mistake to regard the official recognition of our present twenty-seven books by the church as the act which gave them their canonical status. The decisions of the church were in reality the acknowledgement of the intrinsic authority and power of these writings.[13]

---

11 The Canons of the Synod held in the City of Laodicea, 59.

12 Athanasius, *Festal Letter No. 39*, 5.

13 du Toit, "Canon: New Testament," in Metzger and Coogan, ed., *The Oxford Companion to the Bible*, 104.

B. CLASSIC STATEMENTS OF THE DOCTRINE OF REVELATION IN SCRIPTURE

1. Early church fathers: Origen

Origen was one of the first Christian writers to develop a doctrine of Scripture. He was born in Egypt towards the end of the second century. Early in the third century, the Roman emperor inflicted harsh persecution on the Christians there. Most pastors were killed. Origen, who had been training in theology, found himself the senior Christian teacher in Alexandria, even though he was only in his early twenties. When he was forty-five, Origen moved to Caesarea as head of a theological training school. While there, he wrote many volumes. In all his writings, Origen demonstrates a firm commitment to the Bible as the Word of God. One of his works has a section devoted entirely to the divine origin of Scripture. He offers four proofs that the Scriptures are "inspired by the Spirit of God":

(1) *The worldwide impact of the Bible*
Origen notes that the Bible is unrivalled in this respect. Other writers might like to see their opinions changing the face of nations, but only the sacred Scriptures have actually achieved this.

(2) *The worldwide spread of the gospel*
Origen describes the progress of the gospel across many nations. It has taken place in relatively few years, and has happened in spite of the persecution targeted against believers. Origen writes, "we have no difficulty in saying that the result is beyond any human power."

(3) *The fulfilment of the prophets' predictions*
Origen shows most interest in the Old Testament predictions connected with the coming of Christ, especially those whose fulfilment required major changes in international politics. Here is proof of God's control of global affairs in order to bring about the fulfilment of what he had prophesied about Christ in his inspired Word.

(4) *The subjective experience of reading the Scriptures*
If we read the Bible with care, attention, zeal, and reverence, we can

trace its divinity. We feel our minds touched by the divine breath. We then acknowledge that the words of Scripture are no mere human utterances, but the language of God.

2. Reformers and Puritans: Thomas Watson

After studying at Cambridge, Thomas Watson spent sixteen years as pastor of a congregation in the centre of London. In 1662, Watson, along with many other Puritans, was thrown out of the Church of England because its bishops were opposed to a thorough reformation of the church. For the next thirteen years, Watson risked being fined or imprisoned by preaching from time to time at secret meetings whenever he could do so in safety.

In 1675, the British government finally allowed Nonconformists to licence premises for worship. Watson then became pastor of another London congregation. One of Watson's published sermons is entitled *The Scriptures*. Watson begins by giving seven arguments proving the Bible to be the inspired Word of God: (1) it is ancient, and reaches further back in time than any other historical writing; (2) it has been miraculously preserved, despite the devil's attempts to destroy it; (3) its subject matter is beyond the power of human invention; (4) its predictions, sometimes looking many centuries ahead, have been fulfilled; (5) its human authors were willing to speak of their own failings in order to give all glory to God; (6) the Bible has transforming power in the lives of men and women; and (7) the miracles which the Scriptures record demonstrate its divine origin.

Watson insists that Scripture is to be its own interpreter, and that God has appointed pastors in his church to expound the Scriptures for his people. This is not, however, to pin our faith upon mere men: God gives all his people the spirit of discernment so that they can tell whether what is preached is true to God's Word.[14]

Watson then demonstrates that the truth of the inspiration of Scripture implies a rebuke on five types of people: (1) those who take away part of the Scripture; (2) those who neglect the Old Testament; (3) those who reject the Bible as a dead letter on the pretext that they have the Spirit; (4) those who simply do not bother to read the Bible; and

---

14 Acts 17:11.

(5) those who put forward strange interpretations because they fail to compare Scripture with Scripture.

The truth of the inspiration of Scripture also implies eight exhortations: (1) we must study the Bible reverently; (2) we must value the Bible more than gold; (3) we must believe everything the Scriptures say; (4) we must love the Word; (5) we must conform our lives to the commands of Scripture; (6) we must contend for the Bible against those who oppose it; (7) we must give thanks to God for giving us the Bible; and (8) if we have tasted the life-giving power of the Word, we must praise God for his saving grace.

C. ADDRESSING ERRORS ON THE SUBJECT OF REVELATION IN SCRIPTURE—"THE FUNDAMENTALS"

Between 1910 and 1915, a 12-volume series of journals was published in America. They were entitled *The Fundamentals*. They were published in response to a challenge to the traditional view of Scripture. The view that the Bible is the inspired and infallible Word of God was accepted virtually without question in the church until the mid-eighteenth century. Since then, a new approach to the Bible had been gaining support. This new view was anti-supernatural. It denied the possibility of miracles. It ruled out predictive prophecy. It reclassified many of the Bible's narratives as myths. The Bible was regarded as a purely human work and marked by the fallibility afflicting all human works. There was no ultimate authority in the message of the Bible. It was up to us to pass judgement on each part of the Bible to see whether it was true to the Christian spirit.

The people putting forward this new view were still prepared to speak of "inspiration," but they meant something very different from the normal meaning of the word. For these people, inspiration meant that within this unreliable human book it was possible to come up against divine mystery. It was not that the exact words were inspired. The precise words were not important. It was that the writers were inspired men. They somehow possessed the divine Spirit to a remarkable degree, and when you read the Bible, you could sometimes catch something of that mystical Spirit.

When a doctrine is challenged in such a way, it presents believers with a great opportunity to stand up for the truth. That is what the early twentieth-century Christians in America did through *The Fun-damentals*. Altogether 90 articles were published in the series, and 29 of them had to do with the doctrine of Scripture.

James Gray, of Moody Bible Institute, wrote an article aimed at correcting the mistaken view of inspiration. He pointed out that "inspiration" refers to the writings, not to the writers. He explained:

> Moses, David, Paul, John, were not always and everywhere inspired, for then always and everywhere they would have been infallible and inerrant, which was not the case. They sometimes made mistakes in thought and erred in conduct. But however fallible and errant they may have been as men compassed with infirmity like ourselves, such fallibility or errancy was never in any circumstances communicated to their sacred writings.[15]

In another article Leander Whitcomb Munhall, a Methodist evangelist, used the term "verbal inspiration" to teach that the very words of the Bible matter. It is not just that the *thoughts* of Scripture are of an elevated quality, but that the exact words are God-given: "If they were not, then the Bible is not inspired at all, since it is composed only and solely of words."[16] Munhall quotes a number of other writers to support this point. One of them is Dean Burgon, who said,

> As for thoughts being inspired apart from the words which give them expression, you might as well talk of a tune without notes, or a sum without figures. No such theory of inspiration is even intelligible.[17]

Among the evidences for inspiration offered in *The Fundamentals*, two were particularly favoured by the contributors:

(1) *The witness of Christ*. An article by William Caren of Canada makes the following eight points: (i) the Lord never questioned the

---

15 J.M. Gray, "The Inspiration of the Bible—Definition, Extent and Proof," in C.L. Feinberg, ed., *The Fundamentals for Today*, 2 vol. (1958; reprint, Grand Rapids: Kregel, 1990), 138f.

16 L.W. Munhall, "Inspiration," in C.L. Feinberg, ed., *The Fundamentals*, 159.

17 Quoted by Munhall, "Inspiration," in C.L. Feinberg, ed., *The Fundamentals*, 160.

Jewish canon; (ii) he never expressed doubt about anything that the Scriptures teach; (iii) he accepted the narratives of Scripture as historically accurate; (iv) he assumed that the Scriptures are from God; (v) he treated the Scriptures as God speaking; (vi) he took it for granted that the Scriptures are authoritative and not merely human; (vii) he taught the absolute infallibility of Scripture; and (viii) he declared that he himself is the fulfilment of the prophecies of Scripture.[18]

(2) *The structural unity of the Bible.* A.T. Pierson, who succeeded C.H. Spurgeon at the Metropolitan Tabernacle in London, points out that the harmonious teaching of the entire Bible is miraculous in itself:

> Here are some sixty or more separate documents, written by some forty different persons, scattered over wide intervals of space and time, strangers to each other. These documents are written in three different languages, in different lands, among different and sometimes hostile peoples, with marked diversities of literary style, and by men of all grades of culture and mental capacity, from Moses to Malachi. When we look into these productions, there is even in them great unlikeness, both in matter and manner of statement; yet they all constitute one volume.[19]

Pierson stresses that all the diverse parts of Scripture agree. He concludes that there is no possible explanation except that God superintended the production of the Bible: "Its unity is the unity of a divine plan, and its harmony the harmony of a Supreme Intelligence."

When *The Fundamentals* series was being published, the opponents of the historic doctrine of Scripture were liberal theologians. At the start of the twentieth century, the evangelical world was standing firm against the erosion of the biblical doctrine of revelation. However, by the end of the century, some who would still claim to be evangelicals were shifting their position. A view known as neo-evangelicalism became less clear on the inerrancy of Scripture. Neo-evangelicalism

---

18 W. Caren, "The Testimony of Christ to the Old Testament," in C.L. Feinberg, ed., *The Fundamentals*, 59-65.

19 A.T. Pierson, "The Testimony of the Organic Unity of the Bible to its Inspiration," in C.L. Feinberg, ed., *The Fundamentals*, 195f.

wants to accept the authority of the Bible, and yet it separates inspiration from inerrancy. The Bible was held to be infallible in matters concerning salvation. However, its writers were subject to the worldview of their time, so in matters of science and history they may have made some errors. A leading example of this approach was Daniel Fuller, the founder of Fuller Theological Seminary in the USA. Robert Lightner explains Fuller's view of inspiration like this:

> [It] makes sure that we have an authoritative record of all that God wanted to make known. But it was not God's intention or purpose to secure inerrancy in peripheral matters.

This raises the question, on what criteria do we decide what matters are "peripheral"? Lightner gives Fuller's answer,

> "Peripheral matters" include Scriptural data which have nothing to do with faith and life, such as minor historical details, grammatical constructions and the like.[20]

We are on shaky ground here. How can we be certain that we have correctly identified those details called "minor"? How can we be sure that a particular detail does not in fact have a bearing on faith and life? In 1976, Harold Lindsell wrote a book, *The Battle for the Bible*, in which he accused those holding a limited inerrancy view of opening the door to modernism. The danger in the theory of partial inerrancy is that our sinfulness is likely to make us weed out the bits of the Bible which we do not want to hear. The passages rebuking us are the ones which we are likely to downgrade. Those passages that correct wrong behaviour, redirect warped thinking, or shape and alter disobedient lifestyles are the ones which we decide to dismiss.

In response to this evangelical shift, the International Council on Biblical Inerrancy was set up in 1978, with James Montgomery Boice as chairman. Boice has pointed out the fallacy of claiming that historical inaccuracies may still be consistent with infallibility in matters

---

20 Quoted by H.M. Conn, *Contemporary World Theology* (Philadelphia: Presbyterian and Reformed, 1973), 136.

of salvation: "The Bible is a historical book, and Christianity is a historical religion. If the Bible errs in matters of history, Christianity itself is affected."[21]

Moreover, if we reject the doctrine of biblical inerrancy, this has a knock-on effect. It has implications for other doctrines and for aspects of Christian devotion. In John 10:35, Jesus says, "Scripture cannot be broken." Donald Macleod makes this comment on these words:

> The Bible, in the judgment of Jesus…can't be wrong. It can't be false. It can't mislead. It can't deceive. It can't be violated…. Christ has said this book is infallible. He has attested it as the unbreakable Word of God, and it is because of his testimony… that [we] believe in the full, final, infallible authority of Scripture. I cannot see how one can be loyal to Christ and yet defy him on something as fundamental as his view of the status of the Bible…. Belief in the God-givenness of the Bible is simply an aspect of devotion to Christ.[22]

At the beginning of the twenty-first century, we face a new challenge. There is a tendency now to doubt the *sufficiency* of Scripture. Dr. Boice has observed how, in the work of the church,

> …the Bible is often laid aside and reliance is placed instead upon such extra-biblical props as sociological techniques, psychology and psychiatry, and what are called 'signs and wonders.'[23]

He raises the following questions:

> Do we really believe God has given us what we need in this book? Or do we think we have to supplement the Bible with other man-made things? Do we need sociological techniques to do evangelism? Must we attract people to our churches by showmanship and entertainment? Do we need psychology and psychiatry for

---

21 J.M. Boice, *Standing on the Rock* (Grand Rapids: Baker, 1994), 132.

22 D. Macleod, *A Faith to Live By* (Fearn: Christian Focus, 1998), 14.

23 Boice, *Standing on the Rock*, 12.

Christian growth? Do we need extra-biblical signs or miracles for guidance? Is the Bible's teaching adequate for achieving social progress and reform?[24]

Boice insists that the Scriptures are sufficient for all times and in all areas of life. Because they are "the very words of God," they "are useful for dealing with any problem you will face in the church or out of the church, at this time or at any other period of history."[25] We might add this. In the secular west, in the Islamic world, in the nations of Asia, in Latin America, anywhere and everywhere, the Bible says it all.

In the past few years, there has been a new attack on the sufficiency of Scripture in the theory of "trajectory hermeneutics," developed by the Canadian theologian William Webb. He argues that the Bible traces a redemptive movement towards the ultimate ethic, and that we today need to apply the redemptive spirit of a text, not its bare words. Webb argues for what he calls "the X-Y-Z principle." X represents the position held on an issue in the wider cultural world of Bible times. Y is the ethical assessment of the Bible on that issue for its own times. Z is the ultimate ethic towards which biblical statements are progressing. However, the Bible did not reach the ultimate ethic. Therefore, we must go further, in line with the Bible's own redemptive spirit, along the trajectory of the redemptive movement of Scripture. Webb applies this in particular to gender roles and the ministry of women. He argues for complete gender equality without role differentiation because, he claims, that is the direction towards which Scripture is tending, even though it has not yet arrived at that destination.

Webb raises some important questions. We do have to interpret Scripture within our own cultural context in the light of its place within its own cultural context. However, if the Bible is not the revelation of the ultimate ethic, then how can we possibly know what the ultimate ethic is? If we deny the sufficiency of Scripture, we flounder in a sea of speculation.

---

24 Boice, *Standing on the Rock*, 133.
25 Boice, *Standing on the Rock*, 114f.

PART 4: KEY POINTS OF PRACTICAL APPLICATION

Charles Colson became a Christian around the time he was imprisoned in America for his part in the Watergate scandal, which eventually ended Richard Nixon's presidency. After his release from prison, he became involved in a ministry working with prisoners. He admits that, at one time, the question of biblical inerrancy was of no concern to him. However, he became convinced of its importance when he saw the effects of different views of Scripture on the front lines of spiritual warfare in the prisons. This was his conclusion:

> The authority and truth of Scripture is not an obscure issue reserved for the private debate and entertainment of theologians; it is relevant, indeed critical, for every serious Christian—layman, pastor and theologian alike. My convictions have come, not from studies in Ivory Tower academia, but from life in what may be termed the front line trenches, where Christians grapple in hand-to-hand combat with the prince of darkness. In our prison fellowships, where the Bible is proclaimed as God's holy and inerrant revelation, believers grow and discipleship deepens. Where the Bible is not so proclaimed (or where Christianity is presumed to rest on subjective experience alone or content-less fellowship), faith withers and dies. Christianity without biblical fidelity is merely another passing fad in an age of passing fads.[26]

For the application of the doctrine of divine revelation in an inerrant Scripture, we can do better than to quote Charles Colson. Here are four texts from the Pastoral Epistles referring to God's Word. They apply the truth about God's Word to the work of the ministry in particular.

---

26 Quoted by Boice, *Standing on the Rock*, 112.

1. *1 Timothy 5:17*

> Let the elders who rule well be considered worthy of double
> honour, especially those who labour in preaching and teaching.

The word translated *labour* is *kopiao*. It speaks of work that makes you
tired—exhausting effort. The same word is used in Luke 5:5 of the fisher-
men who "toiled all night." We should be toiling at the Scriptures. This
word is also used in 2 Timothy 2:6 of the hard-working farmer. We
should prepare for strenuous effort in the work of the gospel. It follows
from the fact that the Bible is God's unchallengeable revelation. The
Lord deserves the most energetic effort of which we are capable.

2. *2 Timothy 2:15*

> Do your best to present yourself to God as one approved, a
> worker who has no need to be ashamed, rightly handling the
> word of truth.

Since God's Word is the truth, the gospel minister is to be *a worker*.
This word (*ergates*) is used of harvesters labouring in a cornfield. In
Matthew 9:37-38 Jesus said, "The harvest is plentiful, but the labourers
are few; therefore pray earnestly to the Lord of the harvest to send out
labourers into his harvest."

The word is used of grape-pickers in a vineyard. Jesus' parable in
Matthew 20:1-2 begins like this:

> The kingdom of heaven is like a master of a house who went out
> early in the morning to hire labourers for his vineyard. After
> agreeing with the labourers for a denarius a day, he sent them
> into his vineyard.

The same word is used in Acts 19:25 (rendered *workmen*) of artisans
at the smithies. Verses 24 and 25 read as follows:

> A man named Demetrius, a silversmith, who made silver shrines
> of Artemis, brought no little business to the craftsmen. These he

gathered together, with the workmen in similar trades, and said, "Men, you know that from this business we have our wealth."

Paul's exhortation to Timothy in 2 Timothy 2:15 begins with "do your best." This phrase translates the Greek word *spoudazo*. It could be translated "be in a hurry." It is an urgent matter to research the Scriptures so that we can proclaim the gospel message. It is a message for dying sinners. They need to hear it now, and we should be eager to bring it to them. We must exert ourselves, putting every effort into the work.

The actual work of the gospel worker is described as "rightly handling the word." This term (*orthotomeo*) means "to cut straight." It is found in the Greek translation of Proverbs 3:6: "In all your ways acknowledge him, and he will make straight your paths." The idea of cutting a straight path brings to mind the picture of blazing a trail through the jungle and laying the tarmac for a new road. Our task as preachers is to carve out for our hearers a highway through the Bible. We are not to meander in obscurities, but to lay bare the essentials of God's gospel revelation in Jesus Christ.

3. 2 Timothy 4:2

Preach the word; be ready in season and out of season; reprove, rebuke, and exhort, with complete patience and teaching.

Because this word is divine revelation, it must be preached. The verb here is *kerusso*, which links with the noun *kerux*. A *kerux* was a man with a commission to shout out an item of information for all to hear. He operated under the authority of another as spokesman. He had nothing to say except the message his master had given him. He had to be totally dedicated to his task. The true preacher never expresses his personal opinion. He always declares what God has revealed in the Word of Scripture. Moreover, he must be *ready*. He must stand poised. He must never be caught with nothing to say. He must be so familiar with the Word that whenever there is an opportunity to proclaim it, whenever a question is raised or a challenge is posed, he declares unhesitatingly what God says. This readiness is necessary *in season and out of season*. We must be ready when people are clamouring to hear.

We must also be ready when being a preacher is a lonely and costly calling. The following verses (2 Timothy 4:3-5) describe such a time:

> The time is coming when people will not endure sound teaching, but having itching ears they will accumulate for themselves teachers to suit their own passions, and will turn away from listening to the truth and wander off into myths. As for you, always be sober-minded, endure suffering, do the work of an evangelist, fulfil your ministry.

At such times, standing for God's Word may involve suffering, as verse 5 indicates. But we must *fulfil* the ministry of the Word. We must carry it through to completion in successive acts of proclamation.

4. *Titus 1:9*

> He must hold firm to the trustworthy word as taught, so that he may be able to give instruction in sound doctrine and also to rebuke those who contradict it.

God's Word is trustworthy: it is dependable; it is free from error. Therefore, we are to *hold firm* to it. The verb here is *antechomai*. It speaks of loyalty. Jesus used it in Matthew 6:24, where it is translated "be devoted":

> No one can serve two masters, for either he will hate the one and love the other, or he will be devoted to the one and despise the other. You cannot serve God and money.

Notice that the opposite of devoted loyalty, in Jesus' words, is to *despise*. This translates the verb *kataphroneo*, which means to have a low opinion of something. We are not to have a low opinion of the Scriptures. We are not to propagate our own ideas in its place. We must stand on the truth of God's Word with loyalty.

REFLECT

1. What comfort do you derive from the fact that the Scriptures are both inerrant (contain no error in the original autographs) and infallible?

2. How would you respond to someone who declared the Bible to be archaic, incomplete or obsolete?

3. In what ways has the Bible proven its transforming power in your life, or the lives of those you know?

4. List your strengths and weaknesses when it comes to conforming your life to the Word of God.

5. God's Word is applicable to all of life and to any situation. How can you use this truth when counselling others?

REJOICE

Holy Bible, Book divine,
　Precious treasure, thou art mine;
Mine to tell me whence I come;
　Mine to teach me where I am.

Mine to chide me when I rove;
　Mine to show a Saviour's love;
Mine thou art to guide and guard;
　Mine to punish or reward.

Mine to comfort in distress;
　Suffering in this wilderness;
Mine to show, by living faith,
　Man can triumph over death.

Mine to tell of joys to come,
　And the rebel sinner's doom;
O thou holy Book divine,
　Precious treasure, thou art mine.
—*John Burton (1773–1822)*

4

THE DOCTRINE OF REVELATION IN CREATION

How does God make his glory known in the created realm?

The doctrine of revelation in Scripture is the absolute foundation for every other doctrine. That is why we have dealt with it at some length. If we lose confidence in the Scriptures, that will have implications for what we say about everything else. When we do accept the inspiration, inerrancy, and authority of Scripture as the ultimate revelation, then we can say that there is a second form of revelation—in creation. We can say so, only because Scripture tells us so.

PART 1: KEY TEXTS

A. OLD TESTAMENT

PSALM 19:1-4

> 1 The heavens declare the glory of God, and the sky above proclaims his handiwork.
> 2 Day to day pours out speech, and night to night reveals knowledge.
> 3 There is no speech, nor are there words, whose voice is not heard.
> 4 Their measuring line goes out through all the earth, and their words to the end of the world.

We notice three things from this passage:

1. The sky is a revelation of God

The Hebrew word rendered *heavens* is *shamayim*. It is defined by the word *sky*, which translates *raqiya'*. Both terms refer to the visible skies above us. The last time these words occurred together was in Genesis 1, where *raqiya'* is rendered *expanse*. Here are the relevant verses:

> 8 And God called the expanse Heaven. And there was evening and there was morning, the second day.
> 14 And God said, "Let there be lights in the expanse of the heavens to separate the day from the night. And let them be for signs and for seasons, and for days and years,

15 and let them be lights in the expanse of the heavens to give
light upon the earth." And it was so.
17 And God set them in the expanse of the heavens to give light
on the earth,
20 And God said, "Let the waters swarm with swarms of living
creatures, and let birds fly above the earth across the expanse of
the heavens."

It is clear from verse 8 that the two words refer to the same thing. We
learn from verses 14, 15, and 17 that they refer to the place where the
stars are. Verse 20 tells us that it is the place where the birds fly. Now
the psalmist tells us that the sky declares God's glory.

The wind is invisible, but we can see the branches moving on the
trees and sometimes, when the wind is strong, we see branches blown
down on to the road. God is invisible, but we can observe the effects
of his reality.

God's glory is obvious from his handiwork. This word translates the
Hebrew term *ma'aseh*. This speaks of a work accomplished, with the
connotation that it is a remarkable achievement, a massive undertaking. The word is used many times of the intricate work that went into
the construction of the tabernacle and its equipment. It is used of
the needlework in the curtains and the high priest's garments, of the
metalwork for the altars, the candlestick, and the priest's chains, of
engravings in stone, and of the blending of the anointing oil. To take
just one example, here is Exodus 27:16:

For the gate of the court there shall be a screen twenty cubits
long, of blue and purple and scarlet yarns and fine twined linen,
embroidered with needlework (*ma'aseh*).[1]

All this is skilful work. God's skill is seen in the sky. In his skilful works,
there is a declaration, a proclamation. God's publishes his splendour
to the world.

---

1 See also Ex. 28:8,11,14,15,22,32,39; 30:25,35; 36:8,35,37; 37:29; 38:4,18; 39:3,5,8,
15,22,27,29; Num. 8:4.

2. This is true all the time

Verse 2 speaks of day and night, recognizing the two main ways in which we see the sky. First, there is the daytime sky. Sometimes we bask in brilliant sunshine. At other times, the sky is heavy with cloud. Second, there is the nighttime sky. Some nights there is a magnificent display of stars. On other occasions, we gaze up into an eerie mistiness.

The transition between the two halves of the twenty-four-hour period also exhibits divine majesty. There is the transition from night to day. Think of the spectacle of the gradually growing light and beauty of the sunrise. And then, there is the transition from day to night. Amazing colours decorate the sky at sunset. The sky, with all its diverse faces, *pours out speech*, and reveals the knowledge of God. The word translated *pours out* is *naba'*. It means to spring up, to gush forth. In Proverbs 18:4, the same word is translated *bubbling*: "The words of a man's mouth are deep waters; the fountain of wisdom is a *bubbling* brook."

The sky just cannot help itself. By day and by night, the sun, the clouds, the light, the colours, and the stars are just an overflow of revelation of God's abundant splendour. The repetition of the words *day* and *night* emphasize the constant nature of this display of divine glory. From one day to the next, night after night, this revelation is unvaryingly there. No matter the weather conditions, the sky in all its various moods is always a revelation of God.

3. This is true everywhere

There are two possible ways of translating verse 3. One possibility is given above:

> There is no speech, nor are there words, whose voice is not heard.

It means that this eloquent revelation by the sky is not in words. It is not even audible to the human ear. The other possibility goes like this:

> There is no speech nor language where their voice is not heard.

This means that there is no human communication where the voice of the sky is unheard. In other words, there is no such place, because wherever you go, human beings are talking to one another. Personally, I prefer this translation. One of my reasons is that the word translated *voice* (which is *qowl*) sometimes means the sound of thunder, as, for example, in Psalm 77:18: "The crash (*qowl*) of your thunder was in the whirlwind; your lightnings lighted up the world."

Perhaps Psalm 19:3 is saying that the revelation of God in the sky is thunderous: you cannot miss it. On the other translation, to understand it to mean that the voice of the sky does not thunder would be rather overdoing it. Rather, it would mean that it does not make the faintest squeak. However, although the voice of the sky is silent, it is nonetheless thunderous. It is inescapable. It speaks in every place.

Sometimes *qowl* is used of the sound of music. It is used of the sound of instruments, and of singing. One example is 1 Chronicles 15:28: "all Israel brought up the ark of the covenant of the LORD with shouting, to the sound of the horn, trumpets, and cymbals, and made loud music on harps and lyres."

The revelation in the sky is melodious and harmonious, and its song is heard everywhere. Verse 4 continues this theme. The whole planet, to its remotest end, views the revelation of God in the skies. No tribe, however isolated, is beyond its reach. That is why the apostle can quote this verse in Romans 10:18 as an assertion that sinful humanity is inexcusable. No one can say, "I never heard," because the skies are singing of God's glory, daily, nightly, incessantly, everywhere.

B. NEW TESTAMENT

ROMANS 1:19-20

19 For what can be known about God is plain to them, because God has shown it to them.
20 For his invisible attributes, namely, his eternal power and divine nature, have been clearly perceived, ever since the creation of the world, in the things that have been made. So they are without excuse.

In these verses, Paul speaks of the revelation of God in creation. He makes the following points.

1. God is the author of it

Whereas Psalm 19 depicts the sky as speaking, here God speaks through his creation. God "has shown" the revelation to the world. The voice of the sky in the psalm is, in fact, the mediated voice of God himself. James Dunn writes: "God's knowability is not merely a characteristic or 'spin-off' of creation, but was willed and effected by God."[2]

The tense of the Greek verb at the end of verse 19 is aorist. It speaks of a one-off revelation. Paul seems to mean that the act of creation was God's manifestation of himself. Verse 20 then says that what has been true since the creation of the world continues to be true: the attributes of God remain clear in the creation.

2. Not everything about God is knowable

Verse 19 begins with the words, "what can be known about God." The apostle is recognizing that there are depths in the reality of God that human beings cannot penetrate. There are aspects of the divine character for which far more is necessary than the available revelation in creation if we are ever to understand them. Verse 20 clarifies what can be known about God from creation. There are two things:

(1) *His eternal power.* God is always able to do whatever he purposes to do. There is power inherent in his nature without any interruption.

(2) *His divine nature.* This phrase translates the noun *theiotes*. This is the only place where it is found in the New Testament, but a related adjective, *theios*, appears three times. The way it is used helps us to get at what the apostle means here. In Acts 17:29, while preaching at Athens, Paul says, "we ought not to think that the divine being is like gold or silver or stone, an image formed by the art and imagination of man." Here Paul is emphasizing God's unlikeness: he is not like anything else. He is distinct, separate, and unique. Peter twice uses *theios* in 2 Peter 1:3-4:

3 His divine power has granted to us all things that pertain to life and godliness, through the knowledge of him who called us to his own glory and excellence,
4 by which he has granted to us his precious and very great promises, so that through them you may become partakers of the

---

2 J.D.G. Dunn, *Romans 1-8* (Dallas: Word, 1988), 57.

divine nature, having escaped from the corruption that is in the world because of sinful desire.

Verse 3 describes the all-sufficiency of God: he is able to give us all things because he is in possession of all things. He has infinite resources. Verse 4 contrasts the divine nature with worldly corruption. God is free from every hint of corruption. He is a God of absolute purity and integrity. That is the chief way in which God is unique and distinct. It is the source of his sufficiency.

These two attributes are *plain* (verse 19). God has brought out into the open the fact that he is an incomparably holy God, characterized by a unique power. In creation, these attributes of God are in full view. They are revealed to everyone.

3. This revelation in creation is seen in two places

(1) *It is seen in human life itself.* The best translation of the first part of verse 19 would read, "what can be known about God is plain in them." The preposition *en* is used. There is something intrinsic to the human personality that says, "There is a God." Paul will have in mind our moral sense, the conscience. Because we have been created in God's image, we have a feeling of accountability. Sin has spoiled this moral consciousness, but it has not smashed it completely.

(2) *It is seen in the world.* Verse 20 says that God's attributes are perceived "in the things that have been made." Created things give shape and form in the human mind to the divine invisibility. Invisibility is a characteristic feature of God. Paul speaks of Christ as "the image of the invisible God" (Colossians 1:15). He ascribes praise "to the King of ages, immortal, invisible, the only God" (1 Timothy 1:17). Moses, we read, "endured as seeing him who is invisible" (Hebrews 11:27). Created things give a sort of visibility to God—or at least to certain of his attributes. This vision of God is not physical but mental. Human eyes see the things that have been made, and the mind perceives the truth that God made them.

4. Unbelief is inexcusable

Verse 20 ends with the statement that we have nothing to say in our own defence for our unbelief. The problem is not ignorance of the truth, but suppression of the truth, as verse 18 has said. Human beings in sin deliberately tread down the truth about God revealed in creation, until it is so hindered that they are no longer able to embrace it. G.I. Williamson puts it well. He says that the evidence of God's existence

> is impossible to find when one is dead in trespasses and sins. But the evidence is impossible to escape anywhere when one is regenerated by God's Spirit.[3]

Section summary and personal application

REMEMBER

The heavens declare the glory of God, and the sky above proclaims his handiwork. Day to day pours out speech, and night to night reveals knowledge. There is no speech, nor are there words, whose voice is not heard. Their voice goes out through all the earth, and their words to the end of the world.

—*Psalm 19:1-4*

REFLECT

1. How does the created realm reaffirm the wonder of who God is? What characteristics of God do you perceive? How does this strengthen your faith?
2. As science reveals more of the glory of God through the microscopic and the telescopic realms, what does this teach you about the knowability and incomprehensibility of God? How should you respond?

---

3   G.I. Williamson, *The Westminster Confession of Faith for Study Classes* (Philadelphia: Presbyterian and Reformed, 1964), 23.

REJOICE

All creatures of our God and King
Lift up your voice and with us sing,
Alleluia! Alleluia!
Thou burning sun with golden beam,
Thou silver moon with softer gleam!
   O praise Him! O praise Him!
   Alleluia! Alleluia! Alleluia!

Thou rushing wind that art so strong
Ye clouds that sail in Heaven along,
O praise Him! Alleluia!
Thou rising moon, in praise rejoice,
Ye lights of evening, find a voice!
   O praise Him! O praise Him!
   Alleluia! Alleluia! Alleluia!

Let all things their Creator bless,
And worship Him in humbleness,
O praise Him! Alleluia!
Praise, praise the Father, praise the Son,
And praise the Spirit, Three in One!
   O praise Him! O praise Him!
   Alleluia! Alleluia! Alleluia!
—Francis of Assisi (1181–1226), trans. William H. Draper (1855–1933)

PART 2: KEY CREEDS AND CONFESSIONS

THE REFORMATION CONFESSIONS

Revelation in creation was not a doctrine that figured in the early creeds. Neither is it mentioned in the modern confessions we are considering. Some of the Reformation confessions, however, did speak of God's revelation of himself in his works. The *Belgic Confession*, produced in the Netherlands in 1561, describes the universe as "an elegant book."[4] It is comparing the creation to a play. Every created thing, great or small, is a character in the drama. Through the impact of the whole, we are led to the contemplation of God. The very fact of the existence of the created universe, with all its beauty, its order, the clear evidence of design, its immensity and magnificence, is a testimony to the reality of the Creator God. The confessions find this revelation, not only in the existence of the universe, but also in the preservation and government of creation. We can discern the signs of God's ongoing involvement with the things he has made. Every day, in his sovereignty, he directs the stars and planets; he oversees the movements of the animals and the seas. In his providential control, we see a revelation of his power, his wisdom, and his goodness.

However, revelation in creation assumes prior faith. The sheer existence of anything at all may point inevitably to the existence of God. However, to see in the preservation and government of the universe a revelation of God presupposes our acceptance that God preserves and governs all things. Unbelievers are unlikely to conclude from their observation of things that God is providentially ordering the course of creation. For the goodness, wisdom and power of God to be seen in creation assumes that we already believe that God is a God of goodness, wisdom and power. That is probably why the *Baptist Confession of Faith of 1689* alters the order of the *Westminster Confession*, on which it is based. The *Westminster Confession* begins with the revelation of God in creation. It notes the inadequacy of this revelation to give a saving knowledge of God. Therefore, it moves on to the statement of supernatural revelation, culminating in the Scriptures. The *1689 Confession* retains all that. Its wording is precisely the same as *Westminster Confession*, but it prefaces it with the sentence, "The Holy Scripture is the only infallible rule of all saving knowledge, faith, and obedience."[5] To begin with creation is to recognize that God is staring everyone in the face in his works, but only to leave them without excuse. People are blind because of sin. We are unable to see this revelation. The *1689 Confession* begins with Scripture. It knows

---

4   *Belgic Confession*, Article 2.
5   *The Baptist Confession of Faith of 1689*, 1.1.

that it is only when God's saving grace revealed in the gospel has removed our blindness that the revelation in creation can tell us anything at all. Only then can we truly perceive this revelation.

PART 3: KEY HISTORICAL DEVELOPMENTS

This recognition that creation is a closed book until grace opens our sin-blinded eyes has led to some controversy over the validity of speaking of a revelation other than God's Word in Scripture and in Christ. There is a phrase in the *Westminster Confession* referring to the manifestation of God by "the light of nature."[6] Some people have taken exception to this expression.

Robert Shaw suggests that the confession meant that people could conclude that there is a God both from sense observation and through rational thought. Indeed, he says, they can reach no other conclusion. Through their senses, people are acquainted with the works of God, and by reason, they infer the excellence of the God who made them. Shaw claims that the universality of religion is evidence of this natural light within the human constitution that reveals the fact of God. Even professed atheists have qualms of conscience from time-to-time.[7] However, to some people these ideas seem to imply that there is such a thing as "natural religion," which makes divine revelation unnecessary. The concept of the light of nature underlies the various "proofs" put forward for the existence of God. The mediæval Catholic theologian, Thomas Aquinas, stated five ways by which, he claimed, the existence of God could be proved:

(1) *There is the argument from motion.* Observation of the world tells us that things are moving. Whatever moves must have been set in motion by something else, and that thing by yet another, and so on. It is impossible to go back to infinity. If there is no first mover,

---

6 *Westminster Confession*, 1.1.

7 Shaw, *An Exposition of the Confession of Faith*, 2-4.

then nothing moves. Therefore, this first mover is God.

(2) *There is the argument from efficient cause.* Nothing can cause itself, because it is impossible for something to precede itself. Every effect has a cause. Therefore, there had to be a first cause. This is God.

(3) *There is the argument from possibility and necessity.* In nature, things may either be or not be. Any thing that we see had a beginning, but eventually it decays. For now, it is, but it might not have been, and one day it will no longer be. However, if absolutely everything were merely *possible*, then there must have been a time when there was nothing. What exists could only have a beginning because of other things already existing. Therefore, there has to be some being whose existence is not merely possible, but necessary. This being is God.

(4) *There is the argument from the gradation in things.* Among existing things, some are better, others are less good, some are more noble, others less so. This presupposes a standard, a maximum in goodness, nobility, or anything else. This is God.

(5) *There is the argument from the government of the world.* Even inanimate things exist for a purpose. They were therefore designed for that purpose. Only an intelligent being could have designed things. This is God.

From here, Aquinas argued that a certain knowledge of God is attainable by the exercise of the intellect. The human intellect needs the illumination of grace to lift it to a higher knowledge of God. Grace strengthens the natural light of reason. Nevertheless, that natural light is present, independently of God's illuminating grace.

The controversy over revelation in creation in Reformed circles arises from the suspicion that such a doctrine implies that the fall of human nature into sin is not total. To teach that grace merely assists human nature, as Aquinas did, conflicts with the truth that we need to be born again even to begin to see the kingdom of God. Moreover, it seemed to some Reformed thinkers that a doctrine of revelation in creation leads to the idea that fallen human beings can get to know God by their own powers, independently of the Scriptures and Jesus Christ. This is a fair criticism of Aquinas, but was it what the *Westminster Confession* meant?

Professor Berkouwer of Amsterdam has written a book entitled *General Revelation.*[8] This is an alternative term for revelation in cre-

---

8   G.C. Berkouwer, *General Revelation* (Grand Rapids: Eerdmans, 1955).

ation. Berkouwer insists that we must carefully distinguish between natural theology and general revelation. He denies the validity of the former concept, but affirms the reality of general revelation, but only because Scripture so clearly speaks of a revelation of God in creation and providence. This doctrine is not talking about abilities in human nature, but about where God has set the revelation of himself. One focus of that revelation is creation. The revelation is there, whether or not there is any power left in fallen humanity actually able to see it. The fact that, apart from God's saving grace, fallen human beings cannot see it does not take away the fact that the revelation is there. Therefore, we are without excuse.

Berkouwer also refers to Calvin's teaching on this subject. We find his teaching in Book 1, chapters 3-5 of the *Institutes*. Calvin accepts that there is a sense of deity innate in man. The universality of the conviction that there is a God is evidence of this. The strength of this conviction is seen in idolatry. It is very hard for the human being to lower himself and set other created things above him. Yet idolatry does just that. People worship wood and stone. This proves just how inescapable this innate sense of God is.

However, man suppresses the truth about God. Genuine godliness is absent. Yet man is inexcusable, because pride and stubbornness accompany his ignorance. God still desires the perfection of blessedness for his creatures. He has manifested his perfections in the whole structure of the universe. Whenever we open our eyes, we are compelled to behold him. That proves man's shameful ingratitude. We do not burst forth in praise, but swell with pride and suppress the evidences of God. We ascribe wonderful events not to providence but to chance.

So Calvin says, "In vain for us, therefore, does creation exhibit so many bright lamps lighted up to show forth the glory of its Author." The display in creation represents the invisible Godhead, but we have no eyes to see it until we are enlightened through faith. Calvin concludes:

> When Paul says that what may be known of God is manifested by the creation of the world, he does not mean such a manifestation as may be comprehended by the wit of man; on the contrary, he shows that it has no further effect than to render us inexcusable.[9]

---

9 Calvin, *Institutes*, 5.14.

This debate about human ability when confronted by revelation in creation is not just a matter of vague historical interest. It has contemporary significance. In his book *Mission and Meaninglessness*, Peter Cotterell puts forward the thesis that

> there is a divine self-revelation in creation which is not of itself salvific, but which may lead to the abandonment of human religious effort and to a flight to the mercy and grace of God.[10]

Cotterell argues that people who have never heard the gospel, people who have never heard of Christ, may be saved by Christ's passion as they seek God by faith, because they have perceived his eternal power and deity in his creation. Cotterell bases this on Acts 17:27. Verses 24-27 say,

> 24 The God who made the world and everything in it, being Lord of heaven and earth, does not live in temples made by man,
> 25 nor is he served by human hands, as though he needed anything, since he himself gives to all mankind life and breath and everything.
> 26 And he made from one man every nation of mankind to live on all the face of the earth, having determined allotted periods and the boundaries of their dwelling place,
> 27 that they should seek God, in the hope that they might feel their way toward him and find him. Yet he is actually not far from each one of us.

Cotterell reads verse 27 as a clear statement of the saving purpose of God: general revelation may lead people to the grace of God. Hywel Jones has written in response to this position.[11] He reads this text to mean not that many people will seek and find God through his revelation in creation, but rather that *despite* the revelation in creation, people simply grope as in the dark, because their eyes are blinded by sin. Jones acknowledges that revelation in creation might lead people

---

10 P. Cotterell, *Mission and Meaninglessness* (London: SPCK, 1990), 75, quoted by H.R. Jones, *Only One Way* (Bromley: Day One, 1996), 40.

11 Jones, *Only One Way*, 40f.

to a sense of the divine benevolence. However, to know of God's grace we need more than the revelation in creation—*we need Christ.*

PART 4: KEY POINTS OF PRACTICAL APPLICATION

(1) *We may use aspects of the revelation in creation as a theme in our evangelistic preaching.* Not that it is enough to preach on creation alone. But this doctrine may provide a point of contact with the unbeliever. It may enable us to establish a relationship, so that we can go on to proclaim Christ. The apostle Paul did this. We have already mentioned Acts 17. It is noticeable that, having spoken of creation and providence, he went on to preach Jesus. Here are verses 30 and 31:

> 30 The times of ignorance God overlooked, but now he commands all people everywhere to repent,
> 31 because he has fixed a day on which he will judge the world in righteousness by a man whom he has appointed; and of this he has given assurance to all by raising him from the dead.

In Acts 14:15-17 again he uses the revelation in creation as a preparation for the gospel:

> 15 Men, why are you doing these things? We also are men, of like nature with you, and we bring you good news, that you should turn from these vain things to a living God, who made the heaven and the earth and the sea and all that is in them.
> 16 In past generations he allowed all the nations to walk in their own ways.
> 17 Yet he did not leave himself without witness, for he did good by giving you rains from heaven and fruitful seasons, satisfying your hearts with food and gladness.

It is true that there is no reference in this context to Paul preaching

Christ on this foundation of the revelation in creation. However, verse 18 suggests that this was because it was impossible for him to complete his message on that occasion: "Even with these words they scarcely restrained the people from offering sacrifice to them." We may use the revelation in creation, then, as an argument to whet people's appetites to hear the gospel.

(2) *As for ourselves, we may see the revelation in creation with eyes opened by the grace of God.* This should lead us to worship the God of creation.

REFLECT

1. Before you were a Christian, did anyone ever talk to you about creation? If so, how would you take your personal responses from that time and apply them in your discussions with unbelievers today?
2. Do you think that presenting the truth about God from creation is a valid method? If not, why not?
3. Is there a way to highlight God's mercy through creation? If so, how would you go about it?

REJOICE

This is my Father's world, and to my listening ears
All nature sings, and round me rings the music of the spheres.
This is my Father's world: I rest me in the thought
Of rocks and trees, of skies and seas;
His hand the wonders wrought.

This is my Father's world, the birds their carols raise,
The morning light, the lily white, declare their Maker's praise.
This is my Father's world: he shines in all that's fair;
In the rustling grass I hear him pass;
He speaks to me everywhere.

This is my Father's world. O let me ne'er forget
That though the wrong seems oft so strong, God is the ruler yet.
This is my Father's world: why should my heart be sad?
The Lord is King; let the heavens ring!
God reigns; let the earth be glad!
—*Maltbie D. Babcock (1858–1901)*

5

THE DOCTRINE OF CREATION IN ITS ORIGIN

How is the glory of God revealed in his works?

That there is a revelation of God in the creation leads us on to consider the doctrine of creation itself. The doctrine of creation divides into two parts. In this chapter, we will consider the origin of this universe and how God displays his glory in it. In the following chapter, we will examine the present state of the universe.

PART 1: KEY TEXTS

Our study will focus around the biblical vocabulary relating to creation. The Old Testament term normally translated *to create* is *bara'*. The most common form of the verb (Qal perfect) emphasizes that God acted in creation and that his action was completed.

The New Testament word group normally used of creation is *ktizo* (to create) and its cognates, *ktisis* (creation), *ktisma* (creature), and *ktistes* (Creator). They may refer either to the original event of creation or to creation as a present existing reality. In the latter case, they may refer to the creation as a whole or to particular created things.

A. OLD TESTAMENT

GENESIS 1:1

In the beginning, God created the heavens and the earth.

This statement is the starting point of God's entire revelation. The first sentence of the Bible sets the context for everything following. What follows in the rest of Genesis is an account of the events leading up to the call of Abraham, and then the story of the establishment of the covenant. The covenant is then unfolded through the remainder of the Old Testament. It reaches its focal point in Christ, spreads worldwide through the New Testament era, and will reach its climax with the Lord's return.

The Bible, at its most basic level, is the story of God's mercy at work to the ends of the earth through the seed of Abraham. So "these seven words [in the Hebrew text of Genesis 1] are the foundation of all that is to follow in the Bible."[1] Creation is the stage on which the drama of divine mercy is enacted.

Four components make up this text:

1. In the beginning

Beginning translates the Hebrew word *re'sit*, which usually "marks a starting point of a definite duration."[2] This is clear in Deuteronomy 11:12, which specifies a period running "from the beginning (*re'sit*) of the year to the end of the year." Two verses in Job contrast the beginning with the latter days: Job 8:7 says, "though your beginning was small, your latter days will be very great," and from Job 42:12 we learn that "the Lord blessed the latter days of Job more than his beginning." Similarly Ecclesiastes 7:8 says, "better is the end of a thing than its beginning." It is a characteristic of God to be "declaring the end from the beginning" (Isaiah 46:10).

Gordon Wenham points out that "more rarely" *re'sit* "is used absolutely, with the period of time left unspecified."[3] He thinks that is the case here with the beginning of time itself. However, Sailhamer is probably right to see in the use of *re'sit* here a signal that the history now beginning will reach its climax in the consummation at the end of time. This reference to the beginning prepares us to anticipate the glorious end in store. This emphasizes the truth that creation is the stage on which the Lord displays his mercy, and that mercy will finally and fully be seen in all the blaze of its glory at the end of all things. Creation is not an end in itself. It is just a beginning. The end is somewhere else. The end is something else. The end (the goal, the target, the aim, the purpose) for which this beginning is taking place is *Jesus Christ*. Throughout the history of creation, we are "waiting for the mercy of our Lord Jesus Christ that leads to eternal life" (Jude 21).

This text reveals a vital truth. Mere existence is not everything. There is a purpose higher than just being. The purpose of creation is

---

1   J.H. Sailhamer, "Commentary on Genesis," in Gaebelein, ed., *Expositor's Bible Commentary*, on Genesis 1:1.

2   Sailhamer, "Commentary on Genesis," in Gaebelein, ed., *Expositor's Bible Commentary*, on Genesis 1:1.

3   Wenham, *Genesis 1-15*, on Genesis 1:1.

to be a revelation of God, an exhibition of divine mercy. The purpose of human life within the context of this creation is to see that revelation, to experience that mercy.

2. God

"The first subject of the Bible and Genesis is God."[4] The word here translated *God* is *'elohim*. According to the *Theological Wordbook of the Old Testament*, this divine title especially stresses God's sovereignty and his Saviourhood.[5] Wenham emphasizes the first of these divine qualities when he suggests that the use of *'elohim* here "implies that God is the sovereign Creator of the whole universe."[6] However, it is true that the sovereign Creator is also the merciful Saviour. This title occurs many times in association with some of the terms expressing the mercy of God. Here are just three examples:

> Genesis 24:27—Blessed be the LORD, the God (*'elohim*) of my master Abraham, who has not forsaken his steadfast love (*hesed*) and his faithfulness (*'emet*) toward my master.

> Psalm 51:1—Have mercy (*hanan*) on me, O God (*'elohim*), according to your steadfast love (*hesed*); according to your abundant mercy (*raham*) blot out my transgressions.

> Daniel 9:9—To the Lord our God (*'elohim*) belong mercy (*raham*) and forgiveness (*selihah*).

So the use of *'elohim* signals that the God who created is the God who, in the developing context of that creation, will abound in mercy to his people. This very title underlines the fact that creation is just the beginning that establishes the context for the glorious end. The end is the manifestation of God's saving mercy.

---

4   O. Procksch, *Die Genesis übersetzt und erklärt* (Leipzig: Deicherische Verlagsbuchhandlung, 1924), 438, as quoted in Wenham, *Genesis 1-15*, on Genesis 1:1.

5   R.L. Harris, G.L. Archer, Jr. and B.K. Waltke, ed., *Theological Wordbook of the Old Testament* (Chicago: Moody, 2003), 93.

6   Wenham, *Genesis 1-15*, on Genesis 1:1.

As Sailhamer points out, in Genesis 2:4 *'elohim* is explicitly identified with the LORD, the God of Abraham, the God of Israel. He notes that the God of Genesis 1:1 "is far from a faceless deity." He is none other than the God who is the Redeemer of his people. The purpose of this opening sentence is to inform us that the God whom we already know in his mercy is himself the Creator of the universe.

3. Created

The verb *bara'* appears 54 times in the Hebrew Scriptures. It usually has God as its subject. There are just six exceptions (in five verses), and in most of them "to create" is not a suitable rendering:

(1) "go up by yourselves to the forest, and there clear (*bara'*) ground for yourselves" (Joshua 17:15).
(2) "though it is a forest, you shall clear (*bara'*) it and possess it" (Joshua 17:18).
(3) "you scorn my sacrifices and my offerings that I commanded, and honour your sons above me by fattening (*bara'*) yourselves on the choicest parts of every offering" (1 Samuel 2:29).
(4) "make (*bara'*) a signpost; make (*bara'*) it at the head of the way to a city" (Ezekiel 21:19).
(5) "the host shall stone them and cut them down (*bara'*) with their swords" (Ezekiel 23:47).

This word is never used of human creativity, unless perhaps in Ezekiel 21:19. However, even when human beings use their creativity to make something, this differs from God's creativity. A human being can only shape existing materials. When God creates, something entirely new and unprecedented comes into being. That is why Genesis 1 does not speak of any raw materials, out of which God created. They were part of his creation just as much as the finished product. Creation was out of nothing.

4. The heavens and the earth

This phrase refers to absolutely everything that exists without any exceptions at all. The entire universe is the handiwork of God.

We now make some general observations on this verse.

(1) We must ponder the precise status of the opening verse within the context of the following chapter. Some people have seen it as a title or summary, with verse 2 onwards expounding what verse 1 means. Others have seen it as the initial statement, describing the first act of creation, with verse 2 onwards describing subsequent creative actions.

Wenham has presented cogent arguments against the view that verse 1 is a title. If the account of creation itself begins in verse 2, then there is no mention of the bringing into being of matter itself. This would seem to imply that matter was eternal, though in a chaotic state, and that creation was simply God putting it in order. We must therefore read verse 1 as the statement of the first creative event. Only then, for the first time ever, did anything at all begin to exist.

(2) So understood, the Bible's very first sentence is already a polemic against polytheistic paganism. That was the nature of the ancient religious environment in which the faith of Israel was proclaimed. That is apparent in two ways: (i) The reference to creation in a general sense, to the totality of the universe, in the phrase 'the heavens and the earth' opposes Canaanite theology. This did indeed teach that creation was the ordering of pre-existing matter. The Bible insists that matter itself is the creation of God; (ii) There is the reference to the one *'elohim*. Although this noun is plural in form, the verb is singular. Sailhamer makes this comment:

> By identifying God as the Creator, a crucial distinction is introduced between the God of the fathers and the gods of the nations, gods that to the biblical authors were mere idols. God alone created the heavens and the earth.[7]

Sailhamer cites Jeremiah 10:11 as conveying the same message: "The gods who did not make the heavens and the earth shall perish from the earth and from under the heavens." We might also mention Psalm 96:5: "All the gods of the peoples are worthless idols, but the LORD made the heavens."

---

7 Sailhamer, "Commentary on Genesis," in Gaebelein, ed., *Expositor's Bible Commentary*, on Genesis 1:1.

(3) The very first sentence of God's revelation in Scripture is already calling us to worship. It highlights the uniqueness of God, the splendour of his work, the dependency of all creatures. It is truly, as Wenham says, "a triumphant invocation" of God.[8]

GENESIS 1:2

> The earth was without form and void, and darkness was over the face of the deep. And the Spirit of God was hovering over the face of the waters.

We have here a description of the universe immediately after God's first creative act. The raw materials, which are destined to become ordered and beautiful, have been brought into being. So far, everything is in darkness. Water covers the surface of the earth. God's Spirit is hovering. He is poised for action. He is waiting for the moment to begin.

The main issue raised by this verse is the meaning of the phrase "without form and void." *Without form* translates the Hebrew word *tohu*, while *void* translates *bohu*. Wenham suggests that the two terms together mean *total chaos*. He writes:

> ...frightening disorganization is the antithesis to the order that characterized the work of creation when it was complete....The dreadfulness of the situation before the divine word brought order out of chaos is underlined.[9]

It seems to me very improbable that this is the significance of this phrase. Such an interpretation would seem to impugn the character and work of God. Could God really do anything "dreadful"? Surely, there was no one there to be "frightened," except God himself—and that is hardly likely. We need a more positive reading of these words.

Sailhamer seems to be on the right lines when he says that this expression "refers to the condition of the land in its 'not-yet' state." Creation is not yet what it shall be. Sailhamer notes that the rest of

---

8   Wenham, *Genesis 1-15*, on Genesis 1:1-2:3.

9   Wenham, *Genesis 1-15*, on Genesis 1:2.

the chapter will tell the story of the preparation of the land as a place for man to live. So far, it is not habitable. Sailhamer points, pertinently, to Isaiah 45:18, where the word *tohu* is also used:

> For thus says the LORD, who created the heavens (he is God!), who formed the earth and made it (he established it; he did not create it empty (*tohu*), he formed it to be inhabited!): "I am the LORD, and there is no other."

Here *tohu* contrasts with *inhabited*. However, even Sailhamer suggests that *tohu* and *bohu* "describe the condition of the land before God made it good."[10] This, again, seems very questionably to imply that God's initial act of creation was bad.

Actually, however, it is not necessary to give *tohu* and *bohu* a pejorative sense. At this stage, the earth is unformed and unfilled. The rest of the chapter will record its forming and filling. God has not done that yet. However, that does not mean that the earth is not yet good.

It is sometimes alleged that Isaiah 45:18 contradicts Genesis 1:2. Genesis says that God created the earth *tohu*. Isaiah says he did not. However, the exact word in Isaiah is *l'tohu*. The prefix *l'* means *to* or *for*,[11] or *towards*.[12] Isaiah is saying that God did not create the world *for* emptiness. He did not make the earth to be empty. That was not his ultimate intention, even though it began like that. He was not working towards emptiness. Emptiness was the starting point of his route toward fullness. His final goal was that the earth should be inhabited, and that it should be a suitable home for man. Isaiah 45:18 is linked to verse 17 by the word *for*. Verse 17 says this: "Israel is saved by the LORD with everlasting salvation; you shall not be put to shame or confounded to all eternity." In describing the earth as a suitable home for man, the main thing is that it is a fitting location, within which human beings could get to know the saving mercy of the Lord.

---

10 Sailhamer, "Commentary on Genesis," in Gaebelein, ed., *Expositor's Bible Commentary*, on Genesis 1:2a.

11 E.C. Hostetter, *An Elementary Grammar of Biblical Hebrew* (Sheffield: Academic Press, 2000), 37.

12 F.H.W. Gesenius, *Hebrew and Chaldee Lexicon to the Old Testament Scriptures* (London: Bagster, 1857), 237.

GENESIS 1:3-25

3 And God said, "Let there be light," and there was light.

4 And God saw that the light was good. And God separated the light from the darkness.

5 God called the light Day, and the darkness he called Night. And there was evening and there was morning, the first day.

6 And God said, "Let there be an expanse in the midst of the waters, and let it separate the waters from the waters."

7 And God made the expanse and separated the waters that were under the expanse from the waters that were above the expanse. And it was so.

8 And God called the expanse Heaven. And there was evening and there was morning, the second day.

9 And God said, "Let the waters under the heavens be gathered together into one place, and let the dry land appear." And it was so.

10 God called the dry land Earth, and the waters that were gathered together he called Seas. And God saw that it was good.

11 And God said, "Let the earth sprout vegetation, plants yielding seed, and fruit trees bearing fruit in which is their seed, each according to its kind, on the earth." And it was so.

12 The earth brought forth vegetation, plants yielding seed according to their own kinds, and trees bearing fruit in which is their seed, each according to its kind. And God saw that it was good.

13 And there was evening and there was morning, the third day.

14 And God said, "Let there be lights in the expanse of the heavens to separate the day from the night. And let them be for signs and for seasons, and for days and years,

15 and let them be lights in the expanse of the heavens to give light upon the earth." And it was so.

16 And God made the two great lights—the greater light to rule the day and the lesser light to rule the night—and the stars.

17 And God set them in the expanse of the heavens to give light on the earth,

18 to rule over the day and over the night, and to separate the light from the darkness. And God saw that it was good.

19 And there was evening and there was morning, the fourth day.
20 And God said, "Let the waters swarm with swarms of living creatures, and let birds fly above the earth across the expanse of the heavens."
21 So God created the great sea creatures and every living creature that moves, with which the waters swarm, according to their kinds, and every winged bird according to its kind. And God saw that it was good.
22 And God blessed them, saying, "Be fruitful and multiply and fill the waters in the seas, and let birds multiply on the earth."
23 And there was evening and there was morning, the fifth day.
24 And God said, "Let the earth bring forth living creatures according to their kinds—livestock and creeping things and beasts of the earth according to their kinds." And it was so.
25 And God made the beasts of the earth according to their kinds and the livestock according to their kinds, and everything that creeps on the ground according to its kind. And God saw that it was good.

This passage tells the story of the forming and filling of the earth during six days. The six days occur in two corresponding sets of three.

1. The first set: days one and four

On day one (verses 3-5) light is created. Light includes colour. Light is a spectrum, seen in the colours of the rainbow. Light and colour are the source of aesthetic beauty. For God to create light first is for him to indicate the priority which he gives to beauty in his creation.

Corresponding to day one is day four (verses 14-19), when the sun, moon and stars are created. Their purpose is to focus the light and to give structure to time. It is sometimes objected that it is unrealistic for light to be created before the light-sources. Sailhamer argues that this was not in fact what happened. He suggests that the sun, moon, and stars were created at the very beginning, and are included in the words "the heavens and the earth" in verse 1. Verse 3, then, describes the first appearance of the sun through the darkness. Sailhamer then suggests a different translation for verse 14: "Let the lights in the expanse of the heavens separate the day from the night." This would imply that the lights were already there. On day four, their function is being allocated for the first time.[13] This seems to me an ingenious way of solving a difficulty that is itself only imaginary. It is not necessary to read verse 1 as meaning that every single component of the completed universe was in place from the start. To protest that God could not create light before creating light-sources betrays a poor view of the power of God.

In fact, there is an important reason why God did not create the light-sources from the first moment of creation. He is emphasizing that he is himself the true light-source. Even the sun, so central to the solar system to which we belong, receives its light from God as the sovereign Giver. This will become clear at the end:

> Revelation 21:23—And the city has no need of sun or moon to shine on it, for the glory of God gives it light, and its lamp is the Lamb.

> Revelation 22:5—And night will be no more. They will need no light of lamp or sun, for the Lord God will be their light, and they will reign forever and ever.

Such a view would tie in with some observations which Wenham makes about day four:

> The creation of the sun, moon and stars is described at much greater length than anything save the creation of man....The fullness of the description suggests that the creation of the heavenly bodies held a special significance.[14]

The reason is that the sun, moon and stars held an important place in the thinking of Israel's neighbours. They were some of their most important gods. They were often credited with controlling human destiny—as is still the case today. Wenham notes four ways in which

---

13 Sailhamer, "Commentary on Genesis," in Gaebelein, ed., *Expositor's Bible Commentary*, on Genesis 1:14.

14 Wenham, *Genesis 1-15*, on Genesis 1:14-19.

the Genesis account underlines its rejection of this understanding of the heavenly bodies:

(1) *They were created by God.* They are not gods, but creatures. They are not eternal, but transient.

(2) *The sun and moon are not referred to by their normal Hebrew names.* They are called simply 'the greater light' and 'the lesser light.' Their importance is thus reduced. They cannot be equated with any astral deities the nations might foolishly honour.

(3) *Their function is defined simply as lighting the earth.* This is a lowly task compared with the elevated claims that Mesopotamian religion made for these entities.

(4) *The stars are mentioned almost as an afterthought at the end of verse 16.* It is as if the author says, "Oh, I almost forgot, God made the stars too." He is disdainful of the idea that they are the controllers of human destiny, worthy of veneration.[15]

2. The second set: days two and five

On day two (verses 6-8), the sky is created. Corresponding to this, on day five (verses 20-23), God creates the birds to fly in the sky, preceded by marine life.

3. The third set: days three and six

On day three (verses 9-13), we see the appearance of land that is then covered with vegetation. The corresponding day is day six (verses 24-25). Now the land animals are created. Wenham notes that the correspondence between these two days is highlighted in the text by the repetition of the Hebrew verb *yasa'* (to bring forth) in verses 12 and 24.

There are six recurring features in this passage:

(1) *Creation took place by mere command.* Seven times, we read "God said" (verses 3, 6, 9, 11, 14, 20, 24). Each time God's command is followed by a phrase confirming that what was said actually happened. In verse 3 the phrase is "and there was." In verse 7, it is "and God made." In verse 21, we read "so God created." The most frequent phrase is "and it was so" (verses 9, 11, 15, 24). This draws attention to God's amazing

---

15 Wenham, *Genesis 1-15*, on Genesis 1:14-19.

power. He is not dependent on anything else at all. God is in total control, and creation is totally under his control. We see the power of God's Word. The Word of God is creative and effective. Psalm 33:6 emphasizes this: "By the word of the LORD the heavens were made, and by the breath of his mouth all their host."

(2) *The entire universe was good.* As it left the Maker's hand, every single part of creation was good. Six times, we hear that God saw that what he had just made was good. This phrase occurs every day except day two, and twice on day three (verses 4, 10, 12, 18, 21,25). In what sense were the elements of creation "good"? Sailhamer suggests that the word is used in the sense of "beneficial for man." He sees this as the reason why the word is absent from the account of day two:

> On that day there was nothing created or made that was, in fact, 'good' or beneficial for man. The heavens were made and the waters divided, but the land, where man was to dwell, still remained hidden under the deep.[16]

While I think that Sailhamer is partly right in his interpretation of "it was good," I question his explanation of the absence of the formula on day two. Even though man was to dwell on land, the waters would be beneficial for man. Adam Clarke reports some scientific experiments on evaporation. They demonstrated that the quantity of water in creation is precisely what is needed to produce enough water vapour to cool the atmosphere and water the land.[17]

Wenham's explanation for the absence of the words "it was good" on day two seems more probable: "the separation of the waters was not completed until the following day." Also, I think Wenham's explanation of "it was good" adds an important additional emphasis. He describes it as an "appreciation formula," and compares it to an artist admiring his own handiwork.[18] Creation was good in God's estimation.

---

16 Sailhamer, "Commentary on Genesis," in Gaebelein, ed., *Expositor's Bible Commentary*, on Genesis 1:3-5.

17 A. Clarke, *The Holy Bible: A Commentary* (1810-1826; available online), on Genesis 1:10.

18 Wenham, *Genesis 1-15*, on Genesis 1:5.

It was satisfying and glorifying to him. Its very existence brought God satisfaction. This passage highlights several features of God's creation that promote his glory. Verses 11-12 and 22-24 tell of the earth's productive capacity, and of its inbuilt potential for further development. Verses 20-21 stress the abundance found in God's creation. Verses 16-18 point to the orderliness, regularity and predictability of creation.

(3) *God named the things he had created.* On each of the first three days, "God called" the thing he had created by its appropriate name (verses 5, 8, 10). Wenham explains: "in the Old Testament to name something is to assert authority over it."[19]

(4) *Creation took place by division.* The Hebrew word *badal* comes five times in this passage (verses 4, 6, 7, 14, 18). It is translated to *separate.* In creating, God founded distinctions. The LORD established the integrity of different aspects of creation at first. The Creator ascribed to the various parts of his creation their proper functions. The use of created things is not something decided by human whim.

(5) *Living creatures were made "according to their kinds."* Such a phrase comes three times in verses 11 and 12 with reference to the vegetation, twice in verse 21 with reference to the fish and the birds, and five times in verses 24 and 25 with reference to the land animals. This is an aspect of the differentiation built into creation.

Modern biology, zoology and botany have discovered the distinctions between order, family, genus, and species. God created these basic life forms. Wenham's comment is worth noting:

> There is a givenness about time and space which God has ordered by his own decree. The different species of plant and animal life again bear testimony to God's creative plan. The implication, though not stated, is clear: what God has distinguished and created distinct, man ought not to confuse. Order, not chaos, is the hallmark of God's activity.... Things are the way they are because God made it so, and men and women should accept his decree.[20]

---

19 Wenham, *Genesis 1-15*, on Genesis 1:5.
20 Wenham, *Genesis 1-15*, on Genesis 1:12.

(6) *God's creation is blessed by the Creator.* Although a reference to blessing comes only once in this passage (verse 22), it will reappear in verse 28 and again in 2:3. It is a notable feature of the account. The Hebrew word translated *to bless* is *barak*. Its form here is Piel. This usually represents intent. God determined to bless the sea creatures and the birds. He blessed them thoroughly. Sometimes the Piel can express repetition or permanence. God blessed his creatures repeatedly. Their blessedness was a constant state.

Wenham notes that "where modern man talks of success, Old Testament man talked of blessing."[21] What is it to be blessed? The *Theological Wordbook of the Old Testament* says: "To bless in the Old Testament means 'to endue with power for success, prosperity, fruitfulness, long life, etc.'"[22] It is to live a life that fulfils the purpose of creation, and so to find contentment within the creation.

GENESIS 1:31-2:3

> 31 And God saw everything that he had made, and behold, it was very good. And there was evening and there was morning, the sixth day.
>
> 1 Thus the heavens and the earth were finished, and all the host of them.
>
> 2 And on the seventh day God finished his work that he had done, and he rested on the seventh day from all his work that he had done.
>
> 3 So God blessed the seventh day and made it holy, because on it God rested from all his work that he had done in creation.

We notice three things here:

1. The integrated goodness of the completed whole

Verse 31 proclaims the goodness of everything. The word *behold* calls us to gaze with God on his pristine creation and to contemplate with enthusiasm its goodness. It is now *very good*. It is marked by exceed-

---

21 Wenham, *Genesis 1-15*, on Genesis 1:22.

22 Harris, Archer, Jr., Waltke, ed., *Theological Wordbook of the Old Testament*, 285.

ing goodness. It cannot be improved. No one else could do the slightest bit better than the master Creator has done. When the separate pieces of creation were made, God pronounced them "good." Now, as he surveys the finished whole, he pronounces it "very good." Wenham says,

> The harmony and perfection of the completed heavens and earth express more adequately the character of their Creator than any of the separate components can.[23]

2. The summary of the work done

The work is now finished. The Hebrew word *kalah*, used in verses 1 and 2, contains two ideas: the task is thoroughly accomplished, and God has ceased his work of creation.

3. The inauguration of the Sabbath

Verses 2-3 depict God's rest. It is a pattern and example for his human creatures. There is a certain rhythm of life built into creation. We ignore this rhythm to our cost. From the very beginning, one day in seven was set apart from the remainder of the week as an occasion for rest and refreshment. It is part of the very nature of creation that a rest day is necessary. Later verses emphasize this point. Exodus 23:12 stresses that the refreshing rest is for everyone:

> Six days you shall do your work, but on the seventh day you shall rest; that your ox and your donkey may have rest, and the son of your servant woman, and the alien, may be refreshed.

The word *napas* at the end of this verse (translated *refreshed*) means "to catch your breath" or "to renew your soul"; but Leviticus 25:2 reminds us that the Sabbath rest is "to the LORD." The day spent aside from daily labour is an occasion for the contemplation of God's works, and for responding in worship.

---

23 Wenham, *Genesis 1-15*, on Genesis 1:31.

B. NEW TESTAMENT

There are two additional aspects of the doctrine of creation taught in the New Testament.

1. Jesus Christ was the Father's agent in creation

Hebrews 1:1-2 briefly mentions this truth:

> Long ago, at many times and in many ways, God spoke to our fathers by the prophets, but in these last days he has spoken to us by his Son, whom he appointed the heir of all things, through whom also he created the world.

However, we shall look at a text proclaiming this doctrine at greater length.

COLOSSIANS 1:13-18

> 13 He has delivered us from the domain of darkness and transferred us to the kingdom of his beloved Son,
> 14 in whom we have redemption, the forgiveness of sins.
> 15 He is the image of the invisible God, the firstborn of all creation.
> 16 For by him all things were created, in heaven and on earth, visible and invisible, whether thrones or dominions or rulers or authorities—all things were created through him and for him.
> 17 And he is before all things, and in him all things hold together.
> 18 And he is the head of the body, the church. He is the beginning, the firstborn from the dead, that in everything he might be preeminent.

The phrase "his beloved Son" in verse 13 makes it clear about whom verses 15-16 are talking. That title emphasizes the deity of our Lord, and his relationship within the Godhead to the Father. Verse 14 then stresses that the beloved Son is the very one who became the man Christ Jesus and who died for our redemption. We can analyze his role in creation by noting five elements in this text:

(1) *The clause, "the firstborn of all creation."* The title *firstborn* in verse 15 can indicate either priority in time or supremacy in rank. Curtis Vaughan sees both meanings here, but with the emphasis falling on the latter.[24] So God's beloved Son was there before all things (as verse 17 also says), and he is forever over all things. Just because he is the beloved Son of the Father, he must be superior to all created reality. He is distinct from creation. He is unique. He was therefore instrumental in the origin of the creation.

(2) *The three prepositional phrases.* Verse 16 tells us that all things were created *by him (en auto*—literally *in him), through him (di' autou),* and *for him (eis auton*—literally *towards him).*

i) *in him*
This phrase portrays Christ as the sphere in which creation took place. He is like the container holding the creation. Christ sets the boundaries of creation. He holds the universe in his hands, in his power. As verse 17 adds, "in him all things hold together." Christ is the context within which the Father created. The whole of creation is Christ-like. It reflects his nature. His pulse throbs through everything that God has made.

ii) *through him*
Christ is the Mediator in creation as well as in salvation. God created through Christ. The Son was the Father's agent. He was the Father's voice. Genesis 1 tells us that God created by speaking his Word. We know that Christ is the living Word of God. For God to say, "Let there be" was to commission his Son to work in active power.

iii) *towards him*
Christ is the goal towards which the creation is travelling. God's original purpose was that creation should find its ultimate and final explanation in Christ alone. The only reason why anything exists is for the glory of Jesus Christ. Perhaps this throws additional light

---

24 C. Vaughan, "Commentary on Colossians," in Gaebelein, ed., *Expositor's Bible Commentary*, on Colossians 1:15.

on the word *good* in Genesis 1. We have seen that one interpretation of the word is *good for the glory of God*. Another way of understanding it is *good and beneficial for man*. If creation had Christ as
its destiny, then ultimately *good* means suitable for him. The two
understandings of *good* in Genesis 1 come together in him. He is
the God glorified in creation. He is the true man, for whose benefit
creation was made. God made all things as a present for his Son.

(3) *The two verb tenses*

i) *in him all things were created*
The tense here is aorist. The form of the verb *created* is *ektisthe*.
This draws attention to the initial event of creation. When God
first made everything, he boxed it up in his Son. Creation was
not made free ranging, open-ended, and unpredictable. It shares
something of the constancy of Christ.

ii) *all things were created through him and towards him*
Here the tense is perfect. The form of the verb is *ektistai*. This
draws attention to the continuing reality of the created universe.
To this very day, Christ's creative power sustains everything.
Every single day, the movement of creation is towards him. Exis-
tence for his glory is a perennial feature of creation.

(4) *The phrase "all things."* Verse 16 elaborates on this phrase. It
includes heavenly and earthly things, visible and invisible things, and
four specific invisible things: thrones, dominions, rulers and authori-
ties. These are probably four categories within the angelic hierarchy.
In Colossians 2:18 we read: "Let no one disqualify you, insisting on
asceticism and worship of angels." Evidently, there were some at
Colossae inclined towards angel worship. The apostle undercuts the
idea that this could be valid: angels are just creatures. Others at Colossae seem alarmed by demonic powers. That is, presumably, why Paul
reassures them in these words: "He disarmed the rulers and authori-
ties and put them to open shame, by triumphing over them in him"
(Colossians 2:15). Even they are not self-regulating, independent demi-
gods. The demons, too, are mere creatures. Christ is above them all.

(5) *The words "he is the beginning."* This title for Jesus Christ, used in verse 18, echoes the first verse of the Bible. The Greek word for *beginning (arche)* is the same word used in the Greek translation of Genesis 1:1. Just like *ros*, from the same Hebrew root as *resit*, *arche* can mean *head*. Creation exists with Christ as its head. It derives its very being from him. Already in the first sentence of Genesis, there is an anticipation of the Christological fulfilment. A profundity here defeats our finite minds. How can we put this into words?

2. God's pleasure is the ultimate purpose of creation

REVELATION 4:11

> Worthy are you, our Lord and God, to receive glory and honour and power, for you created all things, and by your will they existed and were created.

Our concern is the final phrase of this verse. There is a question about the most appropriate translation. We read that all things were created "by your will." The Greek phrase is *dia to thelema sou*. I would suggest that the translation above is poor. The Authorized Version rendered this verse like this:

> Thou art worthy, O Lord, to receive glory and honour and power: for thou hast created all things, and for thy pleasure they are and were created.

I think the translation "for your pleasure" is to be preferred. We have here *dia* followed by an accusative. The regular meaning of *dia* in this construction is "because of, on account of, for the sake of."[25] "By your will" would be a different construction, *dia* followed by a genitive: *dia tou thelematos*. That would see God's *thelema* as the first cause of creation. However, the construction in this text suggests that God's *thelema* is the final objective of creation. So how should we translate

---

25 D.B. Wallace, *Greek Grammar Beyond the Basics* (Grand Rapids: Zondervan, 1996), 369.

thelema? It is true that *will* is the usual rendering. However, the
Authorized Version translators were right to recognize that *thelema*
can have a secondary meaning—*pleasure*. In fact, in the Greek translation of the Old Testament God's good pleasure is the normal meaning
of *thelema*.[26] Therefore, Revelation 4:11 is saying that the reason why
God created anything was to satisfy his own desire, to bring himself
pleasure. As that purpose was fulfilled, God pronounced his completed creation "very good" (Genesis 1:31).

Section summary and personal application

REMEMBER

In the beginning, God created the heavens and the earth.
—*Genesis 1:1*

He is the image of the invisible God, the firstborn of all creation.
For by him all things were created, in heaven and on earth, visible
and invisible, whether thrones or dominions or rulers or authori-
ties—all things were created through him and for him. And he
is before all things, and in him all things hold together.
—*Colossians 1:15-17*

REFLECT

1. How does the Hebrew title for God, *'elohim* (translated "God"),
   bring daily encouragement and comfort to your life?
2. The Scripture unequivocally *declares* God as Creator, and does
   not attempt to defend this glorious truth. Does this have implications for evangelism?
3. When we gaze upon creation, what can we learn about the God
   of creation? Make a list of what are the observable attributes of
   God in the world.

---

26 D. Müller, "Will, Purpose," in C. Brown, ed., *New International Dictionary of New
Testament Theology*, 3 vol. (Exeter: Paternoster, 1975–1978), 3:1019.

REJOICE

You're the Word of God the Father
>   From before the world began.
Ev'ry star and ev'ry planet
>   Has been fashioned by Your hand.
All creation holds together
>   By the power of Your voice.
Let the skies declare Your glory;
>   Let the land and seas rejoice!

>   *You're the author of creation;*
>   *You're the Lord of ev'ry man;*
>   *And Your cry of love rings out*
>   *Across the lands.*
— © *Keith Getty and Stuart Townend*

PART 2: KEY CREEDS AND CONFESSIONS

A. THE EARLY CREEDS

We have seen already that the *Apostles'* and *Nicene Creeds* define God as Creator and speak of the universality of his creation. In its section on Jesus Christ, the *Nicene Creed* also includes the phrase "by whom all things were made." Although not precisely a creed, there is a creedal summary in Tertullian's work, *Prescription against Heretics*:

> [God is] the Creator of the world, who, by his own Word coming down in the beginning, brought all things into being out of nothing; and this Word is called his Son, and appeared under the name of God in diverse manners to the patriarchs, was heard at all times in the prophets, and at last entered into the Virgin Mary by the Spirit and power of the Father, was made flesh in her womb, and, being born of her, went forth as Jesus Christ.[27]

---

27 Tertullian, *Prescription Against Heretics*, 13.

Tertullian's theology here is thoroughly Christ-centred. By reference to the Word, he holds together the doctrines of creation, the Trinity, revelation and Christ. We can review his summary of the rule of faith in seven statements:

1. God created the world, defined as all things.
2. God created all things by his Word.
3. The Word was sent forth before all things.
4. God created all things out of nothing.
5. The Word by which God created all things is the second Person of the Trinity.
6. The Word by which God created is also the Word by which he gives his revelation.
7. This Word, by which God created and reveals, is also the Word who became incarnate as Jesus Christ.

For Tertullian, creation, revelation and salvation are all part of a single enterprise, united in the Person of Jesus Christ. Creation took place so that God could reveal his saving mercy.

B. THE REFORMATION CONFESSIONS

The teaching of the confessions on creation can be summed up in nine statements.

1. God created everything

Some confessions elaborate on this basic statement by defining *everything*. It means heaven, earth, and all their contents, both visible and invisible, including the world of spirits. The *Belgic Confession* points out that creation means more than mere existence. God gave every created thing "its being, shape and form."[28] The exact proportions of things were the work of the Creator. He alone is the source of all beauty.

2. Creation was the beginning

The confessions are clear that nothing had any existence before God's work of creation. Time itself began with God's creative work. All

---

28 *Belgic Confession*, Article 12.

things proceed from that one beginning. In his exposition of the *Westminster Confession*, Robert Shaw makes an interesting comment on the teaching that the world had a beginning:

> This will now be considered one of the most obvious truths that can be stated, but it is one which required to be confirmed by divine revelation. That the world existed from eternity was generally maintained by the ancient heathen philosophers. Some of them held that not only the matter of which the world is framed existed from eternity, but that it subsisted in that beautiful form in which we behold it. Others admitted that the heavens and earth had a beginning in respect of their present form, but maintained the eternity of the matter of which they are composed. That the world had a beginning is the uniform doctrine of the Scriptures.[29]

3. God created everything out of nothing

Several of the confessions simply, but clearly, affirm this truth. The *Westminster Confession* understands "out of nothing" to be implied by the word *create*. In its statement that it pleased God "to create, or make out of nothing, the world"[30] the clause "or make out of nothing" reads as a definition of the verb *to create*.

4. Creation was the work of the triune God

The confessions generally insist that God the Father, Son and Holy Spirit worked together in unity, equality, and oneness of purpose to bring about the creation of all things. Robert Shaw comments like this on the *Westminster Confession*:

> The work of creation is common to all the three Persons of the Trinity.... We must not, therefore, suppose that in creation the Father is the principal agent, and the Son and the Holy Ghost inferior agents, or mere instruments. In all external works of Deity, each of the Persons of the Godhead equally concur.[31]

---

29 Shaw, *An Exposition of the Confession of Faith*, 60.
30 *Westminster Confession*, 4.1.
31 Shaw, *An Exposition of the Confession of Faith*, 61.

Nevertheless, the confessions recognize that it is the clear teaching of Scripture that the instrumentality of the Trinity in creation is channelled through the Word. This Word is not God's mere command. It is identified with the second Person of the Trinity.

5. God created everything in six days

The English language confessions include this emphasis on the literal meaning of the six days of Genesis 1. The English Puritan, Thomas Vincent, said:

> God created all things in the space of six days. He could have created all things together in a moment; but he took six days' time to work in, and rested on the seventh day, that we might the better apprehend the order of the creation, and that we might imitate him in working but six days of the week, and in resting on the seventh.[32]

Vincent is observing that for God to take six days over creation could seem unexpectedly long. He links God's decision to take six days with our apprehension of the order of creation. By this, he does not mean the order in which things happened, but the orderliness of things. By portraying the orderly fashion in which God's creative work took place, according to a definite pattern, the Scriptures lift our sights and enhance our appreciation of the orderliness of the world in which we live. We are therefore stimulated to adore the Creator.

6. God created everything very good

Robert Shaw interprets the confessions like this:

> Everything was very good; for it was agreeable to the model which the great Architect had formed in his mind from everlasting; it answered exactly the end of its creation, and was adapted to the purpose for which it was designed.[33]

---

32 T. Vincent, *The Shorter Catechism Explained from Scripture* (1674; reprint, Edinburgh: Banner of Truth, 1980), 45f.

33 Shaw, *An Exposition of the Confession of Faith*, 62.

144 SYSTEMATIC THEOLOGY 1

"Very good," then, is a functional description. Creation fulfils its intended purpose. This raises a further question: what was the purpose of creation? The confessions give two main reasons for which God created. These form our next two strands in their teaching.

7. God created everything for the benefit of man

This applies even to the things of the invisible world. God created the angels to be his messengers in serving the elect.

8. God created everything for himself

God's own pleasure is the ultimate motive behind creation. In reality, no lesser reason is required. God gave every created thing its own peculiar function to serve him within creation as a whole. In creation, the glory of God's power, wisdom, and goodness are made manifest. Vincent comments:

> God created all things for his own glory, that he might make manifest—1. the glory of his power, in effecting so great a work, making everything out of nothing by a word...; 2. the glory of his wisdom, in the order and variety of his creatures...; 3. the glory of his goodness, especially towards man, for whom he provided first a habitation, and every useful creature, before he gave him his being.[34]

Williamson points out the contrast with much modern dogma in these assertions of purpose: according to modern philosophy, "there is no ultimate reason for it all."[35]

9. False teaching about creation is rejected

The Reformation confessions name two false views of creation they reject: the teaching of Marcion and the teaching of Manicheanism.

a) The teaching of Marcion

Marcion was born in Asia Minor and moved to Rome around A.D. 140. He believed that there was a complete antithesis between the Old and

---

34 Vincent, *The Shorter Catechism Explained from Scripture*, 47.
35 Williamson, *The Westminster Confession of Faith for Study Classes*, 41.

New Testaments. He held that different gods inspired them. The god of the Old Testament was a god of justice, but not goodness, whereas the god of the New Testament was the god of love, the god of Jesus. Marcion believed in the eternity of matter. He taught that the imperfections in the material world proved that it was not the creation of the good god. The good god was responsible only for the invisible world above us. The material world was the work of the other god. However, the power of this other god was limited. Therefore, the formation of the material world involved him in a struggle. Under the impulse of Satan, the material from which the world was formed resisted this god's attempt to give it shape. Therefore, the work of creation was only of limited success. This included the creation of man. However, the god of love took pity on man, even though he was not his own creature, and sent Christ to rescue him from the imperfections of the created order.[36]

The Reformation rejected such notions. There is only one God. He created everything, visible as well as invisible. It was all very good as it came from the Creator's hand.

b) *The teaching of Manicheanism*

The philosophy of Manicheanism developed in Persia. Its founder, Manes, was born about A.D. 215. He was sixty-five years old when he started propagating his teaching. It was based on Zoroastrianism. Manes saw life in this world as full of terrible contradictions. This led him to a dualistic view of the universe. He taught that there were two separate cosmic kingdoms, the kingdom of light or goodness, and the kingdom of darkness or evil. The primal God, Manes said, rules the kingdom of light, and he is good. Satan and his demons rule the kingdom of darkness. There is eternal opposition between the two kingdoms. At some point, Satan launched an invasion on the kingdom of light. God retaliated by creating the Archetypal Man. However, Satan won the battle, and stole some particles of light. He mixed them with some elements of darkness. God obtained this mixture, and from it, he formed the visible world. His intention in doing so was to liberate the particles of light.

---

36 G.P. Fisher, *History of Christian Doctrine* (Edinburgh: T. & T. Clark, 1896), 58f.

Satan then created Adam, the first human being in the visible creation. From the very first, Adam was imbued with sin, but Satan put the particles of light into him to keep them more secure from God's attempts to retrieve them.

God sent prophets to the human race. They taught humanity about the imprisoned light. The aim was to set the light free to ascend to God and finish forever with any involvement in the material world. If they are not set free in the case of any particular human being, there are further cycles of life after death, so there is always a chance of redemption. Finally, when (or perhaps it is better to say "if") all the light is reunited with God, he will destroy the material universe, and there will again be a complete separation between the two spiritual kingdoms.[37]

To us this may seem a rather far-fetched philosophy. However, it continued, under various names, until the fourteenth century, and its influence lived on even after it ended as a movement. That is why, even in the sixteenth and seventeenth centuries, the authors of the Reformed confessions felt the need to repudiate it.

C. MODERN CONFESSIONS OF FAITH

1. Confession of Faith of the United Church of Northern India

This Confession contains a brief affirmation of creation. It makes two points: (1) God created all visible things; and (2) God created all things by the word of his power. Presumably, the stipulation that visible things are God's creation is not intended as a denial that God created the things that cannot be seen, whether because they are intrinsically invisible, or because they are beyond the reach of human probing. The Indian Christians would certainly have acknowledged God's creation of the invisible realm. However, the people who formulated this Confession were not concerned to speak of things with which human beings can have no acquaintance. Their only interest was to proclaim the faith as it relates to human life. It is in this visible world that human life takes place. From a human point of view, what matters is that our world is God's creation.

---

37 J. O'Grady, *Heresy* (Shaftesbury: Element, 1985), 65f.

2. Confession of Faith of the Huria Batak Protestant
The Indonesian Confession acknowledges that God is the Creator of all things, both visible and invisible. However, it does see the Father alone as the Creator.

3. Confession of Faith of House Churches in China
The Chinese Confession is also brief on this doctrine. It is satisfied to say, "We believe that God created all things."

Section summary and personal application

REMEMBER
In the beginning it pleased God the Father, Son, and Holy Spirit, for the manifestation of the glory of his eternal power, wisdom, and goodness, to Create or make the world, and all things therein, whether visible or invisible, in the space of six days, and all very good.

—*The Baptist Confession of Faith of 1689, 4.1.*

REFLECT
1. Creation, revelation and salvation unite in Jesus Christ—praise God! In your own words, why is this unity of purpose a comfort? Why is it necessary?
2. How would you explain the purpose of creation and what is its significance to you?
3. What is the effect of saying that creation has no ultimate meaning or purpose?

REJOICE
Fairest Lord Jesus, Ruler of all nature,
   O Thou of God and man the Son,
Thee will I cherish, Thee will I honour,
   Thou, my soul's glory, joy and crown.

Fair are the meadows, fairer still the woodlands,
  Robed in the blooming garb of spring;
Jesus is fairer, Jesus is purer,
  Who makes the woeful heart to sing.

All fairest beauty, heavenly and earthly,
  Wondrously, Jesus, is found in Thee;
None can be nearer, fairer or dearer,
  Than Thou, my Saviour, art to me.
—*Joseph A. Seiss (1823–1904)*

PART 3: KEY HISTORICAL DEVELOPMENTS

One issue arising from the doctrine of creation concerns the six days of Genesis 1. Must they be understood literally as six days of twenty-four hours each? There are some Christians influenced by the theory of evolution, who try to harmonize the biblical account of creation with the claims of evolutionary philosophy. Evolutionists claim that the universe originated in a "Big Bang" as many as 20 billion years ago. They say that our solar system began about 5 billion years ago. The origin of life in single-cell organisms is dated to 3 or 4 billion years ago, and the emergence of multi-cell organisms a couple of billion years later. The ancestors of man are reckoned to have appeared on earth a couple of million years ago, and human life as we know it, with its accompanying culture and civilization, is thought to be between 5 and 10 thousand years old.

The issue is this: can these alleged billions of years somehow fit into the pattern of creation portrayed in Genesis 1? Can we understand Genesis 1 in such a way as to accommodate this vast time span? There are six ways in which some Christians try to make the evolutionary timetable and biblical revelation fit each other:

1. Theistic Evolution

This view accepts the entire evolutionary package, with the add-on that God started the whole process. With that common starting point, there are two variations of this theory: (i) *Deistic Evolution* teaches that God set things going, and then withdrew and let it happen; and (ii) *Providential Evolution* teaches that God overruled and oversaw the entire development from the amoeba to the ape to Adam.

2. The Gap Theory

This theory claims that there is a break in time between the first verse-and-a-half of Genesis 1 and the rest of the chapter. The first two sentences of Genesis say,

> 1 In the beginning, God created the heavens and the earth.
> 2 The earth was without form and void, and darkness was over the face of the deep.

The gap theory argues that the billions of years of alleged geological formation come between those introductory words and the next sentence, which begins the account of the first day of the creation week: "And the Spirit of God was hovering over the face of the waters."

3. The Restitution Theory

Like the gap theory, this view postulates a gap between the initial creation of the universe and God's creative work described in Genesis 1. In that gap, the fall of Satan took place. His fall resulted in creation falling into chaos. This theory reads Genesis 1 not as the story of the original creation, but as an account of the restoration of the damaged cosmos.

4. The Day-Age Theory

This asserts that "day" in Genesis 1 does not mean a twenty-four-hour day, but a period of time that is unspecified, indefinite and lengthy.

5. The Framework Hypothesis

According to this view, Genesis 1 is not an account of creation itself. It is the story of God's revelation of the fact of creation to his people.

The six days form a framework within which God revealed creation. They are not the period during which the things mentioned were actually created.

6. The "Ideal" Interpretation

This theory argues that, since God is outside time, reference to "days" when speaking of his work has no point of contact with earthly days, however understood, whether as periods of twenty-four hours, or as aeons of time. The word *day* conveys the idea of an aspect of divine creative activity. Six days highlight six aspects of God's creative work.

John Morris used to be Professor of Geology at the University of Oklahoma. He now works for the Institute of Creation Research, and has written a book entitled *The Young Earth*.[38] He argues that all these approaches are flawed, and that the six days of Genesis 1 must be understood *literally*. He gives nine reasons:

(1) *Facts require interpretation*
Morris points out that the evolutionary timescale is not a scientific fact, but a philosophy on the basis of which facts are interpreted. He observes that there is no dispute about the facts. The fossil record is there. Experiments have discovered how long certain observable phenomena would take to develop from scratch. However, every interpretation contains assumptions, and these determine the conclusion reached as we examine the facts. Morris names the two chief assumptions of the evolutionary hypothesis. The first is *uniformitarianism*. This is the assumption that everything has always happened at exactly the same rate as we observe it happening now. The second assumption is that *everything started from scratch*.

However, there is another interpretation leading from the same evidence to a very different conclusion—the hypothesis that God created everything in six days. This interpretation has two assumptions opposed to those of evolution. The first is *catastrophism*. This assumes that much of the fossil record and many observable phenomena on and below the earth's surface result not from slow, steady development, but from sudden change brought about by the worldwide flood. The

---

38 J. Morris, *The Young Earth* (Colorado Springs: Master Books, 1994).

second assumption is that *things did not start from scratch*. Rather, the Creator made a functionally mature universe. That is part of what was involved in the pronouncement that everything was very good. Everything was in place that would enable things to function immediately for God's glory and for human benefit.

One example of how the universe was functionally mature from the beginning is seen in the light of the stars. Scientists have calculated that it would take billions of years for starlight to reach the earth. However, when God created the stars he also created the track of light visible to people on earth.

(2) *It is impossible to harmonize the biblical and evolutionary accounts of origins*
Morris draws attention to the different order in the appearance of things according to the two accounts. We may illustrate this in the form of a table (see following page, Table 1). To try to harmonize these two accounts is futile. An astronomer by the name of Hugh Ross has made one attempt. He suggested that the days of Genesis 1 overlapped each other. However, this only indicates the lengths to which it is necessary to go in trying to marry the two hypotheses.

(3) *The old-earth hypothesis threatens the gospel itself*
On the evolutionary model, death becomes a merely natural phenomenon. However, the basic assumption of the gospel is that death is the wages of sin. It follows that, before the entrance of sin, the world as a whole was perfect and death was unknown. To adopt the evolutionary approach is to undermine the entire structure of the Bible's storyline.

(4) *Dating methods have been shown to be unreliable*
If uniformitarianism is wrong, no effective dating method can be devised. Even on uniformitarian assumptions, the methods used are unsuccessful. As an example, Morris mentions the attempt to discover the age of a meteorite known as Allende. Scientists claim that it is 4.6 billion years old. A whole spectrum of dating tests was used, and the results ranged from 0.7 billion years to 16.49 billion years—a margin of error of over 2,000%! Morris explains that the conclusion that the correct figure was 4.6 was reached based on a series of guesses, none

Evolutionary Philosophy	The Bible
1. Matter existed in the beginning.	1. In the beginning was God, who created matter.
2. The sun and the stars appeared first and then the earth.	2. The earth was created several days before the sun and the stars.
3. The land appeared before the oceans.	3. The oceans were created before the land.
4. The sun was the first light source for our solar system.	4. Light was created before the sun.
5. The atmosphere was situated above one layer of water.	5. The atmosphere was situated between two layers of water.
6. The first forms of life were marine organisms.	6. The first life forms created were plants.
7. Fish evolved before fruit trees.	7. Fruit trees were created before fish.
8. Insects evolved before fish.	8. Fish were created before insects.
9. The sun predated the plants.	9. Plants were created before the sun.
10. Land animals appeared before sea mammals.	10. All types of sea creatures were created before land animals.

Table 1: *Comparing biblical and evolutionary accounts of origins.*

of which could be proved, or even tested. Certain test results were excluded because they seemed improbable. Yet probability itself was decided by assumptions which themselves were only guesses. The entire evolutionary approach is based in circular arguments. Morris also mentions that archaeologists can date things that they discover based on their historical knowledge. Carbon dating rarely agrees with what historians know. Therefore, they do not take it seriously.

(5) *Some evolutionary conclusions are incompatible with each other*
Evolutionary geologists claim that the fossil record and radioisotope dating suggest that the earth is 5 billion years old. The seas are said to have emerged about 3 billion years ago. However, examination of the salt content in all the world's oceans demonstrates that the absolute maximum possible age of the seas is 62 million years—a discrepancy of nearly 5,000%.

(6) *Many of the implications of the old-earth theory are illogical*
If man really emerged from hominids who themselves first evolved a million years ago, and if population growth rates have always been approximately uniform, then the human population should by now have reached 10 to the power of 8,600. In fact, there are only about 6 billion people on earth today; less than 6 to the power of 13. In addition, Morris asks, why is there no trace of the bones of all the people who have died in the past?

(7) *There is plenty of geological evidence for a young earth*
Here are just a few of the examples Morris gives. There are ripple marks on lower layers of rock—proving that layers formed on top of each other in rapid succession. There is fossil evidence of living things burrowing upwards to escape from a layer of rock laid in a catastrophe. Trees have been discovered fossilized in a standing position, passing through numerous rock layers—proving that successive layers are of a similar age.

(8) *Uniformitarian assumptions cannot incorporate the teaching about the curse on creation in Genesis 3*
For this reason, such an assumption is incompatible with the Bible. On

uniformitarian assumptions, only two options are available. First, to argue that the description of creation as "very good" lies in the future; that evolution is still pressing onwards and progressing towards a perfect world, such as has never yet been seen. Or, to say that from the very beginning, creation was subject to pain, suffering and death, and that these things are "very good" because they are intrinsic to the process of evolution. Neither of these views is consistent with Scripture.

(9) The argument that "day" can mean a long period in Genesis 1 is not borne out by biblical usage
Morris recognizes that the Hebrew word *yom* (*day*) can mean an indefinite period. However, he says, this is not a legitimate interpretation for Genesis 1. He gives the following reasons:

i) Whenever *yom* is modified by a number, it always means a 24-hour day. Morris says that there are 359 examples elsewhere in the Old Testament.

ii) Whenever the phrase "evening and morning" occurs, it is always referring to a 24-hour day. Morris says that there are 38 examples elsewhere in the Old Testament.

iii) Morris refers to the reference to six days in the fourth commandment (Exodus 20:11): "in six days the LORD made heaven and earth, the sea, and all that is in them, and rested the seventh day. Therefore the LORD blessed the Sabbath day and made it holy." As a basis for the Sabbath commandment, this reference to the six days of creation most naturally reads as meaning six days of 24 hours.

It seems to me that Morris has made the case for not attempting to combine Scripture with modern evolutionary accounts of origins.

Some argue that a non-literal understanding of *day* can be defended on different grounds and from a higher motive. It is said that the increased vastness of time that results leads to an enhanced perception of the glory of the Creator. It is claimed that this reading makes no concession to modern philosophy. The evidence offered is that some of the earliest Christian theologians, centuries before the time of Darwin, interpreted *day* in a symbolic fashion. One defender of this viewpoint is Professor Donald Macleod. He writes:

> How can I possibly entertain the notion that these days are creation eras and not 24-hour periods? First of all, because that interpretation has a very honourable pedigree. It is completely false to imagine that it was only adopted by the church as a counsel of despair in the light of the challenge from Darwinism. It was the prevalent view of the fathers even before Augustine, and certainly from Augustine onwards.[39]

However, I think that Macleod is mistaken here. I have looked up every reference to the six days of creation in all 38 volumes of the American edition of the Edinburgh series of the writings of the Ante-Nicene Fathers and the Nicene and Post-Nicene Fathers. I could not find even one who advocated the view that *day* means a long period. Indeed, some (including Basil, Ambrose and Augustine) were adamant, in contrast to the pagan philosophies of their contemporaries, that *day* means 24 hours, and that the earth is only a few thousand years old. It is true that the Church Fathers did sometimes take the six days in a non-literal way, but Louis Berkhof interprets them correctly:

> The opinion that these days were not ordinary days of 24 hours was not entirely foreign to early Christian theology.... But some of the Church Fathers, who intimated that these days were not to be regarded as ordinary days, expressed the opinion that the whole work of creation was finished in a moment of time, and that the days merely constituted a symbolical framework, which facilitated the description of the work of creation in an orderly fashion, so as to make it more intelligible to finite minds.

On the next page, Berkhof continues:

> The prevailing view has always been that the days of Genesis 1 are to be understood as literal days. Some of the early Church Fathers

---

39 Macleod, *A Faith to Live By*, 58.

did not regard them as real indications of the time in which the work of creation was completed, but rather as literary forms in which the writer of Genesis cast the narrative of creation, in order to picture the work of creation—which was really completed in a moment of time—in an orderly fashion for the human intellect. It was only after the comparatively new sciences of geology and palaeontology came forward with their theories of the enormous age of the earth, that theologians began to show an inclination to identify the days of creation with the long geological ages.[40]

It is true that Macleod tries to avoid capitulating to evolutionary philosophy. He admits that the Bible precludes

the notion that man is the result of an evolution, itself guided by natural selection and taking place through minute, chance variations over many millions of years. The Bible portrays man as new; and as the specific product of divine activity. My personal view of the creation week is that within it there were long periods during which the procedures defined in Genesis operated in terms of the Lord's Word, "Let the waters bring forth," "Let the earth bring forth." These processes went on over many millions of years. The waters kept bringing forth and the earth kept bringing forth. But there are specific points in the process where God intervened, initiating a new departure.[41]

However, I very much doubt that this can be carried through consistently. Two New Testament texts are vital for coming to a conclusion on this matter:

Sin came into the world through one man, and death through sin, and so death spread to all men because all sinned (Romans 5:12).

By a man came death (1 Corinthians 15:21).

---

40 Berkhof, *Systematic Theology*, 152-153; Reymond, *A New Systematic Theology*, 392 n.9, makes the same point.

41 Macleod, *A Faith to Live By*, 68.

Is it possible to maintain a millions-of-years process during which not one living creature died? Old earth theories inevitably teach that some species became extinct long before the creation of human beings. In that case, death is no longer the result of sin, but a merely natural problem. It will not do to say that these Scriptures are speaking only of human death, because the Romans text makes it clear that death came into the world as a whole through sin. This biblical link between sin and death makes me unable to hold to any other than the literal interpretation of Genesis 1.

PART 4: KEY POINTS OF PRACTICAL APPLICATION

Gordon Wenham seeks to analyze the picture of God and the world offered by Genesis 1. Some of the points he makes show clear implications. First, *the fact of creation tells us that God has no equals or rivals.* This means that he alone is to be worshipped. Second, *as Creator, God is also Lawgiver.* The Creator's authority is evident in his naming of the component parts of creation, in his appointment of the heavenly lights for a declared purpose, in the command given to the animals to be fruitful and multiply, and in his setting of bounds and defining of roles for his creatures. Wenham writes: "With this goes the corollary that all creatures will fulfil their divinely appointed role only if they adhere to God's directive." Clearly, this applies equally to human beings. Our duty is to live in obedience to the God who made everything. Third, *the world reflects its Creator.* The implication of this is that general revelation in nature leaves human beings without excuse if we refuse to acknowledge and submit to God.[42]

The Scriptures suggest two other applications:

(1) Ecclesiastes 12:1 says, "Remember also your Creator in the days of your youth, before the evil days come and the years draw near of which you will say, 'I have no pleasure in them.'" The contrast here

---

42 Wenham, *Genesis 1-15*, on Genesis 1:1-2:3.

between "youth" and "the evil days" recognizes that old age is often a time of difficulty, tragedy and sadness. The pleasures of life may well be in the past by the time a person is old. However, even youth, with all its joys, falls short of what it should be if the Creator is forgotten. Moreover, to neglect the remembrance of the Creator during the days of youth may be to leave it too late: to remember the Creator early "is shown to be especially important in view of the gradual loss of vitality as age takes its toll of the body and brain."[43] To remember God as Creator is to live in a constant attitude of gratitude. It is to cultivate a life of obedience. It is to take a serious-minded approach to life. It is to be a sincere worshipper. It is to seek God's forgiveness and to trust in his mercy offered to us in his Son.

(2) Psalm 89:12 says, "The north and the south, you have created them; Tabor and Hermon joyously praise your name." Hermon and Tabor represent the north and the south respectively. The parallel phrases "you have created them" and "joyously praise your name" demonstrate equivalence in the psalmist's mind between creation and joy. If the inanimate creation rejoices (metaphorically), so ought we to rejoice (literally) in God's creation. God "richly provides us with everything to enjoy" (1 Timothy 6:17). We glorify him when we take pleasure in his creation. He means us to enjoy the things he has made.

REFLECT

1. Do you give credence to evolutionary philosophies? If not, why not? If so, why?
2. List personal benefits of delighting in God's creation.
3. Creation declares the glory of God. Do you take time out just to enjoy God's handiwork?

REJOICE

Let every creature join
    To praise th' eternal God;
Ye heav'nly hosts, the song begin,
    And sound his name abroad.

---

43 J.S. Wright, "Commentary on Ecclesiastes," in Gaebelein, ed., *Expositor's Bible Commentary*, on Ecclesiastes 12:1-8.

He built those worlds above,
   And fixed their wondrous frame;
By his command they stand or move,
   And ever speak his name.
Ye vapors, when ye rise,
   Or fall in showers of snow;
Ye thunders, murmuring round the skies,
   His power and glory show.
—*Isaac Watts (1674–1748)*

6

THE DOCTRINE OF CREATION IN ITS PRESENT CONDITION

How is the glory of God revealed today?

PART 1: KEY TEXTS

A. OLD TESTAMENT

GENESIS 3:17-19

> 17 And to Adam he said, "Because you have listened to the voice of your wife and have eaten of the tree of which I commanded you, 'You shall not eat of it,' cursed is the ground because of you; in pain you shall eat of it all the days of your life;
> 18 thorns and thistles it shall bring forth for you; and you shall eat the plants of the field.
> 19 By the sweat of your face you shall eat bread, till you return to the ground, for out of it you were taken; for you are dust, and to dust you shall return."

It is obvious that the present state of the earth is quite different from the Creator's original description as "very good." This passage explains the difference as the result of the curse on the ground (verse 17) which followed the entry of sin into the world. The reference to thorns and thistles indicates what the curse means in practice. *Thorns* translates the Hebrew word *qots*. Elsewhere in the Old Testament, this word has various connotations. It may speak of something only fit for rejection, as in 2 Samuel 23:6: "worthless men are all like thorns that are thrown away." Thorns are responsible for turning joy to misery, as Isaiah 32:12-13 indicates:

> 12 Beat your breasts for the pleasant fields, for the fruitful vine,
> 13 for the soil of my people growing up in thorns and briers, yes, for all the joyous houses in the exultant city.

Thorns make land unfit for cultivation. That is why Jeremiah 4:3 says, "sow not among thorns." Thorns may represent bitter disappointment, as in Jeremiah 12:13: "they have sown wheat and reaped thorns." Again, thorns are a source of pain. Ezekiel 28:24 speaks of "a brier to prick or a thorn to hurt."

The Hebrew word for *thistles* is *dardar*. It comes only once more in the Bible, again along with *qots*. Hosea 10:5-8 reads as follows:

> 5 The inhabitants of Samaria tremble for the calf of Beth-aven. Its people mourn for it, and so do its idolatrous priests—those who rejoiced over it and over its glory—for it has departed from them.
> 6 The thing itself shall be carried to Assyria as tribute to the great king. Ephraim shall be put to shame, and Israel shall be ashamed of his idol.
> 7 Samaria's king shall perish like a twig on the face of the waters.
> 8 The high places of Aven, the sin of Israel, shall be destroyed. Thorn and thistle shall grow up on their altars.

In this context, the growth of thorns and thistles represents a situation where glory has departed and been replaced by shame, insignificance ("a twig on the face of the waters"), and destruction. Because of the curse, then, creation is now in a spoiled, flimsy, dangerous condition. People find this world to be a constant source of frustrating disappointment. Creation is far removed from the glory of its origin. The frustrating nature of the world as it is now is brought out by two words describing human experience on earth, the word *pain* in verse 17, and the word *sweat* in verse 19. *Pain* renders the Hebrew term *itstsabown*. This word has been used already in verse 16 of a woman's acute pain in childbirth. It is used only once more, in Genesis 5:29, where again it is connected with the curse as Lamech explains the name of his son, Noah:

> Out of the ground that the LORD has cursed this one shall bring us relief from our work and from the painful toil (*itstsabown*) of our hands.

Itstsabown is derived from the verb *atsab*, which may refer to physical pain, mental discomfort, emotional sorrow, or spiritual anguish. To live as a frustrated human being in a cursed world is to have an ache in your body and grief in your heart, because the world in which we live is so badly damaged. As Ecclesiastes 10:9 recognizes, it is so often the case now that "he who quarries stones is hurt by them." To have to labour in the painful conditions of the present creation is inevitably to sweat. As verse 17 makes clear, this is going to be true every single day. This reminds us that we should not expect too much in the present world. Our sights should be set on the new creation.

B. NEW TESTAMENT

ROMANS 8:18-22

18 For I consider that the sufferings of this present time are not worth comparing with the glory that is to be revealed to us.
19 For the creation waits with eager longing for the revealing of the sons of God.
20 For the creation was subjected to futility, not willingly, but because of him who subjected it, in hope
21 that the creation itself will be set free from its bondage to decay and obtain the freedom of the glory of the children of God.
22 For we know that the whole creation has been groaning together in the pains of childbirth until now.

Two occurrences of the Greek word *nun* bracket this passage. It is translated *present* in verse 18 and *now* at the end of verse 22. We can divide what is said here about the present state of creation into two main themes.

1. Creation's disappointment

The key word is *futility* (verse 20). This translates the Greek term *mataiotes*, a word speaking of emptiness or worthlessness, of something lacking proper purpose. It pictures creation as aimless, just going round in circles, having lost direction. Professor Dunn suggests two ways in which creation has become futile: (1) it fails to function as designed; and (2) it has been accorded a role for which it was never designed.[1] On the first point, thorns and thistles had no place in God's blueprint. The need for ornamental plants and cultivated food to compete with weeds and pests for space, nutrients and air was not God's

---

1   Dunn, *Romans 1-8*, 470.

first intention. As regards Dunn's second point, man now views creation solely in relation to himself, and so abuses it for selfish ends. He gives it a status that effectively turns it into an idol. He treats it as though it is an autonomous entity capable of being studied and worked without reference to God. Three questions arise regarding verse 20.

(1) *What is the force of the word "subjected"?*
This Greek word, *hupetage*, means *put under*. It speaks of something brought under the total control of another. Creation has come under the total control of futility. Futility now dominates the created order. Absolutely nothing goes as it should. Absolutely everything has gone off course.

(2) *Who did the subjecting?*
There are two possibilities, and Bible scholars differ. Some suggest that man is responsible, that sin is the direct cause of this subjection. Others read this verse in the light of Genesis 3:17, and understand Paul to mean that God subjected creation by imposing the curse. This seems more likely. The words "in hope" imply that the subjection was intentionally temporary. While human sin was certainly the indirect cause, the action of God effected the subjection.

(3) *Whose unwillingness is meant?*
Again, there are two possibilities. It may mean that God had to subject creation to futility, but did it reluctantly. Alternatively, it may be that creation is being personified. As Dunn puts it, "creation was not party to Adam's failure but was drawn into it nonetheless."[2] Here it is probably not necessary to choose absolutely between these two options. There may be truth in both.

Creation's disappointment is depicted by a further four words.

i) *Sufferings* (verse 18). The human experience of suffering within this world is a major symptom of the damage done to the creation by sin.

---

2   Dunn, *Romans 1-8*, 470.

ii) *Bondage* (verse 21). Creation is enslaved. It is in a state of helplessness, in the possession of a power greater than its own. Creation inevitably goes off course and can do nothing about it. It never achieves everything for which it was made. Its potential is always restricted. Disappointment has creation in its grasp.

iii) *Decay* (verse 21). The Greek word is *phthora*. Paul uses it again in Colossians 2:22. Here are verses 20-22:

> If with Christ you died to the elemental spirits of the world, why, as if you were still alive in the world, do you submit to regulations—"Do not handle, Do not taste, Do not touch" (referring to things that all perish [*phthora*] as they are used)?

Everything in the world as it is now does indeed perish with use.

iv) *Groaning* (verse 22). The Greek word is *sustenazo*. Literally, this means "groans together." The entire creation is at one in its groaning. Every created object lends its sigh to creation's enormous groan. This word depicts the grieving heart of the world. It is, of course, picture language. Its intent is vividly to emphasize how great is the damage done to creation and how far the created order has been dragged down from the possibilities latent within it at the beginning.

2. Creation's anticipation

Here is a second feature of creation as it is now: it is on the way towards its reconstruction. The apostle is still writing as if creation is a person. There is an element of hope. Creation has a sure and certain anticipation of something better to come. It will at last be restored to what it was in the beginning. That final state is described as "the freedom of the glory of the children of God." It is part of the doctrine of eschatology, and will be considered in that context. For now, we notice that creation's present anticipation of future glory is brought out in two phrases:

(1) *The creation waits with eager longing* (verse 19)

"Waits with eager longing" translates two Greek words. The first is *apokaradokia*. This is a very picturesque word. It portrays someone leaning, straining forward because of his intense desire for an event he is keenly awaiting. Creation is standing on tiptoe to see if the time is yet. The other word is *apekdechetai*. This compares creation's wait to the excitement of a child waiting for some very enjoyable experience, like Christmas, or the school holidays.

(2) *The pains of childbirth* (verse 22)

Creation is depicted as an expectant mother on the point of giving birth. Already she feels the onset of labour. All the sufferings and disappointments of life in creation as it is now are the promise of the birth of the new heavens and the new earth.

These two themes—creation's disappointment and its anticipation—both relate to one set of realities: creation as it is now is full of suffering. We can specify some of those sufferings. There are human illnesses and accidents. There is the grief of bereavement. There are natural disasters, such as earthquakes, volcanoes, storms and famines. There is the inability of the nations to establish peace or eliminate poverty. Yet these very sufferings are the labour pains through which the world to come is in the process of being born out of the wreckage of creation. Our present sufferings are the foundation and inspiration of our hope.

PART 2: KEY CREEDS AND CONFESSIONS

There is nothing in the early creeds, the Reformation confessions, or the modern confessions of faith on this theme. Perhaps those who have drawn up these statements have regarded the present state of creation as so obvious that a specific mention of it is superfluous.

Section summary and personal application

REMEMBER

"By the sweat of your face
    you shall eat bread,
till you return to the ground,
    for out of it you were taken;
for you are dust,
    and to dust you shall return."
—*Genesis 3:19*

For the creation was subjected to futility, not willingly, but because of him who subjected it, in hope that the creation itself will be set free from its bondage to corruption and obtain the freedom of the glory of the children of God.
—*Romans 8:20-21*

REFLECT

1. Solomon declares all is vain, futile and frustrating. What relief or comfort would you offer someone discouraged with life?
2. All earthly things perish. What is the great mercy in this? How would you counsel a believer whose sole focus is on the pleasures of this world (2 Corinthians 4:16–18)?

REJOICE

Lift up the trumpet, and loud let it ring:
    Jesus is coming again!
Cheer up, ye pilgrims, be joyful and sing:
    Jesus is coming again!

    Coming again, coming again,
      Jesus is coming again!

Echo it, hilltops; proclaim it, ye plains:
   Jesus is coming again!
Coming in glory, the Lamb that was slain;
   Jesus is coming again!

Heavings of earth, tell the vast, wondering throng:
   Jesus is coming again!
Tempests and whirlwinds, the anthem prolong;
   Jesus is coming again!
— *Jessie E. Strout (1872)*

PART 3: KEY HISTORICAL DEVELOPMENTS

In recent times, the biblical teaching on creation in its present condition has prompted concern on the part of Christians with environmental issues. Francis Schaeffer raised this concern in 1970 when he wrote *Pollution and the Death of Man*. This was an attempt to offer a Christian view of ecology, which Schaeffer defines as "the study of the balance of living things in nature."[3] Schaeffer's concern is with the way that human activity is leading to such things as water and air pollution, and destructive noise levels, especially in the world's large cities. As a result, the balance of nature is being destroyed.

Basing his argument on Romans 8, Schaeffer advocates "substantial healing."[4] Substantial healing falls short of perfect healing, but it is still evident and real. Schaeffer recognizes that the world will never be totally healed until Christ returns—yet Christians are not just to sit back and wait for that day. By God's help, in the power of his Spirit, and because of the work of Christ, we should be seeking to achieve at least this substantial healing of the planet. In anticipation of the per-

---

3   F.A. Schaeffer, *Pollution and the Death of Man: the Christian View of Ecology* (London: Hodder and Stoughton, 1970), 8.

4   Schaeffer, *Pollution and the Death of Man*, 47.

fection that Christ will establish at the end, we should be seeking to move things in that direction. How is this achieved? Schaeffer's answer is by honouring each component part of the natural world on its own terms. We should not be destroyers of nature, but should treat God's creation with great respect. It may be legitimate to chop down a tree to build a house. However, it is never legitimate to chop down a tree just for the sake of it. As a part of God's creation, even a tree has value. Schaeffer gives the example of a housing development to demonstrate the practical application of his thinking:

> Bulldozers have gone in to flatten everything and clear the trees before the houses are begun. The result is ugliness. It would have cost another thousand pounds to bulldoze round the trees, so they are simply bulldozed down without question. And then we wonder, looking at the result, how people can live there. It is less than human in its barrenness, and even economically it is poorer as the top soil washes away. So when man breaks God's truth, in reality he suffers.[5]

More recently, John Davies of New South Wales, Australia, has published a two-part series on a biblical theology of the environment in the magazine of Third Millennium Ministries. He sees environmental concern as part of our duty of loving our neighbour, with particular reference to those neighbours in the generations yet to be born. Davies notes that the Industrial Revolution has given us the capacity for large-scale environmental degradation. However, it is only in the past few decades that many of the consequences of industrialization have become apparent. A discussion of ecological issues has resulted, and Davies mentions Schaeffer's book as the most notable Christian contribution. Davies structures God's revelation in Scripture around the three themes of creation, rebellion, and resurrection.

The biblical picture of *creation* is that earth and its teeming life was designed to exist under the care of human beings, and to find its value in relation to humanity before God. However, this is not merely a matter of economics:

---

5   Schaeffer, *Pollution and the Death of Man*, 56.

There are the less quantifiable benefits of the richness, the beauty, and the diversity which God's creation brings into our lives, leading us to a greater appreciation of the wisdom and grandeur of God.[6]

The human duty of care for creation still stands, but because of human *rebellion* against the Creator,

The world as we presently experience it is an aberration. Illness and death are abnormal experiences. Pollution, famine, and cyclones are the consequences (direct and indirect) of our rebellion.[7]

Davies sees God's curse as a deliberate pronouncement that all is not well with creation, that the order of things is violated. We have to take seriously the curse and the world's fallen condition. Biblical realism refuses to imagine that we can usher in an environmental utopia. However, we are still to strive to overcome the effects of sin and the curse, at least in partial ways.

Davies recognizes that the frustrations built into a cursed earth are made worse by human greed. Part of caring for a fallen creation is to rethink our attitudes towards economic growth and the expectation of constantly rising living standards.

For the Christian, the *resurrection* gives significance to the entire creation. The resurrection of Christ's physical body is the promise of the renewal of the entire physical environment. Davies argues that the Christian community should be setting the standard in restraining the tendency to environmental degradation. Such degradation is a perversion of God's purposes. Davies calls us to support any initiatives fostering care for God's creation. He challenges us to make personal

---

6 J.A. Davies, "Toward a Biblical Theology of the Environment, Part 1: Introduction and Creation," in *Reformed Perspectives Magazine* (RPM), vol.1, no.15 (June 7-13, 1999), online at www.reformedperspectives.org.

7 J.A. Davies, "Toward a Biblical Theology of the Environment, Part 2: Rebellion and Resurrection," in *Reformed Perspectives Magazine* (RPM), vol.1, no.16 (June 14-20, 1999), online at www.reformedperspectives.org.

adjustments in our lifestyle away from the consumer-driven greed of our generation.

PART 4: KEY POINTS OF PRACTICAL APPLICATION

John Silvius has expressed the practical side of the doctrine of creation in its present condition in terms of stewardship.[8] He lists the following areas of contemporary environmental concern: acid rain, water shortages, water supplies contaminated by toxic chemicals or disease organisms, expanding deserts, drought and famine, the diminishing quality of soil and air, and diminishing quantities of fuel supplies.

Silvius argues that concern for the environment and the earth's natural resources is part of our stewardship in the light of the Christian hope. Silvius says that the Christian steward of the earth must love the Creator and love the creation. Then he must understand his role as the Creator's steward within the creation. A steward is a manager of a home. As the manager of the earth as the human home, the Christian may not live in greedy and careless over-consumption of food, energy, and other resources. To do so would adversely affect our human neighbours, and the rest of God's creatures. Silvius points out that the current reality is that 25% of the world's population consumes 80% of the world's energy and goods. Christians must challenge that situation, and clamour for equitability. In the end, environmental concern becomes an aspect of the demand for international social justice. However, it seems to me, that it is not just for the sake of our fellow creatures that we must care for the environment. We must thoroughly question a merely utilitarian approach to life. There is a remarkable passage in Job 38:25-27:

---

8   J.E. Silvius, "Christian Stewardship of the Environment," in *Creation Social Science and Humanities Society Quarterly Journal*, vol.10, no.3: 24-27.

25 Who has cleft a channel for the torrents of rain and a way for the thunderbolt,
26 to bring rain on a land where no man is, on the desert in which there is no man,
27 to satisfy the waste and desolate land, and to make the ground sprout with grass?

Grass grows even in uninhabited regions of the world. God's urge for beauty is being satisfied. We must nurture beauty in the environment, *chiefly for God's sake*. In a world marred by ugliness because of sin, it is our duty to reject everything making ugliness worse and beauty less.

REFLECT

1. As a Christian, is there a balance between neglecting God's creation and worshipping it? How would you explain a balanced approach?

2. "[We] must nurture beauty…it is our duty to reject everything making ugliness worse and beauty less." How can we nurture beauty in the environment, locally and globally?

REJOICE

All things bright and beautiful,
All creatures great and small,
All things wise and wonderful:
The Lord God made them all.

Each little flower that opens,
Each little bird that sings,
He made their glowing colors,
He made their tiny wings.

The cold wind in the winter,
The pleasant summer sun,
The ripe fruits in the garden,
He made them every one.

He gave us eyes to see them,
   And lips that we might tell
How great is God Almighty,
   Who has made all things well.
—*Cecil Frances H. Alexander (1818–1895)*

7

THE DOCTRINE OF THE DIVINE DECREE

How did God ensure that his glory would be seen in his works?

We know that creation has fallen from its original condition because of human sin. Has this made the world unpredictable, so that even God is no longer in control of what happens? Do things happen by chance, perhaps even taking God by surprise? The doctrine of God's decree is the answer to such questions. This doctrine teaches us that God has ordered everything that will happen. God's decree is rooted in his unique, unrivalled, unchallengeable authority.

We read several times in the Scriptures of decrees made by human monarchs, particularly in the books of Ezra, Esther, and Daniel. A brief survey will help us to get a picture of what is involved in a decree. We shall use the book of Ezra as our example. It tells of a series of decrees made by the Persian emperors. We hear of two decrees made by King Artaxerxes. The enemies of the Jews protested to him about the rebuilding of the temple. They accused the Jews of rebellion and sedition. Artaxerxes therefore made a decree that the history of the Jews should be researched to verify this accusation (Ezra 4:19). On the strength of this information, Artaxerxes ordered his servants to make a decree, halting the work pending a further decree authorizing its recommencement (Ezra 4:21).

However, in the days of King Darius, the prophets Haggai and Zechariah challenged the people to resume the building work. This resulted in an enquiry from the governor of the province: "Who gave you a decree to build this house and finish this structure?" (Ezra 5:3,9). The Jews informed the governor that King Cyrus had made such a decree (Ezra 5:13). The governor then requested King Darius to order a search in the archives to see whether such a decree had in fact been issued by Cyrus (Ezra 5:17). Darius agreed to this (Ezra 6:1). A scroll was duly discovered confirming that Cyrus had issued the decree (Ezra 6:3). Darius therefore issued a further decree, which had two parts. First, he instructed the governor to allow the work on the temple to continue, and decreed that the cost should be covered out of public taxation. Second, he decreed punishment for anyone who failed to comply (Ezra 6:8,11,12). We then hear that the work was completed according to the royal decree (Ezra 6:14).

It is clear that a royal decree had to be obeyed. The king's authority meant that *his word was law*. In the same way, the divine decree is God's word of law for his creation. Every element in the created universe has no alternative but to obey the Lord's decree. He has made decisions governing the material universe. The psalmist celebrates this truth in Psalm 148:3-6:

> 3 Praise him, sun and moon, praise him, all you shining stars!
> 4 Praise him, you highest heavens, and you waters above the heavens!
> 5 Let them praise the name of the LORD! For he commanded and they were created.
> 6 And he established them forever and ever; he gave a decree, and it shall not pass away.

This passage shows that God not only created the universe, but that his decree also controls the orbits of the stars and planets for all time. However, this applies not only to the inanimate creation. Even human plans and activities come within the sovereign decree of the Lord. The Jews recognized this. The completion of the work is recorded in Ezra 6:14.

> The elders of the Jews built and prospered through the prophesying of Haggai the prophet and Zechariah the son of Iddo. They finished their building by decree of the God of Israel and by decree of Cyrus and Darius and Artaxerxes king of Persia.

These words acknowledge that, whatever the world's politicians may decide, behind all their scheming is the sovereign purpose of the God of heaven. Isaiah recognizes that human rulers may well pass unjust decrees: "Woe to those who decree iniquitous decrees" (Isaiah 10:1). The Hebrew word translated *iniquitous* here is *'awen*. Isaiah uses the same word when he quotes the LORD, "I cannot endure iniquity" (Isaiah 1:13). The LORD's decree is always right and just. This is because its main aim is to secure the exaltation of Christ in the salvation of the world. As Psalm 2:7-8 says, speaking prophetically for Christ:

> 7 I will tell of the decree: the LORD said to me, "You are my Son; today I have begotten you."
> 8 Ask of me, and I will make the nations your heritage, and the ends of the earth your possession.

PART 1: KEY TEXTS

For this doctrine, it is more difficult to point to extended passages of Scripture. The evidence is more fragmentary—a verse here and there. It will therefore be necessary to collect a cluster of short statements.

A. OLD TESTAMENT

GENESIS 50:20

> As for you, you meant evil against me, but God meant it for good, to bring it about that many people should be kept alive, as they are today.

These are Joseph's words to his brothers following the death of their father. The brothers are anxious that Joseph may now spot an opportunity to take revenge for their treatment of him. They pretend that Jacob has sent a message requesting Joseph's forgiveness for them. Joseph then reassures them in these words. The Hebrew word rendered *meant* is *hasab*. It means to devise a plan, to frame a purpose. Joseph is expressing his confident conviction that, long before his brothers acted as they did, the LORD had drawn up a plan to get him to Egypt, and into a position of prominence there. This purpose was "for good." The Hebrew word used here, *tob*, is the same as that used of the pristine creation. The good in view is the preservation of human life. John Sailhamer writes:

> Behind all the events and human plans recounted in the story of Joseph lies the unchanging plan of God. It is the same plan introduced from the beginning of the book where God looks out at what he has just created for man and sees that "it is good." Through his dealings with the patriarchs and Joseph, God had continued to bring about his good plan.[1]

---

1   Sailhamer, "Commentary on Genesis," in Gaebelein, ed., *Expositor's Bible Commentary*, on Genesis 50:15-21.

Joseph's assessment of his own experience can be universalized. Whatever happens, behind it there is a divine plan, always intended to promote what is ultimately good. In his mind, the LORD pictured what should happen to achieve the good. Therefore, whatever happens is the LORD's idea coming to reality.

JOB 42:2

I know that you can do all things, and that no purpose of yours can be thwarted.

As in the case of Joseph, Job sees that God's purpose and its outworking are tied together. Whatever happens, it is because the LORD purposed it, and no one can prevent it.

The word translated *purpose* is *mezimmah*. It refers to something worked out with discretion. The LORD has planned his purpose with wisdom. He had a clear understanding of what is for the good. In his decree, he took care to avoid anything detrimental to the ultimate good. The word rendered *thwarted* is *batsar*. It suggests the picture of something out of reach because it is on the other side of a fence. It is impossible for God's purpose to be enclosed so that it becomes inaccessible to him. Once his wisdom has stated what shall be, that is what shall be.

PSALM 33:11

The counsel of the LORD stands forever, the plans of his heart to all generations.

Two terms here refer to the LORD's decreed purpose. *Counsel* translates *'etsah*. The root from which this word comes means to deliberate, to determine, to devise. The LORD determines everything that will happen with deliberate, careful planning. *Plans* translates *mahasabah*, which is connected with *hasab*, used in Genesis 50:20. It denotes a plan prepared in advance before the work begins. Just as a garden designer or a fashion designer will form a mental picture and make sketches of the finished work before starting, so God sketched in his mind from eternity the course his creation would take once he brought it into being. Because God's plans were eternal in their devising, they are also eternal in their outworking. God's decree is like an arch spanning the whole course of history. Willem van Gemeren has said, "Creation and providence are the timely operations of God's purposes. Nothing will thwart his plans."[2]

PSALM 115:3

Our God is in the heavens; he does all that he pleases.

The word *pleases* points us back behind what God does to his motivation. The Hebrew word is *hapets*. It means that God does whatever brings him pleasure and delight. The grand purpose of everything is God's joy. The great purpose was drawn up with the divine happiness in view. God determined that all that happens would serve to make his creation completely attractive to him. This word speaks of an emotional involvement in the planning. The same word is used in a human context of a young man falling in love with a woman. The divine decree is not some cold, calculating plan. It is something to which the LORD is passionately committed. God warms to his purpose. He finds it heart-warming. His plan was devised in the height of emotion.

In our planning, we are often constrained. Circumstances beyond our control mean that we cannot always achieve our own pleasure. There are no such limitations on God, because he is "in the heavens." He is above the reach of hindrances and setbacks. He is free to bring about those things that delight his heart.

PSALM 135:6

Whatever the LORD pleases, he does, in heaven and on earth, in the seas and all deeps.

This verse is repeating the same truth, but with the addition that it is

---

2 W.A. van Gemeren, "Commentary on Psalms," in Gaebelein, ed., *Expositor's Bible Commentary*, on Psalm 33:10-11.

true universally. Nowhere, not even the remotest depths, is outside the control of the LORD's decree.

ISAIAH 14:24-27

24 The LORD of hosts has sworn: 'As I have planned, so shall it be, and as I have purposed, so shall it stand,
25 that I will break the Assyrian in my land, and on my mountains trample him underfoot; and his yoke shall depart from them, and his burden from their shoulder.'
26 This is the purpose that is purposed concerning the whole earth, and this is the hand that is stretched out over all the nations.
27 For the LORD of hosts has purposed, and who will annul it? His hand is stretched out, and who will turn it back?

Verse 26 speaks of a "purpose that is purposed." The noun is the word 'etsah, which we have met in Psalm 33:11. It means a plan determined with deliberation. The verb translated *purposed* is *ya'ats*, the root from which 'etsah comes. The purpose in view is specific and particular, namely the downfall of Assyria. However, the first and last verses of this passage suggest that this specific purpose is just one expression of a far larger, universal purpose. The word translated *purposed* in both verses 24 and 27 is again *ya'ats*. In verse 24 it occurs in parallel with *damah*, translated *thought*. The basic meaning of this verb is "to compare." We may picture the LORD weighing up in his mind various options and then settling on which he will actually bring to pass. The main assertion here is that it is the LORD's purpose which is fulfilled, and no human power can prevent it.

John Watts suggests translating 'etsah as *strategy*, and makes an extended comment on its significance. Here are some extracts:

The idea of God's control of events is common in…the Old Testament…. Yet apparently, Isaiah is the classic and perhaps the first book (and prophet) to speak of [the LORD's] plan on so universal a scale…. God stands in the centre of his view of history as the one who is acting. He has a goal in what he does. He is following a plan…. [Isaiah] sees his time in the light of the living God….

[God's] plan cannot be turned aside…. [Isaiah's prophecy] confronts the events of history with the reality of the living God whose acts and whose plans are becoming visible in the events of the day…. History is the work of [the LORD] of hosts, who is enthroned on Zion. It unfolds according to a plan which he has determined.[3]

In a similar vein, Alec Motyer notes how Isaiah uses the crushing of the Assyrian threat "…as an example of the way the divine hand governs all nations and executes an irresistible world purpose."[4]

ISAIAH 46:9-11

9 "Remember the former things of old; for I am God, and there is no other; I am God, and there is none like me,
10 declaring the end from the beginning and from ancient times things not yet done, saying, 'My counsel shall stand, and I will accomplish all my purpose,'
11 calling a bird of prey from the east, the man of my counsel from a far country. I have spoken, and I will bring it to pass; I have purposed, and I will do it."

Four terms here refer to the divine decree. *Counsel* (verse 10) translates *'etsah* again. *Purpose* (verse 10) translates *hepets*, which is cognate with *hapets* in Psalm 115:3. In the words "I have spoken" in verse 11, we have an indication of the ease with which God gets his will done. At creation, he merely spoke and it was done. In the same way, in the course of history, what he simply says is what happens. The words "I have purposed" render the verb *yatsar*. It might be used of a potter moulding clay. In creating, God brought things into existence out of nothing. By his decree, he shapes what is now there. Each of these terms links with a phrase affirming that God's decree is fulfilled. God's plan stands; it is accomplished (verse 10). It is brought to pass; it is done (verse 11). There are two additional things to note here:

3 J.D.W. Watts, *Isaiah 1-33* (Dallas: Word, 1985), on Isaiah 14:22-27, "Excursus: Yahweh's Strategy."

4 J.A. Motyer, *The Prophecy of Isaiah* (Leicester: IVP, 1993), 146.

1. God declares the end from the beginning

He is able to make known the ultimate destiny of creation, because in the beginning he planned both the destination and the route. He can make known everything that will happen, because he has determined from eternity what shall be. Motyer says that the one unique God "dictates the purpose within history": "He is sovereign, his purpose/plan/counsel is unalterable and is the product not of whim, but of his pleasurable will."[5]

2. Only such a God is worthy of the title "God"

The import of verse 9 is that the LORD is God, the only God. He is the incomparable God. Verse 10 then begins with a participle. This has the effect of making this verse an explanation of what it means to say that the LORD is the unique and incomparable God: namely, he decrees what shall be, and that is exactly what happens.

We may summarize the Old Testament teaching on God's decree like this. God has given the word isolating his plan, his design, for history. He moulds events, with wisdom and care, for his own delight. God is passionately committed to achieving a good outcome. His purpose is unchanging. It affects everything everywhere. His will is done. To say anything less would imply that we are not really talking about God.

B. NEW TESTAMENT

We shall divide the New Testament texts teaching God's decree into two categories.

1. General statements of God's decree

ACTS 15:14-18

14 Simeon has related how God first visited the Gentiles, to take from them a people for his name.
15 And with this the words of the prophets agree, just as it is written,

---

5   Motyer, *The Prophecy of Isaiah*, 370.

16 "After this I will return, and I will rebuild the tent of David
that has fallen; I will rebuild its ruins, and I will restore it,
17 that the remnant of mankind may seek the Lord, and all the
Gentiles who are called by my name, says the Lord, who makes
these things
18 known from of old."

James cites the prophets who foretold the ingathering of the Gentiles.
Their prediction is evidence that God did not make a spontaneous,
last-minute decision to call the Gentiles. God does not make any decisions "on the hoof." He does not merely react and respond to situations
as they arise. He knew from eternity what he would do. Therefore, he
could make his purposes known long ago.

ROMANS 11:36

For from him and through him and to him are all things. To him
be glory forever. Amen.

Here are three prepositions which together state God's responsibility
for absolutely everything: (i) *All things are from him*—God is the origi-
nating point from which all events proceed; (ii) *All things are through
him*—all events take place through God's direct involvement and
agency; and (iii) *All things are to him*—everything is tending towards
God's glory.

EPHESIANS 1:11

In him we have obtained an inheritance, having been predestined according to the purpose of him who works all things
according to the counsel of his will.

Counsel renders the Greek word *boule*. It speaks of a deliberate act of
will, a determined decision. *Will* translates *thelema*, which denotes
God's pleasure in coming to his decision. "The counsel of his will" is
therefore a decision made with delight. *Works* renders *energeo*. It means
that God activates all things powerfully and effectively. He is the ener-

gizing dynamism behind all that happens. "God's unconditional freedom is affirmed, for whatever he has purposed is sure to be fulfilled."[6]

HEBREWS 6:17

When God desired to show more convincingly to the heirs of the promise the unchangeable character of his purpose, he guaranteed it with an oath.

God's purpose (*boule*) is unchangeable in its character. Once God had made his decision in eternity past about the course of events in his creation, nothing could possibly change any single element in that plan.

2. Specific statements of the decree relating to the crucifixion of Christ

The purpose of God in the crucifixion of Christ is an illustration of the larger truth that God's decree governs everything. It is also the ultimate intention of everything else God has planned.

LUKE 22:22

The Son of Man goes as it has been determined, but woe to that man by whom he is betrayed!

The word translated *determined* is *horizo*. It means to mark out a boundary. The Lord's pathway to death had been fenced in for him in advance. God had fixed the boundary of Jesus' earthly life from eternity.

ACTS 2:23

This Jesus, delivered up according to the definite plan and foreknowledge of God, you crucified and killed by the hands of lawless men.

---

6 A.T. Lincoln, *Ephesians* (Dallas: Word, 1990), on Ephesians 1:11-12.

The words *definite* and *plan* translate terms with which we are already familiar—*horizo* and *boule* respectively. *Foreknowledge* renders *prognosis*. It means more than that God knew what was going to happen. It has the sense of pre-arrangement. God knew what was going to happen, because long before he had appointed that the death of Jesus must happen. His death was a matter of "divine necessity,"[7] though, as Matthew Henry rightly reminds us, Jesus himself concurred in the plan.[8]

Robert Reymond finds in Peter's words in this verse "indisputable reason for believing that the cross of Christ was central to the eternal plan of God." Christ's "sacrificial death was an integral part of the divine decree."[9] This is an important observation. It guards against the misconception that the salvation of the human race in Christ was God's second choice when his first plan in Adam failed. Before creation and history ever began, God had mapped out its entire course. Christ and the cross were at the heart of everything which God purposed to achieve.

As Calvin puts it, Jesus Christ "suffered nothing by chance," nor, indeed, because he lacked the power to prevent himself being crucified. Calvin adds: "We must know this, that God decrees nothing in vain or rashly." It follows, Calvin concludes, that "there was just cause for which he would have Christ to suffer," namely to pay the price to deliver us from our sins.

Calvin goes on to describe what is said here about Christ as a mirror of God's universal providence. God foreknows, in his own mind, so to speak, what he will definitely plan, and so determines exactly what he has foreseen. Calvin warns against separating God's foreknowledge from his plan, as if he merely foresaw what was going to happen, but he had no control over it. "It belongs to God not only to know before things to come, but of his own will to determine what he will have done." The alternative, Calvin suggests, is to proclaim that "God sits idle in heaven." However, the Scriptures teach that God governs every-

---

7 R.N. Longenecker, "Commentary on Acts," in Gaebelein, ed., *Expositor's Bible Commentary*, on Acts 2:23.

8 M. Henry, *An Exposition of the New Testament*, Vol. 6: Acts 1-19 (London: Mackenzie reprint), 34f.

9 Reymond, *A New Systematic Theology*, 465.

thing, not excluding the actions of free agents. This, Calvin adds, is not a reason to be carried away with "doting speculations," but to exercise our faith.[10]

ACTS 4:27-28

> 27 In this city there were gathered together against your holy servant Jesus, whom you anointed, both Herod and Pontius Pilate, along with the Gentiles and the peoples of Israel,
> 28 to do whatever your hand and your plan had predestined to take place.

The events surrounding the crucifixion had been predestined to take place by God's hand and plan. *Plan* again translates *boule*. *Predestined* renders *proorizo*, meaning predetermined or decided in advance. God's hand is a common metaphor for God's active power, his intimate control. It was God's decree that put Jesus on the cross. That assures us that the decree is rooted in God's saving mercy.

Section summary and personal application

REMEMBER
In him we have obtained an inheritance, having been predestined according to the purpose of him who works all things according to the counsel of his will.
—*Ephesians 1:11*

REFLECT
1. We have learned that God transforms the evil intent of man into blessing. How is this truth illustrated in the life of Joseph, in the cross of Christ, and in your own life?

---

10 J. Calvin, *Commentary upon the Acts of the Apostles*, 1585 (reprint; Grand Rapids: Baker, 1979), Vol. 1, 96f.

188 SYSTEMATIC THEOLOGY 1

2. What specific comfort do you derive from the knowledge of God's sovereign decree?
3. God's counsel is immutable, and it will always be good. How should you therefore live and confront adverse circumstances?

REJOICE

God moves in a mysterious way
    His wonders to perform;
He plants His footsteps in the sea
    And rides upon the storm.

Ye fearful saints, fresh courage take;
    The clouds ye so much dread
Are big with mercy and shall break
    In blessings on your head.

Judge not the Lord by feeble sense,
    But trust Him for His grace;
Behind a frowning providence
    He hides a smiling face.

Blind unbelief is sure to err
    And scan His work in vain;
God is His own interpreter,
    And He will make it plain.
—*William Cowper (1731–1800)*

PART 2: KEY CREEDS AND CONFESSIONS

A. THE REFORMATION CONFESSIONS

The early creeds did not spell this doctrine out. However, some of the Reformation confessions paid attention to it. We may summarize their teaching on this subject in nine statements.

1. God foreordained whatever happens in time

God's decree relates to the created order of time and space. It relates to the whole duration of time and to the universality of space. Some of the confessions speak of God's decree in the singular, while others use the plural. The decree may be considered as a unity. God made a single decision related to all the events of time. However, it is possible to analyze the decree into component decisions relating to each event. This reminds us that God's decree concerns both the totality of existence viewed as a consistent and coherent whole, and every intricate detail. It is not that God just set the general trend, within which things crop up just as it happens. Nor did God make numerous little decisions and just hope that they would all fit together. Rather, he made a detailed decision about every tiny incident, in such a way as to ensure that all the incidents combine to make up his single determined purpose. Williamson explains:

> Since the Bible declares that the whole system of things is controlled by God, it declares with equal insistency that every single thing, however small and insignificant, is ordered by God ahead of time in his perfect plan.[11]

2. God's decree effectually works and disposes all things

There is no room for unanticipated problems. God is never in the position of having to modify his decree. He brings about precisely what he has planned, with no mistakes.

3. God's decree was made in eternity

The decree is God's definition of his eternal purpose. Every detail was worked out before anything began to be. Donald Macleod says: "Before God spoke the universe into being God thought it. It was in his reason before it was spoken."[12]

In his comments on the *Westminster Confession*, Robert Shaw makes this statement:

---

11 Williamson, *The Westminster Confession of Faith for Study Classes*, 30.

12 Macleod, *A Faith to Live By*, 40.

Everything which has happened and everything which is to happen was known to God from everlasting. To suppose any of the divine decrees to be made in time, is to suppose the knowledge of the Deity to be limited.[13]

4. God's foreordination of all things was a totally free decision

The confessions speak of the decree as an act of the counsel of God's will, and of his will alone. God's will was not under constraint from some power external to him. The decree was not merely the rubber-stamping of what God could see was going to happen anyway. That "would make God dependent upon something outside himself."[14] In which case God would no longer be the highest authority, and so would not be truly God. He acted in sovereign freedom when he decreed whatever would happen. In his freedom, God is absolutely unrestricted. However, the confessions stress that God's free will is both wise and holy. His purpose was not drawn up just based on whim and fancy. As Thomas Vincent said,

> God decreed all things according to the counsel of his will; according to his will, and therefore most freely—according to the counsel of his will, and therefore most wisely.[15]

There is nothing morally dubious in the decree, because it reflects the holiness of God.

5. God's decree is unalterable

God does not change, and so his decree is immutable. God never changes his mind. He never rethinks. He is in total control.

6. The ultimate goal of God's decree is the glory of his name

Robert Reymond has said this:

---

13 Shaw, *An Exposition of the Confession of Faith,* 45.

14 Williamson, *The Westminster Confession of Faith for Study Classes,* 30.

15 Vincent, *The Shorter Catechism Explained from Scripture,* 42.

Just as the chief end of man is to glorify God and enjoy him forever, so also the chief end of God is to glorify and enjoy himself forever.... God loves himself with a holy love.... He himself is at the centre of his affections.... The impulse that drives him, and the thing he pursues in everything he does, is his own glory.... That same concern—to glorify himself—is central to God's eternal plan.[16]

John Piper has worked at this truth very thoroughly. His book, *The Pleasures of God*, is a series of meditations on the fact that "God delights fully in being God."[17]

7. We are not always able to unravel the mysteries of God's plan

God's decree stands, and what happens in time is always in accordance with his decree as he decreed it. This remains true, even though sometimes we may seem to hear something different. We need to remember that not everything has been revealed to us.

8. Three explanations added to the doctrine of the decree

(1) *God is not the author of sin.* Even though God embraced sin in his eternal plan, he is not responsible or accountable for sin. God is holy, and his holiness is not impugned by decreeing to allow sin to happen in his creation. As to why God allowed it, we cannot answer that question. We need here to remember the words of Deuteronomy 29:29: "The secret things belong to the LORD our God, but the things that are revealed belong to us and to our children forever."

(2) *The freedom of intelligent creatures is not violated.* God's foreordination does not mean that we are robots. It is not the case that we are simply programmed to act and react in specific ways. We cannot therefore excuse ourselves for our sins. It would be churlish to refuse to congratulate achievement in others. We never have any reason to complain that God is treating us as sub-human. On the contrary, as Macleod points out, it is certain modern emphases that threaten to deprive us of freedom. Darwinism led to an approach in the human sciences that claimed "that human beings could not help the way they

---

16 Reymond, *A New Systematic Theology*, 343-344.
17 Piper, *The Pleasures of God*, 9.

behaved. Their behaviour was the result of various glands and other biological factors."[18]

Therefore, one of the great problems of modern society has been the elimination of freedom. Macleod quotes Paul Johnson to the effect that the ideas of Karl Marx and Sigmund Freud combined to undermine personal responsibility, and the sense of moral duty. Macleod comments:

> Sociology, criminology, penology and psychology are largely based on the assumption that environment, education and genetic inheritance not only influence, but determine, human behaviour, and that individuals are therefore only minimally answerable for their own conduct.

However, the doctrine of God's decree asserts that

> I am free because God foreordained my freedom. I am not the plaything of pressure and circumstance, or even of internal and endocrinological factors. I am free. I make my own decisions. I am the cause, the ultimate, answerable cause, the responsible cause, of my own decisions.[19]

(3) *The fact of secondary causes is not denied.* The first and ultimate cause of everything is God. His plan is the overarching reality. From it every individual event flows. From it, the overall direction of the whole of creation stems. However, there are also secondary causes. These are causes within the system of things that we belong to, rather than the ultimate cause standing outside and beyond our world. Suppose I fall off my bicycle and break my hip. You might ask me what caused my accident. I would probably not reply, "God knocked me off my bike." I am more likely to say, "I took a bend too fast and skidded on some loose gravel." It is true that the ultimate cause lies with God. In explaining things from an earthly perspective, we refer to secondary causes.

---

18 Macleod, *A Faith to Live By*, 43.

19 Macleod, *A Faith to Live By*, 43-44.

9. God's decree is in Christ
One of the confessions backs up its teaching on the decree by reference to Colossians 2:3. This text refers to Christ, "in whom are hidden all the treasures of wisdom and knowledge." These treasures include God's decree: as early as the planning stage, God, in eternity past, stored up his wisdom in Christ. This means that absolutely everything that exists is Christ-shaped. That assures us that at the heart of everything in existence there stands the divine mercy displayed in Jesus Christ.

B. MODERN CONFESSIONS OF FAITH
The *Confession of Faith of the Huria Batak Protestant* does not mention the doctrine of the decree. The Chinese confession does not address this doctrine specifically, but there is one relevant phrase in its section on the doctrine of God. However, the *Confession of Faith of the United Church of Northern India* makes an indirect reference to God's decree.

1. Confession of Faith of the United Church of Northern India
In the context of its statement on God's creation and government of the world, this confession affirms that "God works all things according to the counsel of his will." Consequently, all things "serve the fulfilment of his wise and good and holy purposes." These words teach that God's will is the shaping factor behind all contingent events. They also assert that history is the fulfilment of what God in his counsel has purposed. Moreover, God's purposes are characterized as wise, good, and holy. These terms make the point that however things may sometimes appear to human perception, the reality is that God's wisdom ensures that what he has purposed is good. Even though evil may occur, God is always working towards the ultimate good. This is because his decree reflects his own character: he is holy, so his purposes are holy. They may never be challenged as lacking in moral integrity.

2. Confession of Faith of House Churches in China
This confession contains only one phrase relevant to the doctrine of the divine decree: "the Father plans salvation." This is actually found in the section on the Trinity, and is only incidentally related to the present subject. However, it does signal the fact that the Chinese

house churches recognize that the Father drew up his plans from eternity. It also bears witness to their conviction that the salvation of his people stands at the very heart of the Father's eternal purpose.

Section summary and personal application

REMEMBER

God from all eternity did, by the most wise and holy counsel of his own will, freely and unchangeably ordain whatsoever comes to pass; yet so as thereby neither is God the author of sin, nor is violence offered to the will of the creatures, nor is the liberty or contingency of second causes taken away, but rather established.
—*Westminster Confession of Faith (1647), Chapter 3*

REFLECT

1. How would you explain God's decree to an unbeliever?
2. What would you say about God's decree to someone grieving over a loss?
3. What mercy and comfort do you find in the fact that God plans our salvation?

REJOICE

The will of God is always best
    And shall be done forever;
And they who trust in Him are blest,
    He will forsake them never.
He helps indeed in time of need
    He chastens with forbearing;
They who depend on God, their friend,
    Shall not be left despairing.

God is my comfort and my trust,
    My hope and life abiding;
And to His counsel, wise and just,

I yield, in Him confiding.
The very hairs, His Word declares,
   Upon my head He numbers.
By night and day God is my stay,
   He never sleeps nor slumbers.
—*Albrecht von Brandenburg (1522–1557)*

PART 3: KEY HISTORICAL DEVELOPMENTS

Recent years have seen the rise of a movement known as *Open Theism*. It began when five Canadian and American theologians collaborated to write a book entitled, *The Openness of God*.[20] One of the participants, Clark Pinnock, followed it up a few years later with another book, *Most Moved Mover*.[21] Most of the contributors have also written briefer accounts of their position.[22] This movement rejects the Reformed doctrine of the divine decree.

Open Theists would insist that the Scriptures we used earlier, to teach the doctrine of the divine decree, are only one set of texts. They do not dispute them. They accept that there are some things which God has planned from all eternity. However, there are other texts, they claim, which show that not everything is pre-planned. According to Open Theism, the Bible is a real story, not the prescribed outworking of a pre-historical decree. There are aspects of the developing history of the world which God has left indefinite. The God of the Bible is one who relates to people in a personal way. He responds to situations. He

---

20 W. Hasker, with C. Pinnock, R. Rice, J. Sanders, and D. Basinger, *The Openness of God* (Downers Grove: IVP, 1994).

21 C. Pinnock, *Most Moved Mover* (Grand Rapids: Baker, 2001).

22 I am basing this summary of Open Theism mainly on two articles: C. Pinnock, "Open Theism: What is this? A new teaching—and with authority!," a lecture given at the University of Calgary, February, 2003, and published at www.fmc-canada.org/who/papers/Pinnock-Open-Theism.pdf; J. Sanders and C. Hall, "Does God know your Next Move?," *Christianity Today* (May 21, 2001): 38-45; and (June 7, 2001): 50-56.

is sometimes surprised by an unexpected turn of events. He can be grieved. He feels pain and pleasure. He may change his mind. He takes account of things when they happen and not before.

In Open Theism, the sovereignty of God is general, not all-encompassing. While his goal is secure, he has no blueprint for the whole of time. He does not micromanage history. His strategies are flexible. True, he has planned some things, and nothing can frustrate his plans, but he has chosen not to predetermine everything that happens. In his love, God gave human beings true freedom. He therefore leaves some of his works contingent on the actions and prayers of people. Human decisions are genuine and their consequences are often unpredictable. God's will is not always done. History is a real interaction between God and man, in which God has invited us into partnership with himself. God reacts to our choices and adjusts his own plans when necessary. The believer's confidence in such a world is that God is infinitely resourceful. He has the wisdom to handle any situation that might arise precisely when it arises.

Open Theism redefines the omniscience of God. He is omniscient in the sense that he knows all that there is to be known. His knowledge of the past and the present is exhaustive, but the future is not yet there to know. The open aspects of the future, including the actions of free creatures, are not yet reality, and so God cannot know them with certainty.

Open Theists see important pastoral implications in this. For one thing, God's will is not always done. The advocates of God's openness do not believe that he wills the tragedies in human experience. This seems inconsistent with the biblical portrait of God as love. A relational God is really influenced by prayer. Prayer is not just a charade. Open Theism implies that passionate human living makes a true difference in the world. To the charge that this leaves God "just fumbling along with the rest of us," John Sanders replies that Openness Theology does not mean that just anything might happen. God is at work to achieve his purposes, but he invites us to collaborate with him in the open part of the future.

One of the strengths of Open Theism is that it takes the Bible seriously. It refuses to explain any texts away in the interests of a preconceived theory. We need to look at the set of texts that, according to

Open Theists, show that not everything is included in the infallible divine decree. We shall take them in biblical order.

1. *Genesis 22:12*

> Do not lay your hand on the boy or do anything to him, for now I know that you fear God, seeing you have not withheld your son, your only son, from me.

These are the words of the angel of the LORD to Abraham after he has passed the test and proved himself willing to sacrifice Isaac. The Open Theists argue that the key word is *now*, and that the statement "now I know that you fear God" proves that God did not know for sure before this moment. However, the Hebrew word for *now* (*'attah*) is connected with the word meaning "time." God's knowledge has now been anchored in time. *The Theological Wordbook of the Old Testament* finds *'attah* derived from a word meaning "to respond." God's knowledge now is a historical response to what has happened on Mount Moriah. However, this does not mean that he did not know before what would happen. It is simply that his previous knowledge was beyond this world of time.

2. *Exodus 4:8-9*

> "If they will not believe you," God said, "or listen to the first sign, they may believe the latter sign. If they will not believe even these two signs or listen to your voice, you shall take some water from the Nile and pour it on the dry ground, and the water that you shall take from the Nile will become blood on the dry ground."

The key words here are *if* and *may*. To the Open Theists it sounds as if God is unsure what will be the outcome of the signs he has given to Moses. However, Walter Kaiser notes that God is really quoting Moses' own sentiments back at him. In verse 1, Moses had said, "they will not believe me or listen to my voice." This is not an admission of divine ignorance, but a concession to Moses.

3. Deuteronomy 13:3

> The LORD your God is testing you, to know whether you love the
> LORD your God with all your heart and with all your soul.

The test is that a prophet who tries to entice the people after other gods
successfully performs a miracle. The Open Theists say that the words
"to know whether" indicate that the LORD would not know the true state
of heart of his people until the test had taken place. However, there are
other ways of reading this text. Calvin cites Augustine, who suggested
that the LORD meant that the test would enable the people to know their
own hearts. However, Calvin prefers to distinguish God's knowledge
from his hidden wisdom, which needed no verification, and his knowledge from experience, which the test would provide.[23]

4. Isaiah 41:21-24; 46:9-10; 48:3-5

> 41:21 Set forth your case, says the LORD; bring your proofs, says
> the King of Jacob.
> 22 Let them bring them, and tell us what is to happen. Tell us the
> former things, what they are, that we may consider them, that
> we may know their outcome; or declare to us the things to come.
> 23 Tell us what is to come hereafter, that we may know that you are
> gods; do good, or do harm, that we may be dismayed and terrified.
> 24 Behold, you are nothing, and your work is less than nothing;
> an abomination is he who chooses you.
> 46:9 remember the former things of old; for I am God, and there
> is no other; I am God, and there is none like me,
> 10 declaring the end from the beginning and from ancient times
> things not yet done, saying, "My counsel shall stand, and I will
> accomplish all my purpose."
> 48:3 The former things I declared of old; they went out from my

---

23 J. Calvin, *Commentaries on the four last books of Moses: arranged in the form of a
harmony* (Grand Rapids: Christian Classics Ethereal Library, 1998), on Deuteronomy
13:3.

mouth and I announced them; then suddenly I did them and they came to pass.

4 Because I know that you are obstinate, and your neck is an iron sinew and your forehead brass,

5 I declared them to you from of old, before they came to pass I announced them to you, lest you should say, "My idol did them, my carved image and my metal image commanded them."

Sanders deals with these three passages together. He alleges that this issue is not foreknowledge but power. This is unconvincing. All three passages stress the expected ability of a god to predict the future. It is true that God predicts because he has the power to do what he has said, but the predictive ability is more to the fore. Geoffrey Grogan comments on the first passage like this:

> The concept of deity is, in some ways, simple, combining super-human power and the claim to human worship. It has many implications, however, and ability to predict is one of these. This is the basis of the argument here. If the gods of Babylonia and other nations have objective reality as deities, they should be able to predict the future and also to so interpret history that past and future are seen to be linked in one divinely controlled plan.[24]

5. *Jeremiah 26:3; Ezekiel 12:3*

> 26:3 It may be they will listen, and every one turn from his evil way, that I may relent of the disaster that I intend to do to them because of their evil deeds.
> 12:3 You shall go like an exile from your place to another place in their sight. Perhaps they will understand, though they are a rebellious house.

We may deal with these two texts together, since they both contain the same Hebrew word, *'ulay*. It is rendered *it may be* and *perhaps* in

---

24 G.W. Grogan, "Commentary on Isaiah," in Gaebelein, ed., *Expositor's Bible Commentary*, on Isaiah 41:21-24.

the two verses respectively. Both prophets are being commanded to preach publicly, Jeremiah verbally, and Ezekiel in an acted parable. Perhaps God's Word will get a positive response. Open Theists claim that the choice of this word indicates God's uncertainty. However, it is better to see it as an indication of the genuineness of God's appeal, even though he knew what the outcome would be.

6. Jeremiah 32:24-25

24 Behold, the siege mounds have come up to the city to take it, and because of sword and famine and pestilence the city is given into the hands of the Chaldeans who are fighting against it. What you spoke has come to pass, and behold, you see it.
25 Yet you, O Lord GOD, have said to me, "Buy the field for money and get witnesses"—though the city is given into the hands of the Chaldeans.

The LORD told Jeremiah to buy a field near Jerusalem. However, the city and its surrounding countryside subsequently passed into the possession of the Chaldeans when they overran Judah as the instrument of God's judgment. Hence, according to Pinnock, the LORD's direction proved to be unwise. Had the LORD known what the future held, he would not have given such an instruction. Now it is certainly true that "the contradiction or absurdity of God's command to buy the field while the Babylonians are conquering the city"[25] is the first thing that strikes the reader. However, merely to highlight the apparent absurdity, as Pinnock does, is to ignore the context of the whole chapter. The subsequent verses predict the restoration of God's people and their return to the land. Jeremiah's purchase of the field is a sign from the LORD and an act of faith in his foreknowledge and sure planning. Charles Feinberg explains:

The fall of the city and the divine command for Jeremiah's purchase of land seemed irreconcilable. The incongruity was plain.

25 G.L. Keown, P.J. Scalise and T.G. Smothers, *Jeremiah 26-52* (Dallas: Word, 1995), on Jeremiah 32:24-25.

Why buy the field when it would soon be lost to the Babylonians?
Yet in spite of the dire circumstances, God had commanded Jeremiah to buy the field and to do it publicly. It was a situation
calling for faith in, and obedience to, the word the LORD had
given him to proclaim.[26]

So, far from being evidence of the LORD's limited omniscience, this
text is actually testimony to his definite knowledge of the future—
even at a time when the likelihood of such a future ever becoming
reality was, to all appearances, remote.

7. Jonah 3:10

> When God saw what they did, how they turned from their evil
> way, God relented of the disaster that he had said he would do to
> them, and he did not do it.

Open Theists claim that God changed his mind when Nineveh repented in response to Jonah's preaching. However, Jonah's words in Jonah
4:2 show us that he recognized that this was the LORD's regular character: "you are a gracious God and merciful, slow to anger and abounding in steadfast love, and relenting from disaster." Therefore, we do
not have here a change of mind, so much as the enactment of the
LORD's definite preference. The Hebrew word translated *relented* in
3:10 is *naham*. Its basic sense has to do with pity or compassion. That
characteristic of God led him to withhold the action he had threatened.
All the LORD's warnings are conditional. Repentance always triggers
his compassion. It had never been his intention to strike Nineveh in
the face of their repentance. In fact, conditional warnings are part of
God's strategy for evoking the desired and determined response. Jeremiah 18 indicates his normal method of procedure:"…if that nation,
concerning which I have spoken, turns from its evil, I will relent of
the disaster that I intended to do to it."

---

26 C. Feinberg, "Commentary on Jeremiah," in Gaebelein, ed., *Expositor's Bible
Commentary*, on Jeremiah 32:17-25.

There is a definition within Jonah 3:10 of the word *relented*: "he did not do it." The alteration was outward. It has nothing to do with the LORD's inmost knowledge of how things would turn out.

In addition to these Scriptures, others proclaim unequivocally God's absolute and detailed knowledge of the future. The following may be mentioned:

i) *1 Samuel 8:9*: "You shall solemnly warn them and show them the ways of the king who shall reign over them." These are the LORD's words to Samuel at the time when Israel was clamouring for a king. The LORD was under no illusions as to how King Saul would turn out.

ii) *Psalm 139:2*: "You know when I sit down and when I rise up; you discern my thoughts from afar." The words *from afar* translate the Hebrew term *rahowq*. Sometimes it refers to a far away time. On several occasions, it is translated *long ago*.[27] Long ago in the past, the LORD knew what the present would be, even in so secret a matter as David's innermost thoughts. On two occasions *rahowq* refers to the LORD's prediction concerning the distant future.[28]

iii) *Psalm 139:16*: "Your eyes saw my unformed substance; in your book were written, every one of them, the days that were formed for me, when as yet there were none of them." Here again David is confident that the LORD had planned his life long before he was born. The LORD's planning was not vague and general. The details of every day were written down.

iv) *Jeremiah 1:5*: "Before I formed you in the womb I knew you, and before you were born I consecrated you; I appointed you a prophet to the nations." Even before Jeremiah was conceived, the LORD knew the way he had appointed for his life.

Several other questions might be raised against the openness of God theology. Here are a few of them: (1) If God is not in total control of everything, is there really any point in prayer? (2) Is there in fact a problem with the idea that God can know in advance what free choices free agents would make? After all, even human beings can sometimes see things coming, as Proverbs 22:3 assures us: "The prudent sees

---

27 2 Kgs. 19:25; Isa. 22:11; 25:1; 37:26.
28 2 Sam. 7:19; 1 Chr. 17:17.

danger and hides himself." (3) Is Open Theism really an answer to the tragedies in human life? Could God not have intervened to prevent sin in the beginning? (4) Does it really turn prayer into a charade to say that God has ordained whatever comes to pass? Has he not also ordained that he will act in response to the prayers of his people?

Open Theism is certainly correct to say that God is loving and responsive. He is not unaffected by human decisions. However, the idea that he is ignorant of what those decisions will be until they become present is hard to sustain from Scripture. It is true that the doctrine of the divine decree can be a problem to our finite minds. However, we must submit our thinking to Scripture, and accept what God has said, even where we cannot understand.

PART 4: KEY POINTS OF PRACTICAL APPLICATION

(1) *This doctrine is a source of immense confidence.* Nothing can happen which God has not planned. That is true in our personal lives, as much as on the global stage. In Romans 8:35-39 the apostle assures us of the implications of God's total sovereign control: it means that we are inseparable from his love.

> 35 Who shall separate us from the love of Christ? Shall tribulation, or distress, or persecution, or famine, or nakedness, or danger, or sword?
> 36 As it is written, "For your sake we are being killed all the day long; we are regarded as sheep to be slaughtered."
> 37 No, in all these things we are more than conquerors through him who loved us.
> 38 For I am sure that neither death nor life, nor angels nor rulers, nor things present nor things to come, nor powers,
> 39 nor height nor depth, nor anything else in all creation, will be able to separate us from the love of God in Christ Jesus our Lord.

(2) *This truth is also a reason for deep humility.* Our freedom is subsumed under God's sovereignty. We are not autonomous. We are responsible to God. We are also accountable for our own behaviour.

REFLECT

1. We are responsible and accountable to God. How does this doctrine of divine decree preclude any notion of autonomy?
2. God sovereignly decrees the means as well as the results. How does this encourage you in prayer and evangelism?
3. Do you struggle with the doctrine of God's decree? What passages come to mind to help you delight in God's sovereign plans and purposes in your life?

REJOICE

A Sov'reign Protector I have,
    Unseen, yet forever at hand,
Unchangeably faithful to save,
    Almighty to rule and command.
He smiles, and my comforts abound;
    His grace as the dew shall descend;
And walls of salvation surround
    The soul He delights to defend.

Inspirer and Hearer of prayer,
    Thou Shepherd and Guardian of Thine,
My all to Thy covenant care
    I sleeping and waking resign.
If Thou art my Shield and my Sun,
    The night is no darkness to me;
And fast as my moments roll on,
    They bring me but nearer to Thee.

Kind Author, and ground of my hope,
    Thee, Thee, for my God I avow;
My glad Ebenezer set up,
    And own Thou hast helped me till now.
I muse on the years that are past,

Wherein my defense Thou hast proved;
Nor wilt Thou relinquish at last
   A sinner so signally loved!
—*Augustus Toplady (1740–1778)*

8

THE DOCTRINE OF PROVIDENCE

How does God fulfil his purpose to display his glory in his works?

The doctrine of providence explains how God's overall control works out in practice, year by year and from day to day. God's decree is his eternal ordination of all things prior to the beginning of time. Providence is the outworking of the decree in all the events of time.

When Paul was on trial before Felix, the representative for the Jewish leaders was Tertullus. He began his oration with these words, recorded in Acts 24:2-3:

> Since through you we enjoy much peace, and since by your foresight, most excellent Felix, reforms are being made for this nation, in every way and everywhere we accept this with all gratitude.

Tertullus commends Felix for his foresight. This translates the Greek word *pronoia*. Actually, Tertullus is being rather flattering. The Jewish historian, Josephus, tells us that Felix was "disposed to act unjustly," and that he contrived the murder of the Jewish high priest.[1] However, *pronoia* came to be used of God's providence. When Jerome translated the Bible into Latin, he used the word *providentia* to render *pronoia*. Both words speak of foresight, or advance understanding. We may say that, in his foreknowledge, God has taken forethought with a view to the wise ordering of the world. God has advance knowledge of everything because of his decree: he planned it all. Therefore, he always acts advisedly. He does nothing rashly.

The word *providentia* occurs several times in the Jewish Apocrypha. In the ways the word is used, we can see a distinction theologians have made between God's *general providence* and his *special providence*. God's general providence is his wise ordering of all the ordinary details of everyday events. One example is found in Wisdom 14:3. A seafarer is about to set sail. Credit is given to the skill of the workman who built the ship. Then this statement is added: "But it is your providence, O Father, that steers its course, because you have given it a path in the sea, and a safe way through the waves." By God's "special providence" is meant the care and protection he displays towards his own people. 4 Maccabees 17:22 makes a reference to this: "Divine Providence preserved Israel that previously had been afflicted."

---

1 Flavius Josephus, *Antiquities of the Jews*, Book 20, 8.5.

Our concern is going to be more with God's general providence. We may analyze providence into three strands.

1. Preservation

In Nehemiah 9:6, we read these words:

> You are the LORD, you alone. You have made heaven, the heaven of heavens, with all their host, the earth and all that is on it, the seas and all that is in them; and you preserve all of them.

The only explanation for the continued existence of the world is that God preserves it. Usually providence carries on in a gentle, behind-the-scenes fashion. Occasionally, remarkable and unexpected events turn out with hindsight to be a plank in God's strategy of preservation. In Genesis 45:5-7, Joseph points to such events:

> 5 And now do not be distressed or angry with yourselves because you sold me here, for God sent me before you to preserve life.
> 6 For the famine has been in the land these two years, and there are yet five years in which there will be neither ploughing nor harvest.
> 7 And God sent me before you to preserve for you a remnant on earth, and to keep alive for you many survivors.

2. Provision

Psalm 65:9 speaks of God's providential provision on a global scale:

> You visit the earth and water it; you greatly enrich it; the river of God is full of water; you provide their grain, for so you have prepared it.

Provision also takes place at a more particular level. Job 38:41 tells us that God "provides for the raven its prey." Provision for the needs of his own people is something for which the Lord takes special notice: "My God will supply every need of yours according to his riches in glory in Christ Jesus" (Philippians 4:19).

3. Government

The biblical teaching that God is King is an assertion of his providential government. He is King over his inanimate creation, including the weather, as Psalm 93:1-4 shows:

> 1 The LORD reigns; he is robed in majesty; the LORD is robed; he has put on strength as his belt. Yes, the world is established; it shall never be moved.
> 2 Your throne is established from of old; you are from everlasting.
> 3 The floods have lifted up, O LORD, the floods have lifted up their voice; the floods lift up their roaring.
> 4 Mightier than the thunders of many waters, mightier than the waves of the sea, the LORD on high is mighty!

He is also King over the nations of the world. Psalm 47:7-8 speaks of this: "For God is the King of all the earth; sing praises with a psalm! God reigns over the nations; God sits on his holy throne."

Chiefly, though, God is King over his own people: "God my King is from of old, working salvation in the midst of the earth" (Psalm 74:12). God is working all things to ensure the salvation of his people throughout the earth.

PART 1: KEY TEXTS

A. OLD TESTAMENT

GENESIS 8:22

> While the earth remains, seedtime and harvest, cold and heat, summer and winter, day and night, shall not cease.

This verse is the Bible's initial summary of the truth of divine providence. As long as earth's history continues, God promises that there will be no cessation of sowing and reaping seasons, of the alternations in the weather, of times of busyness and times for resting, of waking times and sleeping times. God will order things so that human life may continue. The food production necessary to sustain human life will not end. *Cease* translates the Hebrew word *sabat*. It is the same word found in Genesis 2:2-3:

> 2 On the seventh day God finished his work that he had done, and he rested (*sabat*) on the seventh day from all his work that he had done.
> 3 So God blessed the seventh day and made it holy, because on it God rested (*sabat*) from all his work that he had done in creation.

It is found also in Exodus 23:12:

> Six days you shall do your work, but on the seventh day you shall rest (sabat); that your ox and your donkey may have rest, and the son of your servant woman, and the alien, may be refreshed.

God *may* rest; man *must* rest. However, the seasonal rhythms of nature will never take a day off. Wenham writes, "God's assurance that these rhythms will be maintained is a mark of his continuing providential blessing on the world."[2] And Leupold reminds us,

> the regular variation of times and seasons here promised is not to be regarded as merely natural, fixed by nature's ordinance, but as an outgrowth of God's specific promise.[3]

In fact, nothing is "merely natural." Nature itself works according to God's providential arrangement.

JOB 38:16-39:30

This is too long a passage to quote in full or to study in detail. It is the LORD's first speech, when he finally appeared to Job after the frustrat-

---

2   Wenham, on Genesis 8:22.

3   H.C. Leupold, *Exposition of Genesis* (1942; reprint, Carluke: Online Bible, 1995-2005), on Genesis 8:22.

ing discussion between Job and his friends. The LORD does not answer Job's questions. Instead, he responds with a series of questions of his own. They are designed to declare to Job how small and limited he is, in contrast with the LORD's own awesome greatness. Their effect is to remind Job of his inevitable ignorance in a world of baffling complexity, and to assure him that even a world of bemusing paradox is under God's providential control.

We shall look at the outline given by Elmer Smick,[4] and quote a few selected verses to illustrate the emphasis on divine providence in this passage. Smick entitles this section of the Book of Job, "God as Ruler." Verses 16-38 of chapter 38 proclaim God as Ruler of inanimate nature. We see his rule over the depths and expanses (verses 16-18), over light and darkness (verses 19-21), over the weather (verses 22-30), over the stars (verses 31-33), and over the floods (verses 34-38). For example, the verses concerning the weather begin like this:

> 22 Have you entered the storehouses of the snow, or have you seen the storehouses of the hail,
> 23 which I have reserved for the time of trouble, for the day of battle and war?

The LORD is affirming that the secret operations of the climate, beyond the reach of human control as they are, nevertheless answer to his authoritative command.

The rest of the passage proclaims God's rule over animal life, including the areas of nourishment (38:39-41), procreation (39:1-4), wild freedom (39:5-8), intractable strength (39:9-12), incongruous speed (39:13-18), fearsome strength (39:19-25), and the flight of the predator (39:26-30). For example, these verses emphasize God's providence in the chosen habitat of the wild donkey (39:5-6):

> 5 Who has let the wild donkey go free? Who has loosed the bonds of the swift donkey,

---

4   E.B. Smick, "Commentary on Job," in Gaebelein, ed., *Expositor's Bible Commentary*, on Job 38:1–40:2.

6 to whom I have given the arid plain for his home and the salt land for his dwelling place?

Even those aspects of creaturely life which seem sad and shocking take place under the government of God, as 39:13-17 show:

13 The wings of the ostrich wave proudly, but are they the pinions and plumage of love?
14 For she leaves her eggs to the earth and lets them be warmed on the ground,
15 forgetting that a foot may crush them and that the wild beast may trample them.
16 She deals cruelly with her young, as if they were not hers; though her labour be in vain, yet she has no fear,
17 because God has made her forget wisdom and given her no share in understanding.

The whole thrust of this passage is to declare "God's management of the universe."[5] At every level, he is in control. He sustains all things. His signature is across the whole creation.

PSALM 104:3-30

"The theme of Psalm 104 is God's greatness in ruling and sustaining his creation."[6] Leslie Allen calls the Psalm "a sketch rather than an analysis."[7] It paints a picture of the LORD who created the world as also the world's sole Sustainer. "The LORD sovereignly rules over all creation and establishes order by his wise administration."[8]

Here are some areas in which we see God's providential sustaining:

---

5 Smick, "Commentary on Job," in Gaebelein, ed., *Expositor's Bible Commentary*, on Job 38:4-7.

6 van Gemeren, 'Psalms,' on Psalm 104.

7 L.C. Allen, *Psalms 101-150* (Dallas: Word, 1983), on Psalm 104.

8 van Gemeren, "Commentary on Psalms," in Gaebelein, ed., *Expositor's Bible Commentary*, on Psalm 104:19-23.

1. His control of the waters (verses 3-11, 25).

Allen describes the typical ancient Israelite as a landlubber. The sea was traditionally an object of dread. Here, though, "water, the potent enemy of terrestrial life, has been harnessed to become its means of sustenance."[9] So in verses 9-11 we read these statements about the waters:

> 9 You set a boundary that they may not pass, so that they might not again cover the earth.
> 10 You make springs gush forth in the valleys; they flow between the hills;
> 11 they give drink to every beast of the field; the wild donkeys quench their thirst.

2. His provision for living creatures (verses 12-18, 26-28)

All creatures are fed richly. All have somewhere to live. This applies to the animals, birds, and sea-creatures as much as to human life. As verses 14-18 point out:

> 14 You cause the grass to grow for the livestock and plants for man to cultivate, that he may bring forth food from the earth
> 15 and wine to gladden the heart of man, oil to make his face shine and bread to strengthen man's heart.
> 16 The trees of the Lord are watered abundantly, the cedars of Lebanon that he planted.
> 17 In them the birds build their nests; the stork has her home in the fir trees.
> 18 The high mountains are for the wild goats; the rocks are a refuge for the rock badgers.

Some wild animals are terrifying to man, and none more so than Leviathan. But in verse 26 Leviathan is depicted simply as the LORD's pet:[10] "There go the ships, and Leviathan, which you formed to play in it."

---

9 Allen, *Psalms 101-150*, on Psalm 104.

10 van Gemeren, "Commentary on Psalms," in Gaebelein, ed., *Expositor's Bible Commentary*, on Psalm 104:24-26.

3. His regulation of time (verses 19-23)

19 He made the moon to mark the seasons; the sun knows its time for setting.
20 You make darkness, and it is night, when all the beasts of the forest creep about.
21 The young lions roar for their prey, seeking their food from God.
22 When the sun rises, they steal away and lie down in their dens.
23 Man goes out to his work and to his labour until the evening.

"The LORD is in control over the seasons and the alternation of day and night."[11] Allen writes:

Animals prowling at night form a counterpart to man at work by day, all sharing in a divinely programmed cycle of activity. Human work belongs to a God-ordained pattern…. The psalmist marvels at the order he can discern in the natural world.[12]

4. His distribution of life and death (verses 29-30)

29 When you hide your face, they are dismayed; when you take away their breath, they die and return to their dust.
30 When you send forth your Spirit, they are created, and you renew the face of the ground.

Here is Allen's comment:

All creatures, great and small, depend upon the LORD…. He is their father-figure and they are members of his extended family. They are at the mercy of his outstretched hand or averted face. The power of life and death is his.

Our great reassurance in knowing that we are at God's mercy is this:

---

11 van Gemeren, "Commentary on Psalms," in Gaebelein, ed., *Expositor's Bible Commentary*, on Psalm 104:24-26.

12 Allen, *Psalms 101-150*, on Psalm 104.

.

it truly is mercy filling his heart. This psalm, then, reminds us that the
LORD is not remote. He is daily involved in the existence of his creation. His involvement is direct and personal. It is not the involvement
of someone who has wound up a toy, keeping a watchful eye to make
sure that it does not stop. Creation has not been left by God to continue by its own intrinsic power. Rather, it is more like a toy that needs
pushing. The Lord carries the universe day by day.

Allen sums up the message of Psalm 104 like this:

> The world and its phenomena are regarded as windows through
> which divine activity of love and power may be glimpsed.... The
> psalmist... subordinates nature to his basic belief in an unchang-
> ing God. The world's stability is divine stability writ large.[13]

Willem van Gemeren draws us to the picture-language of verses 3-4:

> The Lord's involvement in the world of creation comes to expres-
> sion in the imagery of the chariot, the clouds, the wind, and the
> flames of fire. He controls the elements, as if he rides on a chariot,
> using the wind, clouds, and lightning for his purposes.... The
> Creator-King is, as it were, driving his chariot, symbolic of his
> governance of his creation. All his created works reveal the splen-
> dour and wisdom of the Creator, because he remains constantly
> involved with his handiwork.[14]

Therefore, the universe is not a self-regulating system. It is not a
self-contained entity. Its preservation, regularity, and fruitfulness are
the direct result of the Creator's personal management from moment
to moment. The result is satisfaction for the earth (verse 26). The word
translated *satisfaction* is *saba'*. The same word is used in verse 16, where
it speaks of abundance, and in verse 28, where it means fullness. The
LORD's providence is generously enriching the lives of all creation.

---

13 Allen, *Psalms 101-150*, on Psalm 104.
14 van Gemeren, "Commentary on Psalms," in Gaebelein, ed., *Expositor's Bible
Commentary*, on Psalm 104:3-4.

B. NEW TESTAMENT

MATTHEW 5:44-45

> 44 "But I say to you, Love your enemies and pray for those who persecute you,
> 45 so that you may be sons of your Father who is in heaven. For he makes his sun rise on the evil and on the good, and sends rain on the just and on the unjust."

Jesus points out that the weather is the same for evil and unjust people as it is for the just and good. The sun brightens the day for all people. The rain waters crops indiscriminately. Here is our Lord's answer to a modern error known as "the prosperity gospel" or the "health and wealth gospel." This false teaching claims that by becoming a Christian and being good, you will be on the route to enhanced prosperity. Jesus denies this. God showers his good gifts equally on believers and non-Christians alike. Jesus' words in verse 44 make it clear that this indiscriminate provision is an expression of divine love.

We are commanded to love our enemies—because that is what God does. By distributing his kindness even-handedly, he loves even those who do not love him. In this general, practical way, God loves his enemies no less than he loves his own people.

What is clear from verse 45 is that God is *active* in his provision. God does not just sit back and let it rain or stand back and let the sun shine. He *makes* the sun rise. Every day his universal love is displayed as every human being enjoys the light and warmth of the sun. Similarly, he *sends* the rain. Jesus is here tracing things back to their first cause, namely that God is indiscriminate in his kindness.

MATTHEW 6:26-33

> 26 "Look at the birds of the air: they neither sow nor reap nor gather into barns, and yet your heavenly Father feeds them. Are you not of more value than they?
> 27 And which of you by being anxious can add a single hour to his span of life?

28 And why are you anxious about clothing? Consider the lilies of the field, how they grow: they neither toil nor spin,

29 yet I tell you, even Solomon in all his glory was not arrayed like one of these.

30 But if God so clothes the grass of the field, which today is alive and tomorrow is thrown into the oven, will he not much more clothe you, O you of little faith?

31 Therefore do not be anxious, saying, 'What shall we eat?' or 'What shall we drink?' or 'What shall we wear?'

32 For the Gentiles seek after all these things, and your heavenly Father knows that you need them all.

33 But seek first the kingdom of God and his righteousness, and all these things will be added to you."

Here Jesus teaches that God feeds the birds and decorates the flowers. Therefore, he will not fail to look after the most valuable part of his creation—his people.

MATTHEW 10:29-31

29 Are not two sparrows sold for a penny? And not one of them will fall to the ground apart from your Father.

30 But even the hairs of your head are all numbered.

31 Fear not, therefore; you are of more value than many sparrows.

The providence of God extends to the minutest details of the most trivial circumstances of the tiniest creatures. Not even a small bird can fall to the ground unless God makes it happen. Calvin comments on verse 29 like this:

Christ gives a very different account of the providence of God from what is given by many who talk like the philosophers, and tell us that God governs the world, but yet imagine providence to be a confused sort of arrangement, as if God did not keep his eye on each of the creatures. Now, Christ declares that each of the creatures in particular is under his hand and protection, so that nothing is left to chance.[15]

However, as Matthew Henry says, what Jesus is chiefly asserting here is "that the providence of God is in a special manner conversant about the saints, in their suffering." They are of more value than many sparrows, and therefore the hairs of their heads are all numbered. That denotes "the account which God takes and keeps of all the concerns of his people, even those that are most minute and least regarded."[16]

Don Carson issues this encouragement: "God's sovereignty over the tiniest detail should give us confidence that he also superintends the larger matters."[17]

ACTS 17:24-26

24 The God who made the world and everything in it, being Lord of heaven and earth, does not live in temples made by man,
25 nor is he served by human hands, as though he needed anything, since he himself gives to all mankind life and breath and everything.
26 And he made from one man every nation of mankind to live on all the face of the earth, having determined allotted periods and the boundaries of their dwelling place.

We may make five statements about this passage relevant to the doctrine of God's providence:

1. God is independent of his creation
He is not reliant on his creatures for the things he needs. Since everything is his creation, everything is also his possession. This text pro-

---

15 J. Calvin, *Commentary on a Harmony of the Evangelists* (reprint, Albany: Ages, 1997), 1:376.

16 M. Henry, *An Exposition of the Gospel According to St. Matthew* (reprint, Carluke: Online Bible: Ages, 1995-2005), on Matthew 10:16-42.

17 D.A. Carson, "Commentary on Matthew," in Gaebelein, ed., *Expositor's Bible Commentary*, on Matthew 10:29-31.

claims "the self-sufficiency and complete independence of God."[18] God does not even need our service. The word translated *served* in verse 25 is *therapeuo*. It is normally translated *healing*. The reference is not to service pure and simple, but to service as an expression of gratitude. The idea of service is often misunderstood as a favour man does for God, service that supposedly is actually *contributing* to the divine glory. The truth of God's sovereignty and independence from his creation is the foundation for the doctrine of providence.

2. God is the supreme giver

The Greek word *pas* (*all*) comes twice in verse 25. God gives all things to all people. No one has anything which he has not received from God. This applies to things as fundamental as life itself and the breath needed to sustain life.

The word rendered *breath* here is *pnoe*. It is the gentlest available term for a movement of air. Every single inhalation, however slight, is a gracious gift from God.

3. God is the author of ethnicity

The human race is subdivided into different people groups. Ethnic diversity is an expression of God's driving passion for variety. The word *pas* appears twice more in verse 26. God made all nations in all places. Wherever you go on the face of the earth, the Creator has constituted whatever ethnic group you find there. This variety and diversity is not a valid ground for what is sometimes called "racism." In fact, the very idea of race is "racist." This verse teaches that there is only one human race. God made us all from one blood. We share a common ancestry, stemming from the one pair in the Garden of Eden.

Richard Longenecker notes that the Athenians, to whom Paul is talking here, boasted that they were different from all other peoples. They claimed that they originated directly from the soil of Greece. Paul demolishes such proud notions. Because of our common descent from Adam and Eve, genetic diversity developed gradually along with the migrations of people away from the Middle East. The diversity we see today is the result of divine providence at work over many centuries.

18 H. Schönweiss, in Brown, ed., *New International Dictionary of New Testament Theology*, 2:861.

4. God has determined national duration

Migrations took place. Nations formed. Governments were set in place. The time came when they collapsed. Perhaps the nation was overrun in war. Perhaps a people feeling oppressed rose up in revolution. Perhaps moral disintegration caused systemic weakness. Whatever might be the immediate cause of the demise of a nation, empire, or culture, the length of its survival is determined and pre-appointed by the sovereign Lord. The word translated *periods* in verse 26 is *kairos*. It refers not to mere chronology, but to the power and influence of a nation for its time. We need to take note of the words "determined" and "allotted." Two verbs are used. The first is *horizo*. It means to set the limit, in this case, the temporal limit. The tense is aorist: it denotes a determination of timescale fixed in the past, in this case, in eternity. The other verb is *protasso*. It, too, means to determine something in advance. In this case, the tense is perfect: it denotes that what was determined still stands, and therefore inevitably becomes reality at the appointed time.

5. God has determined national location

The boundaries are fixed geographically as well as temporally. Migrations, ancient and contemporary, are all governed by the providence of God.

COLOSSIANS 1:17

He is before all things, and in him all things hold together.

Providence includes preservation. Here is a vital additional element to the truth of God's providential preservation: it is in Christ that all things hold together. This verb indicates that the creation is kept intact. The unity of the universe is upheld. There is a firmness about things which ensures that they do not fall apart. Everything has its place and remains there immovably. The point of cohesion by which all things are preserved is found in Christ. "Apart from his continuous sustaining activity, all would disintegrate."[19] The verb is in the perfect

---

19 P.T. O'Brien, *Colossians, Philemon* (Dallas: Word, 1982), 62.

tense. It implies that all things were and still are held together. There has never been a moment when Christ could relax his sustaining hold. That would have led to total cosmic collapse. I wonder whether that is the reason for the midday darkness and the earthquakes when he died on the cross. Was creation thrown into turmoil because its centre of unification was under threat?

HEBREWS 1:3

He is the radiance of the glory of God and the exact imprint of his nature, and he upholds the universe by the word of his power.

This verse also emphasizes the central role Christ has in providence. He upholds the entire universe. The word translated *upholds* is *phero*. It means "to carry." The Lord Jesus Christ is carrying creation so that it does not fall to destruction. He is moving it forwards towards its ultimate destiny.

These last two texts emphasize the importance of something which T.H.L. Parker says about providence. He insists

we must resist the temptation to think about providence generally and independently of Christ. It would be possible to draw on certain Psalms and the Sermon on the Mount, for example, to make up a doctrine of God's relation to his creation which has nothing to do with Jesus Christ. But since it is in Christ that this relationship is established, an attempt to understand it apart from him would be a misinterpretation from the start. In Jesus Christ God has set up the relationship between himself and his creation.[20]

---

20 T.H.L. Parker, "Providence," in E.F. Harrison, ed., *Baker's Dictionary of Theology* (Grand Rapids: Baker, 1960), 426f.

Section summary and personal application

REMEMBER

"Therefore do not be anxious, saying, What shall we eat?' or 'What shall we drink?' or 'What shall we wear?' For the Gentiles seek after all these things, and your heavenly Father knows that you need them all. But seek first the kingdom of God and his righteousness, and all these things will be added to you."
—*Matthew 6:31-33*

Rejoice in the Lord always; again I will say, rejoice. Let your reasonableness be known to everyone. The Lord is at hand; do not be anxious about anything, but in everything by prayer and supplication with thanksgiving let your requests be made known to God. And the peace of God, which surpasses all understanding, will guard your hearts and your minds in Christ Jesus.
—*Philippians 4:4-7*

REFLECT

1. The Lord providentially controls life and death. How would you counsel someone on his or her deathbed in light of this?
2. Do you ever doubt God's providential mercy? Read Matthew 6:26–33. In light of this passage, how would you counter doubts?

REJOICE

In shady, green pastures, so rich and so sweet,
  God leads His dear children along;
Where the water's cool flow bathes the weary one's feet,
  God leads His dear children along.

Some through the waters, some through the flood,
  Some through the fire, but all through the blood;
Some through great sorrow, but God gives a song,
  In the night season and all the day long.

Sometimes on the mount where the sun shines so bright,
   God leads His dear children along;
Sometimes in the valley, in darkest of night,
   God leads His dear children along.

Though sorrows befall us and evils oppose,
   God leads His dear children along;
Through grace we can conquer, defeat all our foes,
   God leads His dear children along.

Away from the mire, and away from the clay,
   God leads His dear children along;
Away up in glory, eternity's day,
   God leads His dear children along.
   —George A. Young (c.1855–1935)

PART 2: KEY CREEDS AND CONFESSIONS

A. THE REFORMATION CONFESSIONS

The early creeds are silent on this subject. The teaching of the Reformation confessions may be summarized in eight points:

1. The meaning of providence

The confessions define God's ongoing relationship to his creation using a number of different terms. God governs, rules, and directs his creation. He preserves it and upholds it. He orders it and guides it. Creation is quickened and sustained by the Lord. The picture conveyed by the confessions is one in which God is totally involved in the life of the world. God holds creation in his hand, carrying it, shaping it, caring for it.

2. The scope of providence

God's providence extends to all things. The entire universe is subject to God. This applies to the actions of all God's creatures, from the greatest to the least. Providence may be seen as operating on two levels. God sets the overall cosmic direction. He also manages the smallest details. Robert Shaw quotes the words of one Dr. Dick on this point:

> Some maintain only a general providence, which consists in upholding certain general laws, and exclaim against the idea of a particular providence, which takes a concern in individuals and their affairs.... If God has certain designs to accomplish with respect to, or by means of, his intelligent creatures, I should like to know how his intention can be fulfilled without particular attention to their circumstances, their movements, and all the events of their life.... How can a whole be taken care of without taking care of its parts, or a species be preserved if the individuals are neglected?[21]

Spelling this out in more detail, the confessions affirm that everything that happens is disposed and ordained by God. Indeed, nothing can happen apart from his appointment. Every apparent accident occurs only at God's command. Robert Shaw sums up the scope of providence: it extends to the inanimate creation, the whole animal creation, angels, both good and evil ones, and the affairs of nations, families, and individuals.[22]

3. The character of God's providence

We may distinguish between the moral character and the practical character of God's providence. The confessions describe God's providence in moral terms as just, right, good and holy. Practically, it is wise, but inscrutable. This last term amounts to an admission that we are not always able to make sense of what happens. We therefore submit to a higher wisdom.

---

21 Quoted by Shaw, *An Exposition of the Confession of Faith*, 66f.
22 Shaw, *An Exposition of the Confession of Faith*, 67.

4. The basis of God's providence

There are two aspects to the underlying basis of providence: God's infallible foreknowledge and the free counsel of his holy will. God knows everything that will happen, and God decides everything that will happen. Which comes first? Does God decide based on what he knows, or does he know because he has already decided? We cannot answer this question. Knowledge and decision are simultaneous in God. We have to admit that in the doctrine of providence there are perplexing mysteries. We cannot expect to unravel every mystery to our own emotional satisfaction. This doctrine lifts us up to trust and worship God.

5. The methods of providence

Many of the confessions note that God uses means to accomplish his purposes. Secondary causes come into play, and they operate according to their own nature. Of course, the means are ordained just as much as the end. This even applies to the evil choices and actions of sinners and devils, which God has wonderful ways of turning to good.

Shaw distinguishes between ordinary and miraculous providences. In ordinary providence, God works "by means and according to general laws established by his own wisdom." A miraculous providence is God choosing to work by his own immediate agency without the use of means.[23]

6. Providence and sin

The truths emphasized so far inevitably raise the question of the relationship of God's providence to sin considered as a hostile power, and to the individual sins of fallen angels and human beings. Here, too, we find ourselves in the realm of mystery. The confessions acknowledge that if we truly believe in providence, then we have to say that God's sovereign overruling secured the entry of sin into the world in such a way that it was bound to happen. The confessions vary in how they express this. Some prefer to say that God permitted the fall.[24] Others

---

23 Shaw, *An Exposition of the Confession of Faith*, 69.

24 *Second Helvetic Confession* 8.9: the Latin word which the Confession uses is *sino*, which W. Smith and J. Lockwood define as "to leave, let, allow, permit" [W. Smith & J. Lockwood, *Chambers-Murray Latin English Dictionary* (London: Murray, 1976), 690].

make the point more strongly: God ordained the fall.[25] They often then go on to admit the mystery in this, and to warn us against striving too hard to enter into divine secrets which it is beyond our ability to uncover. The confessions also note that all sins committed since the fall, along with all their effects, are carefully handled by God to promote morally praiseworthy ends.

In discussing the teaching of the *Westminster Confession* on this aspect of the doctrine of providence, Shaw notes two biblical examples of God's providential ordering of sin—the sale of Joseph by his brothers, and the crucifixion of Jesus. In both cases, greater good came about through the means of sinful choices and actions. In advance, God secured those sinful choices and actions with a view to that greater good. However, the confessions are quick to assert that this does not make God the *author* of sin. God is not responsible for sin. Sinfulness comes from the creature, not from the Creator. Such teaching obviously causes us some uncertainty. To us it seems a contradiction to say that God decreed sin and yet that he is not the author of sin. Here is what Robert Shaw says about this:

> To solve the difficulty connected with this point, theologians distinguish between an action and its quality. The action, abstractly considered, is from God, for no action can be performed without the concurrence of providence; but the sinfulness of the action proceeds from the creature. As to the manner in which the providence of God is concerned about the sinful actions of creatures, it is usually stated that God permits them, that he limits them, and that he overrules them for the accomplishment of his own holy ends.[26]

This still leaves unanswered the question of why God chose to accomplish holy ends by that route in the first place. Shaw continues:

The *Westminster Larger Catechism*, Question 19, likewise uses the word "permitted" in relation to the fall of the angels.

25 *The Belgic Confession* 13 and *The French Confession of Faith* 8, speak like this: the original French vocabulary used in both confessions was the verb *ordonner* and its related noun *ordonnance*; cf. *Westminster Confession of Faith* 5.4.

26 Shaw, *An Exposition of the Confession of Faith*, 70.

The full elucidation of this abstruse subject, so as to remove every difficulty, surpasses the human faculties. We are certain that God is concerned in all the actions of his creatures; we are equally certain that God cannot be the author of sin; and here we ought to rest.[27]

This doctrine is bound to leave us with some loose ends which we cannot tie up. The confessions commend a humility that will bow before the secrets hidden from us. They warn us not to persist in questioning what is beyond our understanding.

7. The purposes of providence

What is God aiming at in providentially preserving and governing his creation and all its parts? The confessions mention three things: (1) the creation is providentially ruled so that every part of it may serve man, so that man may be better able to serve God; (2) providence is designed for taking care of the people of God in particular: all things are disposed for the good of the church; as it says in 2 Chronicles 16:9: "the eyes of the LORD run to and fro throughout the whole earth, to give strong support to those whose heart is blameless toward him"; and, (3) the highest appointed end of providence is God's own glory.

8. The benefits of providence

The assurance that God's providence is ruling over all is of great benefit to the believer. It gives us peace to know that God is watching over us with fatherly care. It gives us a sense of safety to know that no enemy, human or demonic, can harm us without his permission. To know that nothing can happen to us by chance is a source of rich comfort. The doctrine of providence leads us to trust that God will provide us with all that we need, both materially and spiritually, and that he will turn every experience through which we pass to our good. We can therefore be patient in times of adversity, thankful in times of success, and confident as we face the unknown future.

It is in times of darkness and mystery that this doctrine really comes into its own. To know that all providences, even difficult ones, are for

---

27 Shaw, *An Exposition of the Confession of Faith*, 70.

a purpose is an incalculable comfort to us. To know that nothing can do us ultimate harm is to see even our trials as blessings. There may be temporal evils but, because of providence, they will always turn out to be for our spiritual good.

B. MODERN CONFESSIONS OF FAITH

1. Confession of Faith of the United Church of Northern India

This confession recognizes two strands to God's providence. It says that God preserves and governs all things within the visible world which he has created. Here are words of comfort for human beings: even in the visible, physical world to which we belong, we are never in a situation where God's preserving and governing providence has been removed. Here, in this life, we live every day within the sphere of divine government. At all times, a loving God is preserving us and sustaining human existence.

This confession also makes the point that God "is in no way the author of sin." Without trying to unravel the mysteries of providence, it insists on the holiness of God, and refuses to deny his goodness by blaming him for the miseries which sin has caused.

2. Confession of Faith of the Huria Batak Protestant

The Indonesian confession describes God the Father, in particular, as "the Provider and the Lord of all things visible and invisible." This statement is affirming God's sovereign providence, not only in our world, but also throughout his entire creation. His providential provision and control extend to things invisible as well. Some things are invisible simply because they are out of the range of human exploration. The remotest galaxies and the deepest depths of the seabed would come into this category. Other things are intrinsically invisible by nature. This would include the realm of angels and spirits. The providential care and power of God hold both types of invisible reality. However, this confession explicitly distinguishes the doctrine of divine providence from fatalism. It also includes a statement rejecting the practices of listening to fortune-tellers and reading one's fate in the lines of their hands. Our destiny is shaped by the providence of a caring, loving God, not by impersonal fate.

3. Confession of Faith of House Churches in China

The Chinese confession uses two words in speaking of God's providence. God controls all things. God sustains all things. These two terms
echo the emphases in the Reformation confessions on God's government and preservation of creation. This confession stresses the fact
that providence rules human history. God is described as "the Lord of
human history," and it is within human history that God manifests his
sovereignty. This is not to restrict the sphere of providence to human
history alone, as if God's sovereignty is not at work in the non-human
part of creation, or in the personal histories of individual human beings.
However, it is in human affairs that God's providence is of most interest
to us, and it is on the historical stage that God's sovereignty is at work
most powerfully. He is indeed King of the nations.

Chinese history has been at times illustrious, and at times excruciat-
ingly painful. In both aspects of their history, the Chinese house
church leaders want to trace the government of God. Even if, for them,
God's providence has at times been most mysterious and inexplicable,
yet they know that the sovereign Lord has put every Chinese government in place, and each government remains in place until he sees fit
to remove it. That fact accounts for the sentiments expressed at the
end of the section of the confession that teaches about the church:

> We are opposed to the church taking part in any activities that
> seek to destroy the unity of the people or the unification of the
> Chinese state.

Since the providence of God has unified the Chinese state in the
course of its history, it is not the calling of the Church to interfere with
the workings of providence. The church bows to the sovereign will of
the Lord of history.

Section summary and personal application

REMEMBER

Men of Israel, hear these words: Jesus of Nazareth, a man attested to you by God with mighty works and wonders and signs that God did through him in your midst, as you yourselves know— this Jesus, delivered up according to the definite plan and foreknowledge of God, you crucified and killed by the hands of lawless men.
—*Acts 2:22-23*

God the good Creator of all things, in his infinite power, and wisdom, doth uphold, direct, dispose, and govern all Creatures, and things, from the greatest even to the least, by his most wise and holy providence, to the end for the which they were Created; according unto his infallible foreknowledge, and the free and immutable counsel of his own will; to the praise of the glory of his wisdom, power, justice, infinite goodness and mercy.
—*The Baptist Confession of Faith of 1689, 5.1.*

REFLECT

1. Can providence exist if it is not particular? What would it mean for God to forego the details?
2. God's detailed providence is a great comfort. Knowing that he works all things for the good of those who love him is a mercy he has given us. List some ways in which this truth has served to comfort you in your life.

REJOICE

Heav'nly Father, Thou hast brought us
    Safely to the present day,
Gently leading on our footsteps,
    Watching o'er us all the way.
Friend and guide through life's long journey,
    Grateful hearts to Thee we bring;

But for love so true and changeless
How shall we fit praises sing?

Mercies new and never failing
Brightly shine through all the past,
Watchful care and loving-kindness
Always near from first to last,
Tender love, divine protection
Ever with us day and night;
Blessings more than we can number
Strow the path with golden light.

Shadows deep have crossed our pathway;
We have trembled in the storm;
Clouds have gathered round so darkly
That we could not see Thy form;
Yet Thy love hath never left us
In our griefs alone to be,
And the help each gave the other
Was the strength that came from Thee.
—*Hester Hawkins (1846–1928)*

PART 3: KEY HISTORICAL DEVELOPMENTS

We shall now look at the writings of two men who celebrated the divine providence—the second-century French theologian, Irenaeus of Lyons, and the seventeenth-century English Puritan, John Flavel.

1. Irenaeus of Lyons

Irenaeus' major work was to oppose Gnosticism, a heresy that invaded the church in the second century. His *magnum opus*, *Against Heresies*, includes an exciting and uplifting doctrine of providence. We shall focus on four passages.

(1) Irenaeus taught that *every aspect of everything in existence is a fruit of God's providence.* There is a purpose to everything. Nothing happens "in vain." Everything that happens is rooted in the purpose of God, and occurs with a view to the usefulness which God intended for it. Nothing happens "accidentally." Nothing simply appears. There are no chance events in God's world. On the contrary, everything happens "with exceeding suitability." Irenaeus wrote in Latin, and the word he uses here is *aptatio.* It is derived from a verb meaning "to adjust to fit." It could be used of tightening a belt to secure a piece of armour. It conveys the picture that every event in the story of the world is a minor adjustment God makes to keep creation neatly tailored in its progress towards the fulfilment of his purpose. Every occurrence is a necessary modification to maintain the world's fitness as the realm within which God is working out his grand intention.

Irenaeus uses a musical image when he says that everything happens "in elevated harmony." Even when, to our limited perspective, things seem discordant, they are still playing together under the leadership of the divine conductor. The universe echoes the sublime exaltation of God.[28]

(2) "God exercises a providence over all things," writes Irenaeus. *Nothing is left outside the sphere of divine providence.* Irenaeus explains this universal providence by saying that the Father "arranges the affairs of our world."[29] Here is a comforting truth: even in the midst of life's struggles, we may rely on our Maker and Father, confident that, right here in this world, we are held in his mighty hand.

The word rendered *arranges* is *dispono.* It implies that God, with great care and deliberation, positions things, and times events with precision. He secures regularity in creation, as opposed to haphazardness. He guards his handiwork meticulously. The word was sometimes used of a person's daily work. To be the managing director of the universe is how God is daily employed. Irenaeus describes God as the ruler. Like a herdsman, God sets the direction with a clear aim in view. Like a horse rider, he steers things so that the correct direction is maintained and the intended destination is achieved. God's providen-

---

28 Irenaeus, *Against Heresies*, 2.27.3.
29 Irenaeus, *Against Heresies*, 2.27.7.

tial activity involves guiding the creation forwards to its appointed destiny, just as a helmsman or navigator guides a ship.

There is a practical application which Irenaeus makes. Providence should bring people to the knowledge of God. This is not something that will just happen incidentally. The experience of providence is something that people ought to seize on to lead them to the knowledge of the Lord himself. We have a duty actively to reap the benefits of the understanding of God's providence. What Irenaeus means is that the very facts of order, purpose, harmony, security and provision in this world are making a statement that there is but one God who rules and governs absolutely everything. These facts are staring all rational people in the face, if they will but take unprejudiced notice. Irenaeus admits that the ravages of sin mean that people are moved only slightly. Nevertheless, there is something moving about a purposefully directed world. There is something inspiring and soul-stirring in the fact of providence. At the very least, this ought to alert God's creatures to the realities of his existence, his unity, his omnipotent greatness, and his universal overruling.[30]

(3) Irenaeus goes on to point out that *the supreme act of providence was the coming of Christ*. This event, at a particular point in history, is supreme evidence of the divine ordering of all the events of history. The wonder of this ultimate providence is that, although the coming of Christ took place at one time, its significance and impact are timeless, in the sense that its saving efficacy reaches to every time. However, only believers benefit from the saving power of Christ, and the providence of God in his coming was directed towards them particularly. Irenaeus recognizes that the original cause of the salvation of God's people was his wise ordering of things. The outworking of that divine wisdom saw to it that the coming of Christ as Saviour took place at the appointed moment as the central event of all history.[31]

(4) Irenaeus writes like this: "*It is the Father of our Lord by whose providence all things consist, and all are administered by his command.*"[32] The two parallel phrases here indicate two important aspects of the

---

30 Irenaeus, *Against Heresies*, 3.25.1.

31 Irenaeus, *Against Heresies*, 4.22.2.

32 Irenaeus, *Against Heresies*, 4.36.6.

doctrine of providence for Irenaeus. The two nouns *providence* and *command* tell us that God exercises his providence by issuing the all-powerful word of command. It is God's almighty Word which keeps all things in being. Irenaeus has a particular type of command in view. The original word is *iussus*, which derives from the verb *iubeo*. This means "to bid someone to be safe and sound." For Irenaeus, God's providence is directed towards human safety in a sound world. The two parallel verbs are *consist* and *administer*. What is it for God to administer the world? It means that he secures its reliability and its harmonious continuation. The Latin verb *consto* suggests that the creation stands firm, settled and constant. We do not live in a world totally unpredictable, entirely random, or unreliably fluid. The providence of God ensures the stability that makes it possible for human life to go on.

2. John Flavel

In 1678, John Flavel wrote *The Mystery of Providence*.[33] It is based on Psalm 57:2: "I cry out to God Most High, to God who fulfils his purpose for me." Flavel sets out to demonstrate how the believer can cope in times of distress. He finds the greatest support and comfort at such times to be the certainty that "there is a wise Spirit sitting in all the wheels of motion," so that even the evil designs of the enemies of God's people will turn to their blessing and happiness. Flavel recommends that in the hard times of life we should reflect on our experiences of God's providence at different stages of our lives. He lists eight evidences that providence is overruling all things for the good of God's people: (1) we have experienced mercies beyond the ability of merely natural causes; (2) sometimes, natural causes have come together in strange coincidences; (3) all attempts to destroy the people of God have proved ineffective; (4) sinners have often been turned out of the way of evil in remarkable fashion; (5) sometimes evils done to God's people have been repaid even here on earth; (6) the Scriptures describe exactly the experiences God's people enjoy; (7) sometimes, things turn out so well just in time; and (8) there are specific answers to prayer.[34]

---

33 J. Flavel, *The Mystery of Providence* (1678; reprint, Edinburgh: The Banner of Truth Trust, 1963).

34 Flavel, *The Mystery of Providence*, 27-42.

Flavel mentions six specific areas of life where the believer may meditate on providence: (1) our birth and upbringing; (2) our conversion; (3) our daily working life; (4) our family situation; (5) the way we have been preserved from evil; and (6) the work of sanctification in our lives.[35]

Meditation on providence, Flavel argues, is a Christian duty,[36] and he gives advice on ways of doing it. First, though, he stresses one important factor. We must ensure that we see God as the Author of all providences. This applies to sad afflictions as well as to comfortable providences. Flavel then gives six pieces of advice for times of distress.[37]

First, he says, we must ponder the sovereignty of God. We must remember that we exist by his will, and that everything that we have and everything that happens to us proceeds from his will.

Second, we must remember the grace and goodness of God. Flavel reminds us that things are never as bad as they could be, and certainly nowhere near as bad as we deserve them to be. We must remember that our afflictions are only for the duration of this short lifetime, and things will be better hereafter. If we are afflicted, we should see it as a mercy that we are not destroyed.

Third, we must perceive the wisdom of God. If we are afflicted, it is because God knows that we need his rod of discipline. It is better to lose some of our cherished things now than to perish forever.

Fourth, we must meditate on the faithfulness of God. He knows that it is better for us to suffer a little now than to suffer eternal punishment. His love does not pander to our fancies. It gives us what we need to do us good.

Fifth, we must recall the all-sufficiency of God. Whatever our afflictions might have taken from us, if we still have God, we have enough. Even though one pipe may be blocked, God is still the fountain, and he remains as full as ever. We always find more in God alone than in any of the comforts we have lost.

Finally, we must see the unchanging nature of God. Our condition in life can change for the worse very suddenly. Two or three days may

---

35 Flavel, *The Mystery of Providence*, 43-109.

36 Flavel, *The Mystery of Providence*, 113-116.

37 Flavel, *The Mystery of Providence*, 128-132.

have brought unexpected sadness into our experience. However, God remains what he was and where he was. The passage of time never changes him. If we can learn to meditate on providence like this, Flavel assures us, we shall retain tranquillity of mind amidst all life's changes and uncertainties. We shall remain stable as the revolutions of things in this vain world circle around us.

Our meditations on providence here are at best partial. However, in eternity we shall have the opportunity for a full and entire survey of all the providences of God:

> O how ravishing and delectable a sight will it be to behold at one view the whole design of providence, and the proper place and use of every single act, which we could not understand in this world…. All the dark, intricate, puzzling providences at which we were sometimes so offended, and sometimes amazed, which we could neither reconcile with the promise, nor with each other, nay, which we so unjustly censured and bitterly bewailed, as if they had fallen out quite against our happiness, we shall then see to be to us, as the difficult passage through the wilderness was to Israel, the right way to a city of habitation.[38]

PART 4: KEY POINTS OF PRACTICAL APPLICATION

(1) *We must get hold of the assurance that God is in control, whatever may happen.* We need never despair. We may not understand what his purpose is, but we do understand that his providence is never without purpose, and that his purposes are always for our ultimate good. Our confidence that God is in control may be boosted by considering obvious instances of his providence. We have been kept safe to live until today, when so many unknown dangers could have carried us out of the world already. God has nourished us daily. God's benevolence is

---

38 Flavel, *The Mystery of Providence*, 22.

indiscriminate: he is so favourable and generous to all people. More-over, God's providence is furthering his own work. The church still exists, the gospel is still being preached, even in difficult times. It is towards his children that God's providence is especially tender. We may find comfort in the knowledge that the hairs of our head are numbered. The power of God keeps us forever. Our hearts need not be troubled.

(2) *We must preach providence.* We must preach it evangelistically. This doctrine is a powerful argument with sinners in calling them to repentance. God has been so kind to them every day. We must urge them to turn to him in gratitude and faith. We must preach this doctrine to believers. They need to hear that God is in control. The realization that this is so will help them to rise above the mysteries of a bewildering life and to trust God without grumbling.

(3) *We must praise God that his providential rule centres in Christ.* The God of providence is the Father of our Lord Jesus Christ. "All of God's dealings with his creation are mediated through the Christ."[39] And

> in his eternal purpose God determined that his Son would have a bride conformed to his image, and that he would have a special people residing in the glorified "new heaven and new earth" state, all to the praise of the glory of his grace. And that purpose he executed in and by his works of creation and providence.[40]

REFLECT

1. The doctrine of providence is one of our greatest joys. It encour-ages us in ministry, evangelism, and life. How has this wonder-ful truth motivated you personally?
2. Would you agree with Flavel that the greatest support and com-fort in times of distress is the certainty of the Spirit who works all things for our good? Why or why not?

---

39 Reymond, *A New Systematic Theology,* 400.
40 Reymond, *A New Systematic Theology,* 414.

REJOICE

Be still, my soul: the Lord is on thy side.
  Bear patiently the cross of grief or pain.
Leave to thy God to order and provide;
  In every change, He faithful will remain.
Be still, my soul: thy best, thy heavenly Friend
  Through thorny ways leads to a joyful end.

Be still, my soul: thy God doth undertake
  To guide the future, as He has the past.
Thy hope, thy confidence let nothing shake;
  All now mysterious shall be bright at last.
Be still, my soul: the waves and winds still know
  His voice Who ruled them while He dwelt below.

Be still, my soul: begin the song of praise
  On earth, believing, to Thy Lord on high;
Acknowledge Him in all thy words and ways,
  So shall He view thee with a well pleased eye.
Be still, my soul: the Sun of life divine
  Through passing clouds shall but more brightly shine.
—*Katharina A.D. von Schlegel (1697–1768)*

APPENDIX I

The Apostles' Creed

A.D. fourth or fifth century

I believe in God, the Father Almighty,
   the Maker of heaven and earth,
   and in Jesus Christ, His only Son, our Lord:
Who was conceived by the Holy Ghost,
   born of the virgin Mary,
   suffered under Pontius Pilate,
   was crucified, dead, and buried;
He descended into hell.[1]
The third day He arose again from the dead;
He ascended into heaven,
   and sitteth on the right hand of God the Father Almighty;
   from thence he shall come to judge the quick and the dead.

---

1   I think that Calvin interprets this statement correctly. He understands Christ's experience of hell to have been his experience of "the dread and severity of the divine judgment" (Calvin, *Catechism* (1538) 20.iv, 23) during the three hours of darkness as he hung on the cross. He defines Jesus' descent to hell as "the fearful agonies with which his soul was tormented," and goes on to quote the words of Christ from the cross, "My God, my God, why have you forsaken me?" (Calvin, *Catechism* (1545), Q. 65-66).

In his *Institutes* (2.16.10–12), Calvin speaks of how the Lord Jesus Christ felt "the weight of divine vengeance," and engaged with "the horrors of eternal death" as "he endured the death which is inflicted on the wicked by an angry God." Again Calvin links this with the cry of dereliction from the cross. He comments, "It is evident that this expression was wrung from the anguish of his inmost soul." From this cry of terror, "we may infer how dire and dreadful were the tortures which he endured when he felt himself standing at the bar of God as a criminal in our stead." His sorrow "was no common sorrow": he engaged with "the power of the devil, the fear of death, and the pains of hell." Smitten and afflicted, "he bore the weight of the divine anger."

Calvin does face the possible objection that this interpretation perverts the order of the creed: the descent to hell preceded Jesus' burial, but is mentioned after it. However, Calvin sees logic in this: "After explaining what Christ endured in the sight of man, the creed appropriately adds the invisible and incomprehensible judgment which he endured before God, to teach us that not only was the body of Christ given up as the price of redemption, but that there was a greater and more excellent price— that he bore in his soul the tortures of condemned and ruined man." The vital importance of this additional phrase in the creed is that "had not his soul shared in the punishment, he would have been a Redeemer of bodies only" [cf. J.F. Bayes, *The Apostles' Creed: Truth with Passion* (Eugene: Wipf & Stock, 2010), 102f].

I believe in the Holy Ghost;
    the holy catholic [universal] church;
    the communion of saints;
    the forgiveness of sins;
    the resurrection of the body;
    and the life everlasting.
Amen.

APPENDIX 2

The Nicene Creed

A.D. 325

We believe in one God,
   the Father, the Almighty,
   maker of heaven and earth,
   of all that is, seen and unseen.

We believe in one Lord, Jesus Christ,
   the only Son of God,
   eternally begotten of the Father,
   God from God, light from light,
   true God from true God,
   begotten, not made,
   of one Being with the Father;
   through him all things were made.
For us and for our salvation
   he came down from heaven,
   was incarnate of the Holy Spirit and the Virgin Mary
   and became truly human.
For our sake he was crucified under Pontius Pilate;
   he suffered death and was buried.
On the third day he rose again
   in accordance with the Scriptures;
   he ascended into heaven
   and is seated at the right hand of the Father.
He will come again in glory to judge the living and the dead,
   and his kingdom will have no end.

We believe in the Holy Spirit, the Lord, the giver of life,
   who proceeds from the Father [and the Son],
   who with the Father and the Son is worshipped and glorified,
   who has spoken through the prophets.
We believe in one holy catholic [universal] and apostolic Church.
We acknowledge one baptism for the forgiveness of sins.
We look for the resurrection of the dead,
   and the life of the world to come. Amen.

APPENDIX 3

The Chalcedonian Definition

A.D. 451

Therefore, following the holy fathers,
we all with one accord teach men to acknowledge
one and the same Son, our Lord Jesus Christ,
at once complete in Godhead and complete in manhood,
truly God and truly man,
consisting also of a reasonable soul and body;
of one substance with the Father as regards his Godhead,
and at the same time of one substance with us as regards his
    manhood;
like us in all respects, apart from sin;
as regards his Godhead,
begotten of the Father before the ages,
but yet as regards his manhood begotten,
for us men and for our salvation,
of Mary the Virgin, the God-bearer[1];
one and the same Christ, Son, Lord,
Only-begotten, recognized in two natures,
without confusion, without change, without division, without
    separation;
the distinction of natures being in no way annulled by the union,
but rather the characteristics of each nature being preserved
and coming together to form one person and subsistence,
not as parted or separated into two persons,
but one and the same Son and Only-begotten God the Word,
    Lord Jesus Christ;
even as the prophets from earliest times spoke of him,
and our Lord Jesus Christ himself taught us,
and the creed of the fathers has handed down to us.

---

1   This title is not meant to elevate Mary, but rather, historically, it was meant to elevate Christ and proclaim the truth that he is fully God and fully man.

The Athanasian Creed

c. A.D. 500

1. Whosoever will be saved, before all things it is necessary that he hold the catholic [universal] faith;

2. Which faith except every one do keep whole and undefiled, without doubt he shall perish everlastingly.

3. And the catholic [universal] faith is this: That we worship one God in Trinity, and Trinity in Unity;

4. Neither confounding the persons nor dividing the substance.

5. For there is one person of the Father, another of the Son, and another of the Holy Spirit.

6. But the Godhead of the Father, of the Son, and of the Holy Spirit is all one, the glory equal, the majesty coeternal.

7. Such as the Father is, such is the Son, and such is the Holy Spirit.

8. The Father uncreated, the Son uncreated, and the Holy Spirit uncreated.

9. The Father incomprehensible, the Son incomprehensible, and the Holy Spirit incomprehensible.

10. The Father eternal, the Son eternal, and the Holy Spirit eternal.

11. And yet they are not three eternals but one eternal.

12. As also there are not three uncreated nor three incomprehensible, but one uncreated and one incomprehensible.

13. So likewise the Father is almighty, the Son almighty, and the Holy Spirit almighty.

14. And yet they are not three almighties, but one almighty.

15. So the Father is God, the Son is God, and the Holy Spirit is God;

16. And yet they are not three Gods, but one God.

17. So likewise the Father is Lord, the Son Lord, and the Holy Spirit Lord;

18. And yet they are not three Lords but one Lord.

19. For like as we are compelled by the Christian verity to acknowledge every Person by himself to be God and Lord;

20. So are we forbidden by the catholic [universal] religion to say; There are three Gods or three Lords.

21. The Father is made of none, neither created nor begotten.

22. The Son is of the Father alone; not made nor created, but begotten.

23. The Holy Spirit is of the Father and of the Son; neither made, nor created, nor begotten, but proceeding.
24. So there is one Father, not three Fathers; one Son, not three Sons; one Holy Spirit, not three Holy Spirits.
25. And in this Trinity none is afore or after another; none is greater or less than another.
26. But the whole three persons are coeternal, and coequal.
27. So that in all things, as aforesaid, the Unity in Trinity and the Trinity in Unity is to be worshipped.
28. He therefore that will be saved must thus think of the Trinity.
29. Furthermore it is necessary to everlasting salvation that he also believe rightly the incarnation of our Lord Jesus Christ.
30. For the right faith is that we believe and confess that our Lord Jesus Christ, the Son of God, is God and man.
31. God of the substance of the Father, begotten before the worlds; and man of substance of his mother, born in the world.
32. Perfect God and perfect man, of a reasonable soul and human flesh subsisting.
33. Equal to the Father as touching his Godhead, and inferior to the Father as touching his manhood.
34. Who, although he is God and man, yet he is not two, but one Christ.
35. One, not by conversion of the Godhead into flesh, but by taking of that manhood into God.
36. One altogether, not by confusion of substance, but by unity of person.
37. For as the reasonable soul and flesh is one man, so God and man is one Christ;
38. Who suffered for our salvation, descended into hell,[1] rose again the third day from the dead;
39. He ascended into heaven, he sits on the right hand of the Father, God, Almighty;
40. From thence he shall come to judge the quick and the dead.
41. At whose coming all men shall rise again with their bodies;
42. and shall give account of their own works.

---

1   See Appendix 1, footnote 1.

43. And they that have done good shall go into life everlasting and they that have done evil into everlasting fire.
44. This is the catholic [universal] faith, which except a man believe faithfully he cannot be saved.

Index

creation, according to kinds, 132; all things were created for Christ, 137; anticipation of, 166–167; application of, 110–111, 117–118, 139–140, 147–148, 157–158, 168–169; beginning of, 121–122; blessed by Creator, 133; by command, 130–131; Christ is the beginning, 138; compared to a play, 112; disappointment of, 164–165, 166; distinctiveness in, 132; effects of the curse, 163–164; evangelism through, 117–118; evolution theory, 148–157; false teaching of, 144–146; for the benefit of man, 144; for the glory of God, 144; for the sake of Christ, 169, 172–174; four ways the Genesis account rejects pagan understanding of heavenly bodies, 130; general revelation, 114–115, 116; God created everything, 141; God is the author of, 108; God's appreciation formula, 131–132; God's pleasure the ultimate purpose of, 138–139; goodness of, 143–144; in six days, 143; interpretation of "day", 154–156; Jesus Christ the agent in, 135–138; naming of, 132; natural theology, 113–114, 116; "not-yet" state of, 125–126; origin of, 119–159; out of nothing, 142; present condition of, 161–174; priority of, 128; purpose of, 121, 126; revelation seen in human life, 109; revelation seen in the world, 109; sets of days, 128–133; status of, 131, 133–134; subjected, 165; substantial healing of, 169–170; the "chaotic state", 124, 125; the beginning, 141–142; the curse, 171; the heavens and the earth, 123–125; the ontological argument, 113–114; the sky declares God's glory, 105; the sky is God's revelation, 104–105; the sky's constant declaration, 106; the sky's scope of declaration, 106–107; the thunderous message of the sky, 106–107; Trinity in, 142–143; united in Christ, 141; unwillingness of, 165; worship of God by, 118
Crosby, Fanny, 25
Cyprian of Carthage, 26, 27
Dabney, Robert Lewis, 29
Darwin, Charles, 155
Davies, John, 170, 171

decree, application of, 187–188, 194–195, 203–205; fundamentally for God's glory, 190–191; general statements of, 183–185; in Christ, 193; made in eternity, 189–190; mystery of, 191; never modified, 189; our confidence, 203–204; our humility, 204; outworking of, 176–177; purpose of, 177, 179; secondary causes, 192; specific statements of, 185–187; totally free decision, 190; unalterable, 190; unity of, 189
Dick, Dr., 225
Draper, William H., 111
Dunn, James, 108, 164, 165
Economic Trinitarianism, 56, 62
Emperor Decius, 26
Emperor Valerian, 26
Eusebius, 88
evolution, comparing accounts of origins, 152; refutation of, 150–157; the "ideal" interpretation, 150; the Day–Age theory, 149; the framework hypothesis, 149–150; the gap theory, 149; the Restitution theory, 149; theistic, 149
fatalism, 229
Feinberg, Charles, 200
Flavel, John, 232, 235, 236, 237, 238
Francis of Assisi, 111
Freud, Sigmund, 192
Fuller, Daniel, 95
Geneva Confession, 22
Getty, Keith, 140
Gill, John, 36
Gnosticism, 232
God, as Almighty, 15; as Creator, 16; as Father, 14–15; as holy, 22; as King, 210; as merciful, 21–22, 30–32; as omnipotent, 21; as omnipresent, 21; as One, 16–18, 22; as passionate, 19–20; as Ruler, 212; as source of light, 129; as sovereign, 20; as Spirit, 18–20; as Supreme Giver, 220; as Sustainer, 213; as transcendent, 22; as without passions, 19–20; authority of, 176; divine plan of, 179, 183; first subject, 122–123; four things he cannot do, 21; his activity, 217; his attributes, communicable, 29–30; his attributes, incommunicable, 29–30; his benevolence, 237–238; his character, 34; his control of the waters, 214; his

www.ingramcontent.com/pod-product-compliance
Lightning Source LLC
Chambersburg PA
CBHW030916150426
42812CB00045B/37